Read. autumn 1943
Re-read Feb. 1944.

W. H. Orme
Yale '97

A Portrait of Jesus

A Portrait of

JESUS

A Twentieth Century Interpretation of Christ

By

SHERWOOD EDDY

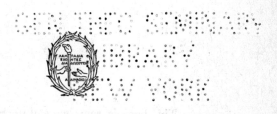

HARPER & BROTHERS
Publishers
NEW YORK *and* LONDON

FIRST EDITION

I-S

This book is complete and unabridged
in contents, and is manufactured in strict
conformity with Government regulations
for saving paper.

TO ALBERT SCHWEITZER

"He comes to us as One unknown, without a name, as of old, by the lakeside, he came to those men who knew him not. He speaks to us the same words: 'Follow thou me!' and sets us to the tasks which he has to fulfill for our time. He commands. And to those who obey him, whether they be wise or simple, he will reveal himself in the toils, the conflicts, the sufferings, which they shall pass through in his fellowship, and, as an ineffable mystery, they shall learn in their own experience who he is."

CONTENTS

PREFACE

THE ALL BUT IMPOSSIBLE TASK OF WRITING A MODERN LIFE OF Jesus was not undertaken lightly. I had been studying the life of Christ for some fifty years, and had copies of the Bible and harmonies of the Gospels filled with notes. But these did not even furnish a beginning of the task. I had to take account of the last century of scholarship and the work of a great body of men of intellectual acumen, of sound learning and of spiritual insight in Germany, England, France, and America, and to read or consult some two hundred volumes. As Schweitzer well says, "It is impossible to overestimate the value of what German research upon the life of Jesus has accomplished. It is a uniquely great expression of sincerity, one of the most significant events in the whole mental and spiritual life of humanity." But this reading also only cleared the ground for the foundation. It seemed that it might be useful, however, to gather the results of modern research scattered in scores of volumes into a single book and make it available for students.

I cannot claim on the one hand that this is a wholly original work, nor on the other that it is a mere mass of borrowings. Even with incessant footnotes it would not always be possible to indicate the source of each thought, or interpretation, or phrase. However, I have included a Bibliography in the last Appendix which gives a partial list of the books that have been consulted. It will be seen in the following chapters that I am under special obligation to the works of Albert Schweitzer, C. H. Dodd, F. C. Burkitt, Martin Dibelius, William Manson, Thomas Walter Manson, Burton Scott Easton, Harvie Branscomb, A. E. J. Rawlinson, E. F. Scott, F. C. Grant, and to the entire series of the Moffatt New Testament Commentaries. Of the lives of Christ and books about Jesus consulted, those by Maurice Goguel, C. A. H. Guignebert, J. Warschauer, Oscar Holtzmann, and Joseph Klausner, were among the most helpful.

It has been an inspiration to work in the library of the Union Theological Seminary with the veteran scholar, Dr. James Moffatt, and to be able occasionally to consult him, as on the chronological table in Appendix III. And it has been helpful to have known personally so many of the writers quoted in this book, including Harnack, Deissmann, Bishop Gore, Dr. William Temple, Streeter, Burkitt, Glover, McGiffert, B. W. Bacon, E. F. Scott, Reinhold Niebuhr, and of the older generation, men like A. B. Bruce and A. M. Fairbairn. In dedicating this life of Jesus to Albert Schweitzer, it is with the conviction that we owe to him more than to any other man of our generation our understanding of the historic figure of Jesus. I do not accept, however, his "thoroughgoing" eschatology nor his "interims ethic."

As the writing of this book had to be done in the midst of a busy life, I have been particularly indebted to my critics who have read a number of the chapters and offered invaluable suggestions, especially to Professors F. C. Grant, Henry Van Dusen, John Knox, and Russell Bowie of Union Theological Seminary, A. T. Mollegen of Alexandria Theological Seminary, and Harvie Branscomb of Duke University. In accordance with the practice in the Authorized and the Revised Versions of the New Testament, pronouns for God and Christ are not capitalized. Moffatt's translation of both the Old and New Testaments is prevailingly followed in this volume, save where some other rendering brings out the special point of the original we have in mind. Just as the four Gospels do not profess to cover the complete life of Jesus, this volume does not attempt to repeat every incident in the record, but, studying brevity at every point, seeks to confine itself to those essentials which shall, as far as possible, enable each student to see for himself the portrait of Jesus in a twentieth century interpretation of Christ.

SHERWOOD EDDY

New York, September 1, 1943

INTRODUCTION

"To make a Portrait of Christ, each man for himself, is the duty of every Christian. It cannot really be done second-hand, by others, if the Figure is to have any vital force or compelling influence." Thus wrote Professor F. C. Burkitt of Cambridge.[1]

IT MAY BE ASKED: WHY ANOTHER LIFE OF CHRIST OR A BOOK ABOUT Jesus, who has already inspired the greatest volume of literature on a single subject ever produced in all history? Why, especially when all the recorded events are only enough to fill a few months of the thirty or more years of Jesus' life? When, after decades of study by a host of brilliant scholars, "the quest of the historical Jesus" has not yielded the solid nucleus of facts which would enable us to write an accurate biography of him, why should we attempt this seemingly impossible task again?

The answer is that it was the recognition of these very difficulties in this period of transition that compelled us to attempt this confessedly difficult task. Historians acknowledge that we can never be certain of the details of historic events in the past, nor of the exact words of any oral teaching such as was given by Gautama Buddha, Socrates, or Jesus. Scholars point out that the four Gospels differ, as do all other historic documents, that no extended saying of Jesus is given in exactly the same words in any two Gospels, and that all four Evangelists handle the material of the others and of the earliest written Sayings of Jesus, where they possessed them, with respect yet with perfect freedom and independence. The writer believes that patient historical criticism must endeavor to find the facts in the life of Jesus, and to discover his original teaching, so far as it is humanly possible, in these differing documents. Yet his own assurance and certainty is in the realm of faith, in personal experience. He be-

[1] J. Warschauer, *The Historical Life of Christ*. The Macmillan Company, p. ix. Quoted by permission.

lieves not only in the Jesus of history but in the living Christ; in his Incarnation, Atonement and Resurrection. Hence he has chosen the title *A Portrait of Jesus: a Twentieth Century Interpretation of Christ*. Our study throughout seeks to be both critical and constructive.

Almost all will agree that in some unprecedented way God was in Jesus, that he had a unique relation to God and experience of God, and that he was able to lead his followers into an intimate relation to their heavenly Father in a remarkable sharing of this experience. The frank object of this book is to widen the circle of those who share this experience of God in this time of desperate human need. Now, if ever, men need to know God, to find the best way of life in order to build a better world. To whom else can we go to find this? It is because we believe that the answer to our deepest problems and our ultimate need is found only in Jesus Christ that this book is written.

We do not have all the knowledge that we crave, but is it not true that we do know all that we need to know historically about Jesus, just as we know about Socrates and about Gautama Buddha, though neither of them wrote anything himself? Even though Christianity is an historical religion, the Gospels are not in a modern sense either biographies or histories. They are not like Plutarch's *Lives* or Caesar's *Gallic War*, but are written by believers for believers with a definite spiritual purpose. Apart from the New Testament, we have only a few bare historic facts about Jesus, as when Tacitus reports, concerning the name "Christian": "The originator of that name, Christ, was executed in the reign of Tiberius by the procurator Pontius Pilate."[2] The Jewish Talmud records that "They hanged Jesus on the eve of the Passover . . . because he practised sorcery and led Israel astray."[3] The existence of a small band of Jewish and Gentile converts leads Josephus to devote a cold and patronizing sentence to the man called "Christ." An early Syriac philosopher[4]

---

[2] *Annals*, xv, 44.

[3] *Bab. Sanhedrin*, f. 43a. The Talmud says that Jesus, the Nazarene, was about thirty-three years of age when he was executed on the eve of the Passover.

[4] Letter of Marabar Sarapion in *Spicilegium Syriacum*.

points to the fact that the Jews killed "their wise King" as an historical example of the persecution of the virtuous.

Now, if, in place of such fragmentary and really insignificant references, and if instead of four brief and varying Gospels and a dozen earlier Epistles, *we had a vast volume of bare facts, including every act of Jesus and every word he ever spoke, recorded with inerrant accuracy, we believe it would not be of decisive value to us.* We must remember that even the twelve intimate companions who heard every word of Jesus and witnessed his every act in his public ministry were at the time little changed thereby, and at the first threat of danger all forsook him and fled. The Apostle Paul, on the other hand, who had never seen or heard Jesus, who had never read a single Gospel, who seldom quotes Jesus' teaching or refers to his acts, and who did not even wish to know him "by what is external," realized all that Christ came to give. This included a Christlike character, power in service which could "turn the world upside down," all that was meant by the grace of God and salvation through Christ, all that could create a new man within and a new society without. It is our conviction that what we need most today is not the priceless privilege of the early Twelve to see and know the historic Jesus, but rather the experience of Christ which transformed Saul into Paul and created the early church.

It is also our conviction, however, that we can most fully share that experience if, like the first disciples, we study "all that Jesus began by doing and teaching." This is why the Gospels rightly hold the first place in the New Testament. Through Paul's own great Epistles, through the four Gospels and by the power of the same Spirit, we also may know "in part" this same historic Jesus, and share the experience of the eternal Christ. Christianity is an historic religion based on the self-revelation of God through his redemptive acts in the Jesus of history. Hence we must begin where the first followers of Jesus began by the lakeside in Galilee. A brief study of the nature and reliability of our sources in the four Gospels should first be made before the narrative can become intelligible. Though we are compelled to relegate this material to Appendix I, it is hoped that this appendix will be read first, as without a clear grasp of the Gospels as historic documents, we cannot understand the life of Jesus.

We shall begin our study of the life of Jesus where, after a brief introduction, the Gospels of Mark and John begin, with the historic fact of the baptism of Jesus by John. And we begin at this point for the same reason that these two Gospels began there. Dr. Klausner, the Jewish writer, in his *Jesus of Nazareth*, shows that silence regarding a great man's early life was the universal custom of the Jews. They were interested in the great man's life only after he had appeared on the stage of history. It was so in the case of Moses, of the prophets, of the great Rabbi Hillel the Elder, and in the case of Jesus. The Jews, even when they became Christians, were interested in Jesus only after his meeting with John the Baptist when he went out on his mission as the Messiah. Dr. Klausner believes that Jesus was born in Nazareth in Galilee a few years before the Christian Era, that thousands and tens of thousands had joined the Zealots, especially in Galilee, "who everywhere led the riots and revolts." "There could not have been better material for a Messianic movement . . . The whole nation looked forward to the coming of the Messiah." Jesus believed himself to be the deliverer of Israel but maintained the Messianic secret until his disciples recognized him and then charged them to secrecy.

We shall study the four Gospels as critically as we would any other historic documents. We shall handle them as freely as the writers themselves dealt with each other's writings, and with their oral and written sources. They regarded these as genuine human material, freely omitting, adding to, or altering their sources without a trace of bibliolatry. The writers no more dreamed that they were writing the Bible of the human race than did the Apostle Paul. But we do not regard the Gospels merely as historic documents. They were written in the interests of faith for a religious purpose, which, however, required dealing with the life of Jesus. Since God had used historic acts to save men—in the life, death and resurrection of Jesus—they instinctively felt that the most effective preaching would be not to talk about those acts but to give a dramatic representation of them. Instead of writing an essay, formulating a philosophy or a creed, they paint a picture, sketch a portrait, or tell a story embodying these acts.

The Gospels are not abstract philosophies but a concrete way of holding up a mirror of the drama of salvation. Since we today supremely need, not meticulous information about Jesus, but salvation, as much as did the readers of the Gospels in Rome, Ephesus, or Jerusalem, we shall try to make such a fresh critical study of the records as may reveal the probable historic facts as well as their saving character, that we also may share the same deep experience which the early Christians enjoyed. Thus our attempted study of the portrait of Jesus is for no other purpose than that which inspired the writing of these imperfect but priceless Gospels and Epistles—good news! Whether writer or reader, however, anyone must pause before a task which is humanly most difficult, especially in the light of Albert Schweitzer's sober word after reviewing the lives of Christ written during more than a century from the time of Reimarus (1694-1768): "Each epoch found its reflection in Jesus; each individual created him in accordance with his own character. There is no historical task which so reveals a man's true self as the writing (or reading) of a Life of Jesus."

There are two worlds of meaning in the two names Jesus and Christ. Both are included in the title of Mark: "The beginning of the good news of Jesus, the Messiah." They suggest the two sources of Christianity, the Hebraic and the Hellenic, which combine two rich traditions, two worlds of thought. Jesus is, of course, the Greek form of the Hebrew Joshua, and Christ the Greek form of the Messiah, or the Anointed. The name Jesus represents to us the historic life of the carpenter-rabbi of Nazareth with all its human conditions and limitations. Christ, the Messiah, was the name ascribed to him in the confession of Peter and used by all the disciples after the resurrection wherein he was "declared to be the Son of God with power." In the New Testament the two names Jesus Christ thus represent to us at once the historic and the transcendent, the human and the divine, his life in time and eternity. In this volume we shall first study Jesus as a man, though this was but the first chapter of the life of Christ, the Anointed of God. In the interpretations of Paul and John we come to the life of Christ after the resurrection. In Jesus the Word had become flesh; in Christ God was manifesting himself in the acts of the apostles and in the life of his disciples from that day to the present. Our spiritual certainty is not in the historic; it is in the realm of faith and experience. Hence, as the title of this book, *A Portrait of Jesus: a Twentieth Century Interpretation of Christ* implies, we include throughout this volume a study of both Jesus and Christ, of the first century and of the twentieth.

A Portrait of Jesus

THE BEGINNING OF THE GOOD NEWS
Mark 1:1-13; Matt. 3:1-17; 4:1-11; Luke 3:1-22; 4:1-13

The beginning of the gospel of Jesus Christ (Mark 1:1).
John appeared baptizing in the desert and preaching a baptism of repentance for the remission of sins (Mark 1:4-5).
Now it was in those days that Jesus arrived from Nazareth
in Galilee and was baptized in the Jordan by John. And the
moment he rose from the water, he saw the heavens cleft and
the Spirit coming down upon him like a dove; then said a
voice from heaven, "Thou art my Son, the Beloved, in thee
is my delight." (Mark 1:9-11.)

THE OPENING WORDS OF MARK CORRECTLY DESCRIBE HIS WRITINGS
as "glad tidings" about Jesus, the Kingdom he came to establish and the salvation he achieved. From first to last this joyous
good news is the substance of the four Gospels and the significance
of Jesus' life and teaching, even when it goes through tragedy
and beyond it. Luke (3:1), characteristically, as historian, probably as the result of his personal researches, helps us to date the
appearance of John the Baptist at approximately 28 A.D.[1] The
volcanic arrival of John the Baptist in the desert, calling Israel
to an unprecedented baptism of repentance, was only a preparation for the mightier Coming One or Messiah, and it was the
occasion of Jesus' first public appearance. John was a prophet and
"more than a prophet," who shook the nation, bursting forth
four centuries after Malachi.

Two generations later, Josephus records John's powerful following and his tragic end. As an ascetic of the desert, a hermit
clad in a prophet's robe of camel's hair in the traditional likeness

[1] "The fifteenth year of the reign of Tiberius" would be about 28 A.D.;
Pontius Pilate was procurator of Judea 26-36 A.D.; Herod Antipas was tetrarch
of Galilee 4 B.C.—39 A.D.; and Philip, son of Herod the Great, reigned as
tetrarch 4 B.C.—33 A.D. See Chronological Table, Appendix III.

of Elijah (II Kings 1:8), against the dark background of the
hopeless national political situation he thunders the doom of
"coming wrath." John's flaming message is one of judgment with
the "axe already laid at the root of the trees" which are to be
"cut down and cast into the fire." He repeats the apocalyptic
hopes and fears which had been current in Judaism for more
than a century, believing apparently that the present order was
about to end and that the Great Judgment was soon to be accomplished. The long discipline of the Law and the prophets had
prepared the people for the expected apocalyptic appearance
of the eagerly awaited Messiah.

Amid many conflicting rumors, the nation was on tiptoe of
expectation. There was a common idea that the Messianic deliverance would take place in the desert as in the case of the
first exodus under Moses. Many devout Israelites were praying
for the coming of God's Kingdom. Josephus tells us of various
Messianic pretenders during the first century. In this charged
atmosphere, the nation was shaken first by John and then by
Jesus in one mighty spiritual movement.

Matthew and Luke quote the Sayings of Jesus,[2] as indicating
John's early expectation of the great judgment and the coming
of a supernatural being, hailed by contemporary Jewish apocalyptic writings. The Coming One would baptize with the Holy
Spirit and with fire, which consumes and purifies. No wonder
Luke says of John "the people's expectations were roused," and
all were wondering whether this was the Christ, the Anointed
One, whom they were eagerly awaiting. Perhaps John's expectation, widely different from that of Jesus, made him impatient
with Jesus' more spiritual and less catastrophic methods when
he asked, "Are you the one who was to come, or should we look
for someone else?" The people eagerly seized upon the more
violent and immediate apocalyptic hope: "*All* Judea and *everybody* in Jerusalem went out to him there and accepted baptism,
acknowledging their sins," including taxgatherers, soldiers, and
even Pharisees and Sadducees who were scathingly condemned
as "a brood of vipers." Nothing like this had been known under

[2] Explained in Appendix I.

the prophets. The whole nation seemed to be swept by this unprecedented movement, and even the Pharisees dared not deny
that John's baptism was from God himself.

This meant the thrilling tidings that the chosen people had
been awaiting for weary centuries. "From the days of John the
Baptist until now, the Kingdom of Heaven suffereth violence
and the violent snatch it to themselves (as they press to win
entrance into it). For all the prophets and the Law prophesied
until John; and if you will receive it this is Elijah which was to
come" (Matt. 11:12). After centuries of slumber a new prophet
had stabbed the nation awake with the message of the impending
visitation of the wrath of God. In those dark and despairing
days under the iron heel of Rome, most Jews had been driven
to think that their only hope lay in a miraculous act of God.
The coming of the Kingdom or Reign of God had become the
concern of the national and individual conscience. Men must
repent, which meant to turn from their sinful past with a complete change of mind and of viewpoint. Without utter moral
reformation the sinful people could not enter the new Messianic
era. No such powerful awakening had been known in Israel since
the great days of the heroic nationalistic Maccabees (175-135 B.C.).
The preaching of John had been not only prophetic and apocalyptic but fiercely ethical. He had been called to "make the way
ready for the Lord" like the great Prophet of the Exile.

No other great intellectual or moral movement in history began more simply than Christianity, when "Jesus came from
Nazareth of Galilee and was baptized of John." Yet the public
appearance of the Baptist marked a turning point in the history
of religion, and the baptism of Jesus marked an epoch in his own
spiritual life and vocation. The baptism of the greater by the
lesser was one of the many awkward things which Mark's naïve
integrity records. Jesus had hitherto lived quietly in his native
village. Now apparently he heard the imperative call of the inner
voice, and felt the irresistible urge to enter this national movement which was so providentially preparing his people for their
great mission. From this day, this unknown God-fearing young

mechanic was to become a "prophet like unto Moses," mighty in word and deed.

To grasp even faintly the spiritual meaning of Jesus' experience at his baptism, we must read the simple words of the Evangelists, looking within and behind their symbolic character. There was evidently an overwhelming experience of spiritual vision, symbolized by the opened heavens. Jesus felt powerfully possessed or anointed by the Spirit of God. The immediate witness was given to him within, typified or symbolized by an outer voice of God as speaking from heaven: "You are my Son, my Beloved! You are my Chosen!" And there was an unprecedented sense of vocation as God's chosen one. Mark probably rightly interpreted the experience of Jesus at his baptism as revealed to himself alone and not to the multitude. The concrete and miraculous terms of Mark's Gospel and of Luke's materialistic description of the Spirit in bodily form, must not blind us to the inner spiritual nature of this great experience. Had God audibly thundered from heaven with all these visible signs, the people with their crude expectations would have seized eagerly upon Jesus' miraculous Messiahship and would have made his spiritual work impossible. There was no clear word recorded "Thou art the Messiah." Rather there was such an overwhelming spiritual experience that it drove the young carpenter immediately into the seclusion of the desert to clarify his divine call; but the recurring doubt in the temptations, "*If* thou art the Son of God," showed that the whole experience had come to Jesus as truly man, tempted as we are, not as some superhuman heavenly being. Jesus' baptism and the temptations that immediately followed were closely related. In the baptism we have God's choice of Jesus as Messiah; in the temptation we have Jesus' choice of God as the sole object of his loyalty, that is as his King.

Isaiah and Jeremiah had felt imperatively called of God; Buddha's illumination had come to him in a moment under the sacred bo tree; Saul became Paul, a new man, on the Damascus road; Mohammed on his night of vision, in 610 A.D., felt called to his prophetic work. Though there was no hint or need of a personal conversion in Jesus' case, the profound experience at his baptism set him forever apart. The baptism was doubtless the occasion of summoning to consciousness all the spiritual forces which were hitherto latent in the soul of Jesus. Out of this overwhelming experience, *Jesus felt called to proclaim the Reign of God and to be himself the deliverer of his people*. This was the beginning of the good news of God's instant willingness to redeem Israel. Probably Jesus' sense of divine vocation or of Messiahship began now to dawn upon him, together with an overpowering and undeniable realization of God's love and nearness. Of the latter he was never afterward in doubt. Certainly he felt called for a unique work for the saving of Israel. Henceforth he walked forward unhestitatingly as the light broke upon him, in the path of God's will for his life, even when later he had to descend to the dark valley of the shadow of death. Looking back upon the event, forty to fifty years later, the Evangelists believed that Jesus was here declared to be God's chosen Messiah and thus endowed with the Spirit as the Saviour of men. Frequently the later experience of the church is read back into earlier events in the record.

Whether in the mind of Jesus or of the early church, the anointing of the Spirit in connection with the voice from heaven, may contain a reference both to the Davidic Messiah and to the Suffering Servant which were destined to be combined and united *only* in Jesus' own person and in his interpretation of his Messianic office. In the second Psalm, with its lofty idealism, the Davidic King as the Lord's Anointed is to be the ruler of the world: "Thou art my Son; this day have I begotten thee." The great Prophet of the Exile (Isa. 42:1-4) also depicts the Suffering Servant who is to bear our iniquities and by whose stripes we are to be healed:

> Here is my Servant whom I uphold,
> My chosen one, my heart's delight,
> I have endowed him with my Spirit,
> To carry true religion to the nations . . .
> He shall not be broken nor grow dim,
> till he has settled true religion upon earth.

It is probable that the church later saw in Jesus' baptism his call to be both the Messiah and the Suffering Servant who was to be crucified. Luke's conception may be paraphrased: "Thou art Messiah; I am well pleased with thee, I chose thee and now anoint thee with the Spirit." If so, the baptism was conceived as the divine call to Jesus' public ministry and to his vocation as the Messiah. Baptized in his humiliation as though a member of the sinful nation, he is the one destined to be the Lord's Anointed in glory, when God shall have declared him to be "installed as Son of God with power by the Spirit when he raised him from the dead" (Rom. 1:4).

The early church found difficulty in accepting the fact that Jesus submitted himself to John's baptism of repentance when they counted him the supreme incarnation and embodiment of perfect holiness, "without spot of sin." It seems impossible to think of Jesus as entering upon his Messianic vocation when he "had the surest moral judgment ever known upon earth," unless he was wholly unconscious of any cloud ever intervening to mar his unbroken relationship to his heavenly Father. As M. Loisy writes: "The baptism of repentance did not render guilty those who came to receive it without sin: a righteous man might avail himself of it as a means of expressing the will to live a pure life, without acknowledging sins which he had not committed." As A. E. J. Rawlinson remarks: "Our Lord, from his boyhood onwards, will have been conscious of standing in a peculiar relation towards God, and of being destined to some great vocation; as he 'increased in wisdom and stature' and grew to manhood at Nazareth, he may have been led already to conceive that it might be his destiny to be Israel's Anointed King." If he recognized John as his Elijah, he surely could not stand aloof from the national response of repentance.

It became him "in all things made like unto his brethren," as the representative of Israel, to be identified with his sinful people, he who was one day to bear their sin. With Isaiah and Daniel he is in this act confessing the sins of his people, in this which is up to this time the profoundest experience of his life.

When he accepts his Messianic vocation, he is at once tempted. All the temptations which immediately follow are concerning the meaning of the Messianic role to which he is now called. He emerges from the baptism by his Elijah with the consciousness of supreme endowment with the plentitude of spiritual authority and power. The passages which leap to his memory in Isaiah, which for him was a single whole, both of the Davidic Messianic King and the ideal Servant of the Lord, are united by the idea of spiritual anointing, which he has received immediately from God: "I have put my Spirit upon him." Here is the one passage in the Old Testament where a person could be anointed (i.e. made a "Christ") with an unction not of oil but of the Holy Spirit. This experience of his is to be repeated for his disciples at Pentecost when they too are to receive their anointing of power.

If the Son of David was also the Suffering Servant, then all Davidic military and political associations must fall away as impossible, and Jesus perhaps even now begins to see in bold outline and to enter upon his exclusively spiritual and sacrificial vocation depicted in Isaiah, chapter fifty-three. All the tempters' promises if he is the Son of God are seen to be base betrayals. The Son of Man conception of Daniel and Enoch will finally suggest to him a *future* Kingdom after the great sacrifice of the Suffering Servant. Now he is destined "to proclaim glad tidings to the poor and meek." He will shrink not only from satanic suggestion, but from all demonic or human testimony of his Davidic Messiahship which is bound to be misleading. Henceforth no one knows the Father but the Son, who is the Suffering Servant, but only after the resurrection do the disciples see the significance of the Servant passages.

2

THE TEMPTATION OF JESUS

Matt. 4:1-11; Mark 1:12-13; Luke 4:1-13

Then Jesus was led into the desert by the Spirit to be tempted by the devil. He fasted forty days and forty nights and afterwards felt hungry. So the tempter came up and said to him, "If you are God's Son, tell these stones to become loaves." He answered, "It is written, *Man is not to live on bread alone, but on every word that issues from the mouth of God.*" Then the devil conveyed him to the holy city and, placing him on the pinnacle of the temple, said to him, "If you are God's Son, throw yourself down; for it is written, *He will give his angels charge of you; they will bear you on their hands, lest you strike your foot against a stone.*" Jesus said to him, "It is written again, *You shall not tempt the Lord your God.*" Once more the devil conveyed him to an exceedingly high mountain and showed him all the realms of the world and their grandeur; he said, "I will give you all that if you will fall down and worship me." Then Jesus told him, "Begone, Satan! it is written, *You must worship the Lord your God, and serve him alone.*" At this the devil left him, and angels came up and ministered to him.

As WE FIND JESUS TRULY A MAN ON EVERY PAGE OF THE SYNOPTIC record, he must have been tempted all his life. But these temptations were of necessity condensed, focused, dramatized in the account of this special period in the wilderness in a symbolic forty days, similar to Moses' forty days on Mount Sinai and Elijah's fast of the same period. So far as they are historic, the accounts of the baptism and the temptation must have been told by Jesus himself, probably in his period of retirement with the disciples, representing the impression Jesus retained of his time of solitude. The persistence of the story of the temptations in the Christian tradition, when there was a tendency to exalt Jesus as Lord and remove him from a purely human category, goes a long way to authenticate the nucleus of the account. There is a human and universal quality in the temptations that vouches for Jesus' utter humanity. But the account as we have it is embellished in symbolic and dramatic literary form and probably colored by the ideas of the early church.

Jesus is "driven" into the wilderness, and as true man is led by the Spirit into the maelstrom of temptation. Luke reminds us that it was when Jesus was full of the Spirit that he was tempted, and after the ordeal he returns in the power of the Spirit. Even then temptation left him only "for a season." It was a Jewish conception that God tries and tests not the wicked but the righteous; for thus God proved Abraham and tested Job. And continuing temptation marks our Christian experience today. We shall find that certain passages of Scripture were dwelt upon by Jesus at various periods of his life, and at this time it was evidently the great passages in Deuteronomy, chapters six to eight, where God had led his people forty years in the wilderness that he might prove them; and he suffered them to hunger that he might make them know that man does not live by bread alone. The focus of the inner conflict was between Jesus' spiritual sense of duty and the newly awakened conviction that he was in a unique way God's Son, or his Anointed Messiah. How could a carpenter of Nazareth be the Messiah? And how could a loving Father want to destroy the nations for the political and military glory of the Jews, as portrayed in apocalyptic literature? To Jesus' clear spiritual vision these conflicting dreams of glory appear as temptations from the personalized source of evil considered as Satan, who is counted as the usurping enemy of God. Throughout his ministry there was a mightier storm and stress at work in Jesus' own soul than he ever allowed to penetrate to the surface, or was ever able to convey to his dull, unimaginative disciples. We have never even grasped his full humanity.

The later Jews had probably been influenced in their beliefs concerning evil by the dualism of the Persian religion of Zoroaster. He had taught the existence of two principles, good and evil, or light and darkness, embodied in two personal beings,

Ormazd and Ahriman—the God of evil being in eternal conflict with the God of light and goodness. Satan's rule over the
world was already a dogma in the apocalyptic of Jesus' period.
The personified principle of evil is found in other religions and
it seems to be a dramatized form of all human experience.
Gautama Buddha on the night of his great renunciation is
tempted by Mara, the spirit of evil, with the promise of universal
rule if he will abandon his plan of salvation. After his enlightenment he is assailed for seven weeks by a personal Tempter and
by lust, craving and discontent. Jesus feels that all Messianic
dreams of glory and glittering political and military promises
are of evil, and from the wilderness to Calvary, he always replies
to these temptations: "Get thee behind me; for thou mindest
not the things of God but the things of men." From this time
on, as Jesus confronts the Messianic hopes of the people, we are
struck by his reticence, reserve and rationality. He is both spiritual and supremely sane. Whenever the Messianic conviction
dawned or grew upon him, he seems to have locked it for the
time deep in his heart as a "Messianic secret" and sternly charged
Peter and the Twelve to tell no man of it. Jesus may have been
conscious of a unique spiritual experience of Sonship before he
felt the vocation of Messiahship.

Following Matthew's order in the temptations as both logical
and dramatic, we find the recurring doubt in the twice-repeated
"*if* thou art the Son of God" and the threefold use of "*if*." At
first sight, the three temptations were to the wrong use of miracle,
of magic, and of might (or worldly power). Ethically they were
an appeal to the three lusts of human nature: the lust of the
flesh, the lust of pride, and the lust for power. And all three
temptations were Messianic; they all bear on his vocation; they
are designed to undermine the relation between Jesus and God.
The Messiah must not suffer hunger for he was to feed his people in abundance; the Messiah should perform the miracles
promised in apocalyptic literature; the Messiah had been promised the rule of the nations, and his Kingdom was to extend in
blessing over the whole earth. Jesus' obedience to God is attacked in the challenge to turn stones into bread; his trust in

God in the invitation to leap from the Temple; his loyalty to God in the offer of the kingdoms of the world on conditions utterly opposed to God's will and his righteous character.

Jesus' circumstances were in direct contradiction to all these Messianic dreams. He is driven in stark fact to solitude in the desert to ask what he is to do if he is the chosen instrument for the deliverance of God's people; then in imagination he stands upon the pinnacle of the Temple whence a dramatic appearance of the Messiah would sweep the people into his train after a triumphal entry into Jerusalem; and finally Jesus is lifted up in a vision of the world, according to Luke, or he is carried in fancy to Mount Tabor which rose high above Nazareth, where in his boyhood the vision of God's great world may first have dawned upon him. According to Josephus, one could not look down from the southern pinnacle of the Temple into the precipitous depths below without turning giddy. The sovereignty not only of the Jews but of all the world had been promised to the Messiah who was to destroy God's enemies and to rule, not from Rome but from Jerusalem, the city of the Great King, whither the heathen would henceforth resort. These and a thousand glittering promises now tempted Jesus after his recent experience at his baptism.

Stated more specifically, the three temptations seem to have been:

1. To satisfy a bodily appetite wrongfully, either for himself or for his people, or to try to live by physical means alone, independently of God. Jesus is moved by his own pangs of hunger which remind him of the poverty-stricken condition of the lower classes in Palestine to use his Messianic office as a means of securing economic relief. Surely the Messiah could turn stones into bread, and if he could thus minister to the bitter need of men, what glorious results might follow if he would only meet popular expectations. But Jesus feels that he must seek no miracle that would free him from facing every problem and privation that other men must meet; he must satisfy no craving of his own body or even of the poor of the land by supernatural means, for he must fulfill the conditions imposed in Deuteronomy (8:3).

"He suffered thee to hunger . . . that he might make thee know that man doth not live by bread only but by every word that proceedeth out of the mouth of God."

2. Jesus is tempted to use Messianic powers to win political triumph. If he will but yield to popular expectation, and appeal to public favor, he may achieve a brilliant and rapid success. Surely a special calling of God would be accredited by signs. The Ninety-first Psalm promised supernatural protection to the man who dwells in communion with God, and Judaism had often applied this Psalm to the Messiah: "He will give his angels charge of you" (Ps. 91:11-12). A Jewish *midrash*, or interpretation, contained this tradition: "When King Messiah is revealed, he comes and stands upon the roof of the Holy Place; then will he announce to the Israelites and say, 'Ye poor, the time of your redemption is come.'" Many such traditions were current in Jesus' apocalyptic time, for Luke tells us of the common people: "They supposed that the Kingdom of God was *immediately* going to appear."

Throughout his ministry Jesus was brought face to face with the popular craving for Messianic signs and wonders. If Jesus had announced that the Messiah had come already, with suitable signs characteristic of God's Anointed, the nation would have burst into flame. When Israel lacked bread in the wilderness, God had mercifully supplied their need with manna; now the Galileans lacked bread. The Pharisees always demanded a sign from heaven, for "an evil and adulterous generation seeketh after a sign." Galileans, Pharisees and the early disciples all had an earthly vision of the Kingdom of God that had been aroused by the prophets and yet more by prevalent apocalyptic literature, and this had recently been intensified by the Baptist himself, so that the pressure of this temptation upon Jesus must have been acute and poignant.

3. Jesus' third temptation seems to have been to use wrong or worldly means to achieve his great end of gaining the kingdoms of the world for God. For the sovereignty of the world had been promised to the Messiah. How could the dream of the sovereignty of the world have been awakened in an artisan of

Nazareth save by a Messianic revelation and the experience of his baptism? Perhaps Jesus was tempted to utilize political means, which might be considered satanic, for the fulfillment of his Messianic office. He could not but think of the recent popular Maccabean heroes as the idols of the people, and the Zealot fanatics as superpatriots whose methods were so palpably appealing to devout Jews by the use of military force. And there were all the pagan kingdoms of the world which were founded on force. Six million Jews living in a closely knit organization were now almost the only remaining live and virile nationality in the Roman Empire. The exploits of the Maccabees had shown their courage and possibilities. Such a program would have been immediately and immensely popular. At first sight it seemed to be a challenge to a mighty faith and thousands in Israel succumbed to it. But Jesus sees that the battle of God's spiritual Kingdom must be fought only with its own weapons. If he follows the path of the gentle "meek upon earth" he will be a stumbling block to the patriots of his nation.

Power itself is the product of spirit. It never exists without an alloy of physical force, but it is always more than compulsion. The prophet and priest had been more powerful than the soldier in Jewish history. But the temptation is ever repeated to wield power for the ultimate welfare of men. Perfect goodness can be symbolized in history only by powerlessness, hence Jesus must be a Suffering Servant, not a Messianic conqueror. God alone, who is all powerful, all wise, and all loving, can perfectly combine power and goodness, so that power is not an evil of itself. But all power in history is ever in peril of becoming an instrument of injustice, as in the case of the Maccabees before Christ, of Julius and Augustus Caesar worshiped as gods, and in all dictatorships in the world today.

But in seeking to follow Jesus, we must not be Christian Pharisees, nor try to reduce Christianity to an oversimplified moralism by the literal imitation of Jesus. Vocationally, Jesus was called to be the Messiah, the Saviour of the world; we are not. He was the Christ; we are called to be Christlike in spirit, to grasp the underlying principles in these temptations and of all Jesus' life and teachings, but not to be enslaved by "the letter that killeth." For Jesus to enter politics, like the Sadducees or the Zealots, would be a betrayal of his divine mission. We, on the other hand, are not called to stand gazing into heaven waiting for his return, but we may be led by the same Spirit that drove him into the wilderness, to enter politics or the grim world of economic injustice to seek reforms. By some means the money-changers must still be driven from the Temple for they are far stronger and more ominous than in Jesus' day. We today must have "the mind of Christ," instead of being in bondage to the literal practice or imitation of the historic Jesus.

Referring to the temptations, Dr. B. S. Easton says:

> The perfect naturalness of the narrative is inimitable; exaltation on discovery of the Messianic vocation, retreat from solitude without a thought of care for the body, waning of the ecstasy, the resultant hunger and depression, which give a fit moment for the intrusion of diabolic suggestion. *And the temptations exactly summarize the ministry.* They exhibit the refusal to take thought for self, or to accede to demands for a sign, or to seek popularity through lowering the moral standard. The hypothesis of a secondary origin (in the early church) for these verses seems excluded. . . . Such a task was beyond the powers of anyone in the apostolic or post-apostolic age. The story was probably told by Christ, in conjunction with that of the baptismal experience, in the last part of the ministry.[1]

And we note that Jesus completely rejects all three temptations without compromise. *He is called only to do God's will, in God's time and way; to seek God's ends by his means alone.* To this one end he devotes his whole life. And there is "one clear call for me" to follow in his steps. It simplifies all life to know that for the rest of my life, in time or eternity, *I have nothing to do but the will of God.* All the temptations of my life will be to prevent my seeking and doing his will. They will be subtle suggestions to live the self-centered not the God-centered life. To each one of them I must say "Get thee behind me. I have come only to *do thy will, O my God.*"

[1] B. S. Easton, *The Gospel According to Luke*, p. 49; and see his excellent *The Gospel Before the Gospels*, pp. 153-162.

Stripped of their Messianic occasion and symbolic language, there is a universal human quality in these realistic temptations. Today as in the time of Jesus and in every age, men are first tempted to doubt God; then if they surmount this first temptation, they are often led to tempt God by fanatic faith, to lose their sense of humble dependence and sane moral obedience. Men are always moved to seek popular favor instead of the single will of God. They are often blinded to seek wrong ends, or else right ends by wrong means. As in the case of all three of the temptations of Jesus, we are constantly induced to take specious and impatient short cuts. But God has all the time there is and eternity as well, and we are fellow workers with him. Like Jesus, we must also suffer temptations of the body, the mind and the spirit, and be tempted in all points like as he was. And it will be found that all temptations in the end, for Jesus and for us, are aimed at an evasion of the Cross.

How did Jesus meet temptation? Three times he falls back upon Scripture, using the Word of God as the Sword of the Spirit. His feet are always on the firm ground of sane human experience or the solid rock of the Law and the prophets. Three times he meets the Tempter with these great bedrock passages in Deuteronomy which are the inspired commentary of the wanderings of the Israelites in the wilderness. The sixth chapter of Deuteronomy was especially familiar to the Jews, and the first portion of Jesus' own daily prayer was taken from the Shema (Deut. 6:4-10, 16; 8:3; Mark 12:29f).[2]

A few years ago the writer stood in a little synagogue in Naza-

[2] "Listen, Israel: The Eternal, the Eternal alone, is our God. And you must love the Eternal your God with all your mind and all your soul and all your strength. These words you must learn by heart, this charge of mine: you must impress them on your children, you must talk about them when you are sitting at home and when you are on the road, when you lie down and when you rise up. You must tie them on your hands as a memento, and wear them on your forehead as a badge; you must inscribe them on the door-posts of your houses and on your gates . . . . You must not put the Eternal your God to the proof . . . . He made you feel your need of him, he let you hunger and then fed you with manna . . . that he might make you know that man lives not only by food but by every word that comes out of the lips of the Eternal."

reth and saw a Jewish boy of twelve poring over the roll of the prophets. He thought of another boy in the synagogue of Nazareth long ago, never owning his own copy of the Scriptures, poring over the rolls of the Law, the prophets, and the Psalms. It is not necessary to insist that all quotations are the authentic words of Jesus himself, but according to the Gospel of Matthew alone, Jesus quoted in his discourses fifty-eight times from seventeen different books of the Old Covenant: some fifteen times from Isaiah, eleven from Psalms, ten from Deuteronomy, and six from Jeremiah. Throughout, his teachings are punctuated with quotations from the Psalms, the major and minor prophets whose truths were hidden away in his heart in the silent years at Nazareth.

Jesus lived and had his being in the sacred Scriptures. Their truth was daily manna to his hungry soul, as the very bread of life, as the strength and nourishment of his character. If he needed such nourishment, much more do we. If we recall the saints all down the centuries, and the characters we would like to resemble, we shall find that more of them were nourished upon the Scriptures and prayer than by any other means. As one has said, if we spend sixteen hours a day dealing with tangible things and often not five minutes a day trying to find God and adjust our lives to him, it will not be strange if the tangible things of the world will seem two hundred times as real as God is.

We might trace throughout these studies how Jesus met the recurring temptations all through his life by falling back upon the truth which makes him free, by the help of God, and by thought and prayer in times of seclusion. He never compromises or dwells upon the evil as "good to eat, delightful to see and desirable to look upon" (Gen. 3:6), but turns instantly and absolutely from temptation as "dead to sin and alive unto God." Finally by the gradual momentum of habit, though ever in utter dependence upon God, he wins one victory at a time, until even in the supreme agony he is able to say, as characteristic of his whole life, "Not my will but thine be done." The temptations show that Jesus is "one who has been tempted in every respect like ourselves, yet without sinning" (Heb. 4:15). The truth was not that Jesus was unable to sin but that he was able not to sin. He was the only reformer or religious leader who was satisfied to allow the Spirit of God to work in him unhindered by the slightest self-will. The temptations summarize Jesus' ministry. The Epistle to the Hebrews states that Christ was tempted in order that he might sympathize with those who are tempted, and that he might win for them the power to overcome temptation. His victory was not for himself but for us. As D. S. Cairns said: "For the first time in history there appeared on earth One who absolutely trusted the Unseen, who had utter confidence that Love was at the heart of things, utter confidence also in the Absolute Power of that absolute love and in the liberty of that love to help him."

3

THE GALILEAN SUNSHINE
JESUS BEGINS TO DO AND TO TEACH
Mark 1:1, 14-15; Luke 16:16

The beginning of the good news of Jesus, the Messiah . . .
After John had been arrested, Jesus went to Galilee proclaiming the glad tidings of God; he said, "The time has
now come, God's reign is near: repent and believe the good
news." . . . The Law and the prophets lasted till John;
since then the good news of the Realm of God is preached.

THESE REMARKABLE PASSAGES ARE NOT ONLY THE TEXT AND THEME
of Mark but of the three Synoptic Gospels as well. The
writers feel that this is the crisis of history; the time has come;
Jesus proclaims the dawn of the new age. No words can convey to
the prosaic contemporary in the twentieth century what this thrilling message meant to "the whole of Judea and all the people of
Jerusalem" just aroused by the Messianic expectations of John
the Baptist. "From that day Jesus began to preach, saying,
'Repent, the Reign of heaven is near'" (Matt. 4:17).

We shall find in these studies that the Kingdom of God is the
theme of the first three Gospels, of the Sermon on the Mount,
and of much of the teaching of Jesus, and that his acts whether
of preaching, forgiving sins, healing or seeking to make men
whole in body, mind, and spirit, are related to this one great
reality of the rule of God. We believe that the rationalists and
humanists of the nineteenth century who conceived of Jesus
as a benevolent teacher preaching the Fatherhood of God and
the brotherhood of man, and sowing the seed of a Kingdom
which was to develop across the centuries, misconceived and mis-
interpreted him, and that we must go back to make a fresh study
of the historic Jesus and of his conception of the Kingdom of God
both as a present spiritual reality and a future consummation.

The prophets had foretold a new age under the divine government of God. The apocalyptists who succeeded them had delineated the divine plan in successive stages of human history, artificially subdivided into ages, seasons, days and hours, subject to the government of God. Jesus in his intuitive conviction of history was what we would call a personal, moral and spiritual determinist who believed that the course of things is ordained by a living God of infinite power, wisdom, and goodness. He was now heralding the Messianic age which, as the consummation of the ages (Heb. 9:26), was to inaugurate the Kingdom of God. We shall find, however, that his view contains a sanity, and depth, and moral content far beyond the prophets and apocalyptists. He was no bigoted nationalist, no military zealot, no religious fanatic. All who will do the will of God are counted his brethren. The Kingdom is dependent not upon race but upon character, conduct and faith. It will include the outcast Samaritans and the Gentiles. For "many shall come from the East and the West and recline with Abraham, Isaac, and Jacob in the Kingdom of Heaven, but the sons of the Kingdom shall be cast forth." This is the amazing message with which Jesus appeared in Galilee, probably in the spring of the year 27 A.D., shortly before the harvest, apparently intending to make a tour of Galilee until the Feast of Tabernacles, September or October of that year.[1]

Many admit that it began to be a different kind of world from the time that Jesus proclaimed this Kingdom of Heaven. Yet they agree with many modern scholars that Jesus was essentially mistaken as to the nearness and character of the visible rule of God on earth. At the outset we are confronted with this initial difficulty. If, as Dr. Burkitt says, the overwhelming impression which Jesus made upon his followers was so creative and

---

[1] Maurice Goguel in *The Life of Jesus* thus fixes the chronological framework of Jesus' ministry: At the close of 26 A.D. or the beginning of 27, he is with John the Baptist at the Jordan. In the spring of 27 he leaves the Baptist and returns to Galilee. Here he begins his own ministry which he carries on until September of that year when he leaves Galilee and comes to Jerusalem. See Chronological Table, Appendix III.

dynamic that the religion of which his worship is the center became the creed of the civilized world, was this whole spiritual
movement founded upon a mistake? Did Jesus in proclaiming
the Kingdom die in error and Paul found the church upon a
superstition?

The results of historical criticism forbid our knowing with certainty how much of the early expectation of the Son of Man coming on the clouds of heaven to reign on earth was due to the
teaching of Jesus himself, and how much must be attributed to
the hopes and wishful thinking of the Evangelists and the writers
of the first Epistles. Jesus said he did not know the day nor the
hour, but the writer of the First Gospel, "Matthew," seems to
have more assurance when, in adding to the simple question
recorded by Mark, "When shall these things be?" (regarding the
destruction of the Temple and Jerusalem), he asks the question
which betrays his own consuming interest: "What will be sign of
your arrival and of the end of the world?" According to the more
sober and historic Mark, this was not the subject of Jesus' warning. If, however, the expectation of all the early Epistles of the
New Testament, the chief burden of the Sayings of Jesus, and
the dominant theme of the Synoptic Evangelists were the Kingdom of God and its early realization, it is difficult to believe that
all his hearers and the early writers completely misunderstood
him and that they did not derive this hope from Jesus himself.
It is highly probable, however, that his followers would not grasp
the whole of his thought, and would almost inevitably intensify
the bright hopes of the early realization of the Kingdom and of
his eagerly expected advent in the dark days of persecution that
followed his death.

The disciples had understood him to say: "Truly I tell you,
you will not have covered the cities of Israel (on this preaching
mission) before the Son of man arrives"; "I tell you truly there
are some of those standing here who will not taste death till they
see the coming of God's Reign with power"; "Then shall be
seen the Son of man coming in the clouds with great power and
glory. . . . I tell you truly, the present generation will not pass
away, till all this happens" (Matt. 10:23; Mark 9:1; 13:2, 26, 30).

As we study the record from a harmony of the Gospels, we can almost see Matthew make his natural mistake as he takes over Mark's sober account and heightens it. So doubtless did they all—and so, be it remembered, do we make our own mistakes and probably shall continue to do so. If, however, from the advantage of our historic viewpoint, we see this great problem in perspective across the centuries, *we shall find five senses in which we may view the coming of the Kingdom of God,* some of which may have been in the mind of Jesus himself:

1. *The Kingdom or rule of God was surely present in Jesus himself.* In him, after long centuries of prophecy and preparation, God's will at last was fully done. The Reign of God was not merely a future catastrophic coming on the clouds; in him it was already in their midst. If he by the finger of God casts out whatever malignant forces oppose God's rule, then in him "the Reign of God has reached you already" (Luke 11:20). In the foretaste of the spiritual triumphs of the mission of his disciples, he had seen evil overthrown and Satan, as it were, falling from heaven. Even we, far from the realization and from the vision of the triumph of God's purpose in the world, see that something happened under Tiberius and Pontius Pilate, and the civilized world rightly divides all history at this point between B.C. and A.D. Jesus absolutely accepts the yoke of the Kingdom in his own person. All life means for him the doing of God's will: "My meat is to do the will of him that sent me." He offers all men what he has tried and proved in his own experience. His call is: Follow me, take my yoke upon you and learn of me, drink my cup, be immersed in my baptism of suffering. This is the foundation of all his teaching about the Kingdom, of all his efforts to bring men into it, of all his claims that he makes upon men for their own acceptance of the yoke of the Kingdom.

All his teaching and preaching are directed to producing in his followers those qualities of trust, loyalty and obedience toward God which he himself experienced and exemplified, which are the condition of their entrance into the Kingdom. The great issue of all life is man's choice between God and some other ruler of life, for no man can serve two masters. Henceforth his followers are to say "No" to self and to seek only God's Kingdom in the doing of his will, as it is done in heaven—and in Jesus himself, where God's rule is already present. The Kingdom is present not only in Jesus; he offers it as a present possession to his followers as treasure hid and found, as a pearl beyond price that costs all that one has. To those who are poor in spirit or persecuted, "the realm of Heaven *is* theirs."

2. *Undoubtedly Jesus made a genuine offer to Israel and could say "all things are now ready."* God was instantly ready to pardon, to receive, to renew and restore his people and to achieve his spiritual reign among them. If they had "all" responded to Jesus' infinitely more searching and difficult call as they had to John the Baptist, who can doubt that the promises would have been fulfilled? Surely God was eager to pour out his promised Spirit upon all flesh. Jesus had not made unconditional prophecies; there were moral conditions to be fulfilled. It was Israel—and mankind—that failed God; it was not Jesus that failed or the purpose of God. God was eager to give; man would not receive. The Old Testament had said the Kingdom might come soon; Jesus says it is at hand now. God had always been ready to rule and to bestow his unimagined blessings, if only men had been willing. Now that a man was ready, the Kingdom could come. In the will of God the Kingdom was indeed at hand; now at last a Son of Man responded perfectly to the eternal willingness of God. The Reign of God need not tarry; it was already present potentially. Jesus' divine offer brings a crisis in history.

3. When man rejected God's offer in Christ, *God's Kingdom, in part, had to come to sinful man in judgment.* A God of holy love judges and redeems; so Christ judges and redeems. God is love but that does not mean mere sentimental benevolence. In the mystery of Calvary "now is the judgment of this world." In the clearly prophesied destruction of Jerusalem and of the Temple, when there was left not one stone upon another, we have the visitation of God. And, as truly as at the destruction of Jerusalem, so in this awful World War and its lowering aftermath, are not God's judgments once more abroad in the earth? Must not we also repent, turn again to God and cut the cancerous

growths from our civilization which had begun to rot? Those who have spiritual vision, or "eyes to see," may even now read the signs of the times as the men of Jesus' day refused to do, demanding apocalyptic portents instead of moral reformation. As long as man sins, God must come to him in judgment as well as in blessing.

4. But the primary promise of the coming of God's rule was not in temporary judgment but in blessing. *There was a symbolic or partial coming of the Reign of God at Pentecost,* in the holy remnant of prepared Israel, within Jesus' own generation of those standing there, as he had promised. There was a partial realization of the Kingdom also in the founding by his followers of the ever-imperfect church of Christ upon earth. It is as fatal to identify this imperfect church with the perfect rule of God in any ecclesiastical organization or any period of history as to identify it with any political state or economic system. None of these are or ever can become the Kingdom of God. There was also a partial and imperfect realization of the rule of God in the hearts of men, as leaven hidden, as seed growing across the silent centuries, in the church militant and triumphant. If God as a Father rejoices when one sinner repents, this invisible Kingdom must be to him a glorious and majestic spectacle. The spiritual universe must be even now, in the eyes of God, more vast and various and infinitely more sublime than is the material universe to the human telescope. But none of these partial and symbolic realizations are the final coming of the Kingdom of which Jesus primarily spoke.

5. *There is the final triumph of the rule and realm of God beyond history if not within it.* The Kingdom certainly did not come "quickly." We shall trace in the record evidences of the agonizing adjustment of Jesus to the rejection of himself as God's Suffering Servant, as we see signs of heartbreak as he wept over Jerusalem, and finally cried, "My God, my God, why hast thou forsaken me?" And we may not stand afar off as idle bystanders or cynical critics and gape upon his agony. We shall ourselves have to enter into that dark valley of the shadow, into the mystery and tragedy and heartbreak of life, darkened by man's sin—

by *our* sin. We can ask no cup of myrrh to deaden our senses, no escape from reality by glib literalism, or bibliolatry, or superstition. Each who would follow him must take up his own cross; each must die his own death to his sinful self. This is the imperative, the inescapable nature of the call of this Son of Man to our common humanity.

In the Fourth Gospel, we shall find that in one sense Christ has come already; that he that believeth *hath* eternal life now, and that each of us may pass through the portal which men miscall "death" into the larger endless life beyond. But all this individual experience of eternal life now and forever, priceless though it is, is a world removed from the mighty social hope of the full realization of the Kingdom of God and even of the Lord's Prayer: "Thy Reign begin; thy will be done *on earth*." Even heaven could offer no moral escape for God, or for us, from responsibility for this sin-stained earth. Jesus did not seek to escape it, nor may we in this here and now.

After patiently tracing and admitting all the historic "mistakes" as to those early apocalyptic visions, the full believer does not for one moment surrender his glorious hope of the final consummation of the Kingdom of God. As we humbly join the Apostle Paul at the table of the Lord's Supper with our fellow disciples, as sinful as those in Corinth, we yet celebrate our eucharist, we "proclaim the Lord's death until he comes." We do not surrender our faith in the future—no not for an hour! As we "see Jesus," we hold the sure and certain hope of the ultimate triumph of God. For the humbly thoughtful, that will not be in some visible reign in Jerusalem, nor in cruel apocalyptic vengeance. Probably it will never be fully realized in man's history, which ever bears a stain. But God who inhabiteth eternity is beyond history as well as within it. And we are children of God in time and in eternity. We today may look to God with the same unfailing faith and hope that Jesus did. We also have received a Kingdom which cannot be shaken. We also share in the final triumph and, as a little flock, expect the Father in his good pleasure to *give* us the Kingdom. Meanwhile, within history, we also, as God's fellow workers, humbly seek to build

our ever-advancing and ever-imperfect social order, more and
more like "the pattern in the Mount" which we see undimmed.
Our ever-new social planning can, at most, only symbolize and
prove a dim analogy to the reality of God's Kingdom. As realists
disillusioned by all our mistakes, and knowing full well that we
shall make many more, we yet run with patience the race that is
set before us, "our eyes fixed upon Jesus as the pioneer and perfection of faith." We look, therefore, to "this same Jesus" who
saw his hope of Israel's repentance fade, who yet steadily endured
the Cross, thinking nothing of its shame, and is now seated at
the right hand of the throne of God (Heb. 12:1-2).

It is in this perspective both of time and eternity that we admit
to ourselves every historical mistake in the record as to the day
or hour or manner of the coming of the rule of God. We too
enter the dark valley with Jesus himself. But, as we catch a
glimpse of the blinding light and the undimmed hope beyond,
we are able, by faith just as he was, to believe in his proclamation
of the Reign of God. In one sense, then and even now, it is "at
hand" and ever "near." The gate is still narrow and the road
is rough to everyone who will enter and strive henceforth to do
the will of God. Our goal is God's will, God's realm. We find in
Jesus the lost secret of life. With and beyond all historical criticism, we can take the mighty promise and proclamation of the
doing of the will of God on earth, and of the Reign of God
beyond history, at its full face value. That is why we study *his*
portrait and *his* life. Faith is the foretaste of victory for us as
it was for him.

We thus see the mystery and the reality of the Kingdom of
God. It was present in Jesus; it was genuinely offered as the rule
of God to Israel and to man; but when that offer was rejected
and God's Messiah was crucified, the Kingdom came in part in
judgment at Calvary, in the destruction of Jerusalem, in man's
sinful strife and ever-recurring wars. It was realized in part in
the experience of Pentecost, in the ever-imperfect church of sinful man, in the unseen realm of God's spiritual Kingdom throughout the world; and finally, without abandoning one jot or tittle
of the fullness of the promise, we believe that God's Kingdom

will yet be realized in part in history but fully and completely beyond history.

At the very beginning of our study, we are confronted, however, with a paradox such as we always find when the human touches the divine. Jesus was sure of the reality of the coming of the Kingdom of God, but he knew not the day nor the hour. He knew not the temporal but he was certain of the eternal. Throughout the Synoptic records, we shall find that Jesus was truly a man, *always man,* limited and subject to all the conditions of our human life. He appeared to share the world view and move in the thought world of his time and place, as taught in the little synagogue school. Apparently he believed in the traditional cosmology of a flat earth and in an earth-centered universe created in six literal days as in the creation poem of Genesis. We shall never know whether he, as well as his reporters, the Evangelists, believed with the whole Judeo-Greco-Roman world of his day in a universe of demons; but we shall find in the records what we would call today cases of epilepsy diagnosed as demon possession.

With his contemporaries apparently he believed that the one hundred and tenth Psalm was by David, when a whole roll or section of the Psalter was dedicated to David. It was a time when all laws were ascribed to Moses, almost all Psalms to David, all proverbs to Solomon, and all the later books to early heroes like Daniel or Enoch. As we have seen, apparently he believed in the early coming on the clouds of heaven of the Son of Man, if all his hearers and all the writers of the New Testament during the first century, including the Apostle Paul, so understood him. As we proceed, we must be honest with ourselves as to whether we find Jesus truly a man of the first century, and not try to make him a modern humanist, or scientist, or philosopher of the twentieth by the common practice of reading our own thoughts into Jesus. If we try to imprison him here, he will pass us by and return to his own time, for it is only there in that setting that we can understand him.

The Call of the First Disciples
Mark 1:16-20; Matt. 4:18-23; Luke 5:1-11; John 1:35-51

Now, as he passed along the sea of Galilee, he saw Simon and Simon's brother Andrew netting fish in the sea—for they were fishermen; so Jesus said to them, "Come, follow me and I will make you fish for men." At once they dropped their nets and went after him. Going on a little further he saw James the son of Zebedaeus and his brother John; they too were in their boat, mending their nets; he called them at once, and they left their father Zebedaeus in the boat with the crew, and went to follow him (Mark 1:16-20). Then he made a tour through the whole of Galilee, teaching in their synagogues, preaching the gospel of the Reign (Matt. 4:23).

DID EVER A GREAT RELIGION SPRING FROM SUCH HUMBLE beginnings? The scene is vivid, poetic, beautiful. He who has just been baptized, anointed and possessed by God for his great work, calls the first four followers who are to be the heralds of his Messianic mission. They are to proclaim with him the good news of God's Reign which is now at hand. This young carpenter-rabbi[1] begins not with prepared scribes or Pharisees, but with humble fisherfolk. He believes in the common man. He begins at the bottom a movement that is to be broad-based, universal, for a common humanity. Yet his was not a proletarian class movement; his first followers were drawn neither from the elite nor from the slums of crowded cities. They were hard-working, intelligent, skilled artisans. These hardy Galileans with their fiery independence formed the backbone of the rebel movement that shortly afterward captured and held the fashionable city

[1] Delitzsch shows that rabbis of this period frequently supported themselves by other work, believing in the dignity and duty of labor. Galilean fisherman were poor: "This fishing was not a lucrative business." Poor himself, Jesus begins with the poor.

of Tiberias. It was but an hour's walk from Nazareth to Sepphoris where in Jesus' boyhood these patriotic Galileans had
risen to throw off the Roman yoke. As a result their city had
been destroyed, the inhabitants sold into slavery, and two thousand men had been nailed to wooden crosses outside of Jerusalem.
That was the stuff of which these Galileans were made.

Jesus himself described two of the fishers he called that day as
"sons of tumult" who would have called down fire from heaven
upon opponents who withstood them. As they left John to follow
Jesus, they could probably conceive but the barest fraction of
Jesus' purpose or of their own destiny. Yet these four were a type
of all who were to follow them. If a Christian is one who responds
to all the meanings he finds increasingly in Christ, these men
were honestly taking the first steps in an endless journey as
genuine disciples or learners of Jesus. Yet even these were prepared men, two of them having apparently been followers of
John the Baptist (John 1:35-40). This had not been their first
meeting with Jesus, but rather the first call to leave their occu-
pation and cast in their lot with Jesus' inner group who were
to proclaim the Messianic Kingdom. Jesus saw deeper possibilities in their lives than they had ever dreamed for themselves.
He saw that they were capable of becoming leaders and winners
of men.

At the first glimpse of the presence of God's power and holiness in Jesus, Peter impulsively cried out "Lord, leave me; I am a
sinful, an unworthy man." As doubtless in the case of all four
young men, for crude, honest, blundering Peter this was a moral
crisis in his awakening soul. Jesus must have made a powerful
and compelling impression to have men so irresistibly convinced
of his holiness and of their sin, of his fullness and their deep
need, that they would leave all to follow him. We shall find that
the whole record bears increasing witness to the extraordinary
psychic and moral influence of Jesus' personality. Doubtless quite
a period of time and many meetings are telescoped into Mark's
dramatic "straightway." Thirty-five times in his sixteen brief
chapters, Mark characteristically uses this impatient word as,
like a Roman soldier, he marches straight to his goal of Jesus'

Messianic good news in his swift narrative. But every page of the record shows how Jesus' transcendent qualities of mind and spirit constantly awakened in his followers a growing realization of the presence of God in life, at first in his life and in time in theirs also. We are sure that Jesus never left Peter as he asked him to do, and doubtless Peter has been following him ever since. All unconsciously in his heart there had begun a process of the reintegration of his personality round a new center. Simply and spontaneously Jesus had begun the spiritual education or re-education of Simon.

It is not lightly or casually that Jesus has chosen these men. He studies them, he weighs them, he tests and selects them one by one: "Man lumps his kind in the mass, God singles them unit by unit." Then as a group, after a long night in prayer, he calls them that they might be with him and that he might send them forth to preach, to proclaim God's coming Kingdom (Mark 3:13-15; Matt. 10:5-7). He will walk and talk with these rough men day by day, win their faith and friendship, bear with their heavy ignorance and human weakness, and slowly lead them on. Beholding Jesus they will be, at long last, changed into his likeness. Slowly—so slowly that their growth will always be imperceptible to themselves and even discouraging—but just as surely, their characters will be changed. For the disciple shall be as his Lord, for he is foreordained to bear his likeness. It will be an interesting character study to trace the growth of impulsive, blundering Peter. We shall find him, and these first four followers, a type of the ultimate transformation in character development for a multitude of men all down the centuries. And in watching Jesus at work upon Peter, we shall be studying not only Jesus and Simon but ourselves. By this Galilean lakeside we are in the very school of life.

The Galilean scene is simple, natural, yet touched with lyric beauty. These men are not pale scholars, chosen from cloistered monastery or Essene community; they are in the open sunshine of nature and the common life of man. From beginning to end we shall find this Man dealing not primarily with professional rabbis, priests, or clergy, nor with religion as a thing apart, but

with life itself. He challenges, he enters, he deals with every walk
of life, to lift each task to a high calling as a spiritual vocation.

Quite simply and naturally, as any other man, we shall find
Jesus following God's providential leading as to the time and
place and manner of his public ministry. The hour for its initia-
tion was indicated by the arrest of John the Baptist by Herod
Antipas. Jesus now began where John had left off. He could not
previously join the Baptist in his completely different mission;
neither could he compete with him while his work was unfinished.
Jesus had apparently made contact with several of John's prepared disciples and went with them from the wilderness to their
homes in Capernaum. He had begun choosing his disciples one
by one and two by two. The sacred number of twelve was probably connected with eschatological expectations, corresponding
to the twelve tribes of Israel. While the ascetic Baptist had sought
the wilderness for his message of judgment, Jesus, characteristically, entered the populous towns and synagogues, as his great
Apostle was to enter the cities of the Empire. Though the teaching function had fallen into the hands of professional scribes,
Jesus chose untutored common fishermen, and spoke with authority to the heart of men. And, again providentially, he began
his public work in the strategic center of Capernaum, not in
the little isolated hamlet of Nazareth, where he was prejudicially
known as a carpenter.

The beauty of this Lake of Tiberias, or Sea of Galilee, eight
by thirteen miles in extent, is proverbial, and the profusion of
bright wild flowers in Galilee resembles those of Switzerland.
This lake in Jesus' day was surrounded by nine populous cities
of some fifteen thousand inhabitants each. Capernaum lay on
the great trade route to Damascus, being a garrison town and
the seat of customs in a thriving community throbbing with life.
The principal scene of Jesus' short activity was the northwestern
shore of this populous lakeside. Jesus lived in the home of Simon
and Andrew, and Capernaum became for the time "his own
city." From here he conducted his preaching tours through the
synagogues and towns of Galilee until he was driven from them
to the open hillsides. Here the multitude thronged about him

to hear his good news, and here he taught them, sitting in Simon's fishing boat near the shore.

Thus, with incredible simplicity, Jesus "began to do and to teach" with four, with twelve, and then among his multiplying followers, until, across the centuries, seen and unseen, they become a great multitude which no man can number. And we shall find that in the same way he still enters human lives; he calls men wherever he finds them as he begins or continues their spiritual education. Not many like the first four, "straightway" leave all to follow him. Not many become visibly apostles or religious leaders; not all are found in orthodox ecclesiastical bodies; for "other sheep" he has in other folds, neither Jewish, nor Christian, nor always even consciously religious. Yet his influence, like leaven, tends to permeate the whole of life.

The call to leave all and join his heroic group will in the end lead to death and martyrdom. If they proclaim the Kingdom with him they will not have where to lay their heads and there will not be time to bury their dead. Jesus, resembling Garibaldi, says in substance to his little heroic band: "I promise you forced marches, short rations, bloody battles, wounds, imprisonment and death—let him who loves home and fatherland follow me." These men were to be not only disciples or learners but to be "apostles," delegates who spoke by his authority and who were to be invested with his power. What must have been his faith in man and man's potentialities to begin with these crude fishermen the founding of an eternal spiritual Kingdom and the Christianizing of the world!

We cannot trace even briefly the growing influence of Jesus upon Peter, or his unobserved entrance into other lives, not only in the New Testament but across the centuries and in world literature. In a strange way men find in him both the ideal and the real. He seems to become the universal Jesus. It is true that men read their own best thoughts into him, but they also find in him their own unattained and undreamed best. As in an individual and different way he meets the need of his multiplying disciples, each finds in him the answer both to his deepest need and highest aspiration. He has meaning for prophets, for poets and for common men from the first century to the twentieth.

To Augustine, Jesus Christ became both a liberator from enslaving lust and the Lord of Thought; to Dante he was the glorified Redeemer; to Savonarola, he was the ruler of cities and communities in the godless Renaissance; to William Blake he was the incarnation of that divine energy ever creating life and beauty and fellowship, not only in Jerusalem but "in England's green and pleasant land"; to Francis Thompson, even in the slums he was the Hound of Heaven, the ever-present Lover who would not let him go; to John Ruskin, Jesus was the living Master who puts men to work and sustains them while they labor.

Browning could say of Jesus as the supreme manifestation of divine Love:

> Believe in me
> Who lived and died, yet essentially
> Am Lord of Life.
> I say, the acknowledgment of God in Christ
> Accepted by thy reason, solves for thee
> All questions in the earth and out of it.

Tennyson found in Jesus "truth embodied in a tale," "the creed of creeds in loveliness of perfect deeds." In prose he said: "I am always amazed when I read the New Testament at the splendor of Christ's purity and holiness, and at his infinite pity." Not all his unanswered questions were solved but, as a contemporary of Darwin, Huxley and Spencer, he fought his doubts and gathered strength, believing that "Christianity with its divine morality, but without the central figure of Christ the Son of Man, would become cold." Though nature seemed to him "red in tooth and claw," he still could say, "Yet I doubt not through the ages one increasing purpose runs." And in the end:

> For tho' from out the bourne of Time and Place
> The flood may bear me far,
> I hope to see my Pilot face to face
> When I have crost the bar.

The work which this carpenter of Nazareth began at that lakeside among Galilean fishermen has never ended. Rather it has become the midstream of spiritual history:

> That God, which ever lives and loves,
> One God, one law, one element,
> And one far-off divine event
> To which the whole creation moves.

We should like to place in evidence a thousand *Gesta Christi*, or triumphs of Christ, but space will confine us to one modern example, the last of many which accidentally have come to the writer's attention. Sir Gordon Guggisberg, a Canadian of Swiss descent, was considered by many to be the handsomest man in the British Army. He represented the Army in cricket and was chosen to play for all England in Association football. He was a keen soldier, a brigadier general, but like all men he had to learn that he was a sinner and he was finally divorced by his wife for unfaithfulness. At the outbreak of the first World War, suffering in a London hospital from a fractured skull, he exercised secretly each night in great agony in order to regain his strength and enter the war.

His first war work was that of camp commandant. Daily he shaved before his mirror, which bore a card with the motto: "For God, for King, for Country." He said: "God meant nothing to me, the King meant a bit, the country everything." After the war he became governor of the Gold Coast in Africa. A living witness for Christ, the bravest man the writer ever knew in the first World War, said to him: "You love your country because you have served it all your life; you have taken every opportunity of seeing the King; but you have never sought or even wished seriously to know God." When Guggisberg asked how one could know him his friend replied: "Some of us believe that Jesus of Nazareth knew more of God than any other man, so we put aside some time each morning to study his thought of God, and to let his Father speak to us, which he will do if Jesus told us the truth about him." Guggisberg replied: "Damn it! I'll try it. It's worth it if it's true." Six months later, he was a great Christian, and he gave his entire life to the service of the Africans whom he loved, and whom he counted a noble people with tremendous possibilities.

Guggisberg called A. G. Fraser of Oxford to found a system of higher education for the colony under a democratic commission, chiefly of Africans. Some of the graduates as scholars at Oxford and Edinburgh outstripped many of their British and American contemporaries. Guggisberg formed the most liberal constitution for the Gold Coast and became the most progressive and devoted governor in all Africa.

When Guggisberg asked the saintly Charlie Andrews to lunch with him at the exclusive Army and Navy Club in London, the doorman kept Andrews waiting outside as a "tramp," for in his voluntary poverty, like that of St. Francis, he was poorly dressed. But Sir Gordon introduced him to all the admirals, generals, and governors as they passed his table, and looking after him as Andrews left, he said: "I feel as though I had been honored to give luncheon to my Lord."

Brigadier General, Sir Gordon Guggisberg, K.C.M.G., D.S.O., laid down his life in the service of Christ. He died poor because he had given all his possessions to aid the Africans to whom he was devoted, who in turn had elected him to the highest rank of their own ruling chiefs. This man is typical of a great host of men across the centuries whose lives have been changed. Just as Jesus summoned the first four disciples by the lakeside in Galilee, Christ ever since has been calling men, even as he calls us today: "Come, follow me and I will make you"—fishers of men, and much more, for it doth not yet appear what we shall be.

A Typical Day in Capernaum

Mark 1:21-45; Matt. 8:2-4, 14-17; Luke 4:31-44; 5:12-16

They then entered Capernaum. As soon as the sabbath came, he began to teach in the synagogue; and people were astounded at his teaching, for he taught them like an authority, not like the scribes (Mark 1:21-23). On leaving the synagogue they went straight to the house of Simon and Andrew, accompanied by James and John. Simon's mother-in-law was in bed with fever, so they told him at once about her; he went up to her and taking her hand made her rise; the fever left her at once, and she ministered to them. When evening came, when the sun set, they brought him all who were ill or possessed by demons—indeed the whole town was gathered at the door—and he cured many who were ill with various diseases, and cast out many demons; but as the demons knew him, he would not let them say anything. In the early morning, long before daylight, he got up and went away out to a lonely spot. He was praying there when Simon and his companions hunted him out and discovered him; they told him, "Everybody is looking for you," but he said to them, "Let us go somewhere else, to the adjoining country-towns, so that I may preach there as well; that is why I came out here." And he went preaching in their synagogues throughout the whole of Galilee, casting out demons (Mark 1:29-39).

THE VIVID DESCRIPTION OF THIS TYPICAL DAY IN JESUS' BUSY LIFE in Capernaum is characteristic of the first three Gospels which are "a succession of pictures in which a painter represents a complete history. . . . They tell their story by pictures, and they are themselves a series of portraits exhibiting their great subject in so many different aspects. Mark's Gospel is the ground sketch." We may compare this day in the life of Jesus with a day in the life of any other man. On this typical day, the Evangelists tell of Jesus' ministry of teaching in the synagogue, the interruption of a man mentally deranged, the story of Simon's sick mother-in-law, and finally of "all that were sick" in the town who were laid at his feet. At sunset, at the end of the Sabbath, it was now legal to bring their broken, diseased or deformed in body, mind, and spirit to this new prophet and healer, whose fame had already begun to spread like wildfire throughout Galilee. The enthusiasm in Capernaum is in contrast to the rejection in Nazareth.

After the loss of the Temple the synagogue had become the center of Jewish life, where services were held each Sabbath morning and afternoon, on festival days and certain weekdays. There on weekdays children were taught to read and understand the Scriptures; and there or at home Jesus himself had probably learned to read. Here also local law courts were held; for the synagogue was a lay institution and preachers were mostly laymen, as Jesus was. Jesus began in the synagogues and taught there until he was expelled. His preaching was not prophetic, beginning with "Thus saith the Lord," but rather Messianic: "It was said of old time . . . but I say unto you." His was a new inner authority and moral certainty. And Jesus' word was incarnated in deed for he made men whole. The synagogue was the strategic center where Jesus could proclaim his message of the Kingdom. He spoke, however, with the immediate and compelling authority of one who knew God fully and not like the hairsplitting scribes with their dry-as-dust quotations from differing "authorities."

His one message throughout the synagogues of Galilee was to prepare the nation by preaching "the good tidings of the Kingdom of God." It was therefore a painful and tragic intrusion when a psychopathic subject, a member of that numerous class suffering from insanity, epilepsy, hysteria or other mental derangements, shrieked out, hailing Jesus as the Messiah: "Jesus, what business have you with us? You are God's holy one." Luke here freely copies and amends Mark who has a fondness for demon and marvel. Matthew omits the incident and will never record a demoniac's confession of the Messiah, while the Fourth Gospel with obvious aversion records no instance of demon expulsion. At every point we thus see the natural human differences among the four Gospels and the freedom with which the Evangelists handled their materials. Mark, whose text was "The beginning of the good news of Jesus, the Messiah," records the unveiling of the secret of Jesus' Messiahship in the following order: (1) to Jesus himself at his baptism; (2) to the insane, as at Capernaum in Peter's earliest record: (3) to Peter at Caesarea Philippi; (4) to Peter, James and John when he was transfigured; (5) to all the prepared disciples; (6) Symbolically, to the initiated at his triumphal entry into Jerusalem; (7) and finally before the rulers in the Sanhedrin as the Christ, the Son of the Blessed One (15:2).

Unlike the Old Testament, the later Jews, influenced by Babylonian and Persian dualistic ideas, together with all the surrounding Syrian, Egyptian and other Hellenistic peoples—just as in China and India today—believed that the world was filled with myriads of disembodied spirits or demons, all under the leadership of the Prince of Evil, Beelzebub, or Satan. Demons were believed to cause plagues, diseases, accidents, and temptation to sin. This sufferer from what we would probably call hysteria or some form of insanity, under the influence of Jesus' compelling personality and of the mass psychology of the crowd, interrupts the whole service and cries out in agony. That Jesus did cure such mental cases whether by natural or supernatural means is one of the best attested facts in history. His enemies admitted the indisputable facts, but claimed that he performed these cures by Beelzebub, while the Talmud states that they were performed through the practice of magic, or exorcism. We find such phenomena not only in the scriptures but in nearly all ancient literature.

On the first Sabbath of Jesus' public ministry in Capernaum, as soon as they returned from the synagogue to Jesus' new home in the house of Peter, they told him that Simon's mother-in-law had what we would call a high temperature, perhaps from the prevalent malaria with which the region was infected. When Jesus raised her up, the news spread in this oriental town, where nothing was private, until at the first moment permitted by the

Law, the populace came pouring out to his door, bringing to
him their sick and afflicted. The Jewish Sabbath ended at sun-
down and the first day of the next week had now begun. All
day Jesus had been proclaiming his all-important message; but
they still had left one brief crowded sunset hour for the healing
of their ills. Mark says they brought all that were sick and he
healed many; the later Matthew says *many* were possessed and
he healed *all*; while Luke adds that he cured "every one." This
is typical of the developing tradition, oral and written, in these
free human documents. The Evangelists were not attempting to
write an inerrant Bible but faithfully trying to record an oral
tradition in the greatest human book of all time.

This narrative raises the whole question of the healing miracles
of Jesus. Whatever the explanation, nothing is plainer or better
attested than that healings commonly occurred. That does not
mean that we would accept the diagnosis or explanation of a
cure recorded by an Oriental of the first century who had never
heard of the laws of nature nor dreamed of medical science.
Oriental countries and ancient times had an obvious leaning
toward the miraculous and the demonic, while the modern mind
has an equally strong antipathy to these things. A growing
body of accurate knowledge of the close relation between mental
and bodily states, however, and of the power of individual and
mass suggestion may furnish us with a hopeful approach to the
understanding of these records.

In the earliest Sayings of Jesus, he condemns the basing of
faith in him upon miracles. He protests that only an evil and
adulterous generation, unfaithful to God, demands signs and
wonders as the ground of their faith. He says that the Ninevites
were converted not by miracles but by Jonah's prophetic preaching. The Queen of Sheba was won by the wisdom of Solomon,
not by miracles; but in the Son of Man they were confronting
One who was greater than Jonah or Solomon. Yet if men would
not hear Moses and the prophets, neither would they be persuaded
if one rose from the dead; for faith implied not magic but moral
discernment. Jesus repeatedly tried to escape the notoriety of his
reputation as a healer, charging the persons who had been

healed by faith to be silent on the subject of their cure. Thus he was far in advance of his generation in his attitude on these matters. When the Fourth Gospel makes the claim that miracles are signs of the Messianic office, it reflects the belief of the primitive church of the second century. Though many of the healings recorded are undoubtedly historical, they are always kept in a subordinate place by Jesus himself, who in this matter seems nearer to our own day than to his.

Alan Richardson in *The Miracle-Stories of the Gospels* shows that these phenomena can only be understood against the theological background of the New Testament Evangelists. To them God is always the personal, active, overruling, living God. He is the source of all power and ultimate purpose in nature and history. His omnipotence could of course work miracles or do anything. We moderns, on the other hand, have such a sense of law and order, of the uniformity of nature and of second causes, that the materialistic, the mechanistic and scientific aspects of the universe are obvious and imperative, while the spiritual and the divine often seem dim and unreal. To the modern Christian, under the primacy of the spiritual, both should be real. The background of the Old Testament is the miracle of the Red Sea and the Exodus with its symbol of the Passover; while that of the New Testament is the resurrection with the sacrament of the eucharist, "Christ our Passover," as the symbol of God's working in history for our salvation.

While Jesus protested against the demand for signs to the spiritually blind, and against being a mere wonder-worker, he believed that his making men whole was God's manifestation of the Messianic powers of the age to come. If he by the finger of God made men whole, then the Kingdom had come upon them. He said the Spirit of the Lord was upon him for the recovering of sight to the blind and to set at liberty them that are bruised. To John the Baptist he sent word of what his followers heard and saw: "The blind see, the lame walk, lepers are cleansed, the deaf hear, and the dead are raised," both spiritually and physically, as the signs of the new age of the Kingdom for those who had eyes to see (Matt. 11:4-6; Luke 4:18; 7:22; Isa. 61:1).

The Evangelists preach the miracle stories as good news, as truth embodied in a tale. The healing of the centurion's servant is the gospel in action to the God-fearing Gentiles and Jesus' healing of the Syrophoenician woman is "the promise of the Children's Bread to the Gentiles" (Matt. 8:5-13; Mark 7:24-30). The stilling of the tempest is a sermon on Christ the Lord of the winds and waves; the barren fig tree is barren Israel; the feeding of the multitude is not giving them a miraculous meal but sacramentally making Christ known in the breaking of bread. All the miracles are preached and recorded by the Evangelists not as opaque facts but to try to tell us who Jesus is. As to which miracles really happened and how they occurred, the individual must give the answer. The scientific historian may help us to find the plain facts, but faith must discover the luminous truth. Not for the credulous but for the believer Jesus came, and for the believer Christ lives. Believing, he will discover in his own experience "who he is." He is not only the Jesus of history but the Christ of faith.

Sir William Osler gave little medicine but seemed to arouse the forces of the patient's inner life for physical recovery, to the limits of the natural. Jesus used spiritual means alone by stirring all the forces of the inner life and arousing faith to attain the limits of the possible. To Jesus and his followers the universe was plastic, and there was available all the power of the living God who was not limited by man's knowledge or experience. God was not enslaved by man's imperfect understanding of his "laws." Whether they were natural or supernatural, the disciples and Evangelists were sure of Jesus' wonderful words and works. The interpretation of both might differ in the first century or the twentieth. It may be, for instance, that after Jesus had restored an insane man to sanity, a herd of swine rushed over a cliff, but we are not obliged to accept the interpretation of the disciples that demons caused the destruction of the swine. The Gospels may faithfully record both the fact and the mistaken interpretation of Jesus' followers, but we need not credit Jesus with this interpretation. Here the tool of historical criticism is our invaluable aid, as it is constantly for a truer understanding of the historic Jesus.

Not only modern medicine but every vital religion has its cures that actually take place. We have not yet learned the limits of the power of suggestion and autosuggestion. From the shrine of Aesculapius, the god of medicine in Greece, and from the temples of India to the innumerable cures recorded on pilgrimages to the "Holy Coat" of Treves,[1] or pictured in the medieval stained glass of Canterbury, or at Lourdes as witnessed by scientists like Dr. Alexis Carrel, or in the contemporary experience of Christian Science healing, we have an unbroken record of such cures. Multitudes have testified and thousands of witnesses have confirmed the evidence of such an experience of healing. In a law-abiding universe, however, we usually attribute to natural causes what was once counted miraculous. We can never be certain from our record exactly what took place at Capernaum, for the best first century eyewitness, which for Mark's narrative was probably Simon Peter himself, would probably omit the features essential for a modern understanding of a case. But how do we know what was or was not possible in the presence of the personality of Jesus? Here was an incalculable divine power. Jesus' mighty works were not necessarily a breach of the natural order, they were perhaps a manifestation of a higher order.

In the Christian sense, we understand by a miracle, not a violation of the laws of nature—for the event may have a natural or rational explanation—but an occasional evidence of direct divine power in a striking act which points to the goodness of God. Primitive peoples with no sense of natural law or cosmic

[1] The record of this shrine of the oldest Christian church in northern Europe is notable. For instance, according to the testimony of German physicians in 1891, the sight of this relic viewed with deep emotion and quickening faith effected in eleven certified cases cures that were medically inexplicable, including atrophy of the optic nerve, lupus, paralysis of the arm, complete loss of the use of the arms and legs, St. Vitus's dance, a serious abdominal complaint, blindness, chronic intestinal disorder, cancer, caries of the spine, and chronic inflammation of the spinal marrow. Such cases, both ancient and modern, could be multiplied indefinitely.

order would account all electric phenomena or the triumphs of modern medicine as miraculous. Albert Schweitzer tells his simple patients in Africa that Jesus heals them. Jesus' words and deeds seemed equally divine and marvelous to his contemporaries, for both seemed to be of God; and he himself ascribes them both to his Father in heaven. Jesus himself seemed to be the great miracle. His person was always more impressive than his deeds. Unlike Gautama, he was not laboring toward self-attained perfection, but letting God wholly possess him and pour through him the divine life into man's abysmal need and emptiness. Both his works and words are in harmony with his personality and with God. They seem but the natural expression of his compassion and of his character.

Matthew Arnold, as a typical humanist and rationalist, makes the dogmatic declaration: "Miracles do not happen." Indeed they do not happen to "the wise and prudent," but Jesus "thrilled with joy in the holy Spirit" as he realized that God reveals his spiritual power "to the simple minded" (Luke 10:21-24). The laws and the conditions of this eternal spiritual realm are doubtless the same yesterday, today, and forever. Jesus knew them spiritually; some of us are just beginning to learn them. Jesus must still marvel at our unbelief which will permit God to do no mighty work and still hinders his rule.

The several nature miracles in the Synoptic Gospels are in a class by themselves, and must be critically examined and appraised. No breach in the order of nature is necessarily involved in any of them. For instance, when the disciples found Jesus asleep, in perfect peace during the tempest, and when he urged supreme faith in the moment of danger, his "Peace, be still!" may have been directed to their troubled hearts rather than to the sea. When the storm seemed to subside abruptly, as the storms on the Sea of Galilee often do, the incident might easily have become a legend, embedded first in the oral and later in the written tradition. So some of the seeming miracles might be naturally accounted for. But Jesus' deeds of mercy can never be explained away so as to deny or ignore the mighty works of healing by which he made men whole, and by which Christ continues to do so among believers in multitudes of cases. The leper whom Jesus is said to have healed (Mark 1:40-45) is the obvious type of the moral leper of sinful humanity, who in the presence of this man cries in his desperate need, "If thou wilt, thou canst make me clean." Man's challenging faith evokes the response of the divine "I will, be thou made clean." The leprosy of the Bible, however, which included various skin diseases that made one ceremonially unclean, was apparently curable and was different from modern leprosy which was known in Egypt from 1550 B.C. and in India from 1400 B.C. to the present.

The story of Jesus' compassionate touch moved St. Francis to kiss the loathed leper in his day, and has led to the founding of modern leper asylums throughout the world. As the distinguished Jewish scholar, Dr. Montefiore, says of Jesus' works of mercy:

> Here we begin to catch the new note in the ministry of Jesus; his intense compassion for the outcast, the sufferer, who by his sin or by his suffering, which was too often regarded as the result of sin, had put himself outside respectable Jewish society, who found himself rejected and despised of men, and believed himself rejected and despised by God. Here was a new and lofty note, a new and exquisite manifestation of the very pity and love which the prophets had demanded.

We can never prove what happened to that leper in Galilee, but, what is more important, we can validate the fact that across the centuries, countless moral lepers have been led to seek his compassion and have been made pure. Whether the means are natural or supernatural, human or divine; whether the malady is physical or spiritual, Jesus consistently reveals that God is ever ready to reassert his rule over sinful and sick humanity which had become estranged from him. And the great means by which this divine fullness enters man's emptiness has been human faith in immediate contact with this Man of Galilee, of whom we see a vivid picture on this typical day in Capernaum.

> In the early morning, long before daylight, he got up and went away out to a lonely spot. He was praying there when Simon and his companions hunted him out and discovered him; they told him, "Everybody is looking for you," (Mark

1:35-38). He answered them, "I must preach the glad news of the Reign of God to the other towns as well, for that is what I was sent to do." So he went preaching through the synagogues of Judaea (Luke 4:43-44).

The strain of the long day in Capernaum, when the whole town poured out with all its woes and chronic ills had been terrific, and Jesus doubtless felt the deep need of renewal for his whole being. There was also the pressing problem of his possible diversion from his real purpose of proclaiming and preparing for the coming Kingdom to become a mere wonder-worker or healer of men's bodies. So in the dark before the dawn Jesus goes out to a solitary place for prayer, for spiritual re-creation and for redirection in his mission. Following his forty days in the wilderness, despite the incompleteness of our record, we shall trace these special periods for prayer all through his life, even to whole nights in prayer. These periods enabled him to draw every breath in unbroken fellowship with the Father, and to abandon himself in his service of preaching and healing, without for a moment losing touch with God.

Simon hastens to seek him out, saying on finding him: "*Everybody* is looking for you." The whole town will now be at his feet, and a wave of popularity might lift his whole mission on a tide of triumph. But this is only a reappearance of his temptations to yield to popular demand, to give the people bread, and to minister primarily to men's superficial physical needs. He always recognizes the primacy of the spiritual and sees the depths of need in man's sin-sick soul. Jesus consistently sets his face toward his one work of proclaiming the good news of the approaching Reign of God: "I *must* preach the glad tidings of the Reign of God—everywhere—for that is what I have been sent to do." After this typical day in Capernaum he must now press on through other towns in his tour of Galilee in the human hope of Israel's acceptance of God's visitation. "And he was followed by great crowds from Galilee and Decapolis and Jerusalem and Judea and from across Jordan."

4

GROWING OPPOSITION

Mark 2:16-28; 3:1-6; Matt. 9:2-17; 12:1-14; Luke 5:17-39; 6:1-11

When some scribes of the Pharisees saw he was eating with sinners and taxgatherers, they said to his disciples, "Why does he eat and drink with taxgatherers and sinners?" On hearing this, Jesus said to them, "Those who are strong have no need of a doctor, but those who are ill: I have not come to call just men but sinners." As the disciples of John and of the Pharisees were observing a fast, people came and asked him, "Why do John's disciples and the disciples of the Pharisees fast, and your disciples do not fast?" Jesus said to them, "Can friends at a wedding fast while the bridegroom is beside them? As long as they have the bridegroom beside them they cannot fast. A time will come when the bridegroom is taken from them; then they will fast, on that day. No one stitches a piece of undressed cloth on an old coat, otherwise the patch breaks away, the new from the old, and the tear is made worse: no one pours fresh wine into old wineskins, otherwise the wine will burst the wineskins, and both wine and wineskins are ruined." Now it happened that he was passing through the cornfields on the sabbath, and as the disciples made their way through, they began to pull the ears of corn. The Pharisees said to him, "Look at what they are doing on the sabbath!" (Mark 2:16-24.) And he said to them, "The sabbath was made for man, not man for the sabbath: so that the Son of man is Lord even over the sabbath." (Mark 2:27-28.)

THE HISTORICAL MARK CLEARLY DIVIDES THE TWO PERIODS OF Jesus' Galilean ministry. They are indicated by the present division of his first two chapters. The first records success and popularity among the common people; the second reveals growing opposition from the religious and secular rulers and leaders. In the first period Jesus begins preaching in the synagogues of Galilee, acclaimed by a multitude who heard him gladly upon every possible occasion. He then chooses an inner group who leave all to follow him in his Messianic mission. The representatives of orthodox Judaism, however, could not approve of an outsider who claimed to speak with immediate authority greater than any prophet, or even than Moses himself. Their jealousy was aroused by his immense popularity, by his mighty works of healing, and by the fervid devotion of his loyal followers. Not only were the Pharisees moved to send down a deputation from Jerusalem, but soon Herod and the secular authorities were alarmed as well.

When Jesus is practically driven from Galilee, he concentrates on training the Twelve and the inner group to carry on his eternal work. His divine Messianic mission drives him throughout his brief career, and he finally sets his face toward his dark fate in Jerusalem. When the clouds gather, it seems as if everyone were turning against him. Even John the Baptist asks what is the matter, whether he is the Coming One or must they look for another who will more violently and suddenly fulfill John's prophecies. His own family count him mad and try to take him home. The religious leaders of all parties not only oppose him but finally unite to have him put to death. Later he pronounces his woes against the very cities which had first received him, and in the end he weeps over Jerusalem. He arraigns the men of his generation who are childish and fickle, who complain of John as having a devil and of himself as a glutton and a drinker of wine.

Mark in this second chapter in a few bold strokes shows the four causes of the swiftly developing opposition to Jesus in five typical cases:

1. Jesus is bitterly criticized by his shocked opponents because of his free forgiveness of sins. This forgiveness is wholly apart from the fulfillment of legal conditions. It is as free as the grace of God, without sacrifice or ceremonial, without authority of Temple or synagogue, without benefit of priest or scribe. His enemies feared that if this dangerous practice and preaching should continue, it might destroy all their privileges under the Law, all exclusive barriers, all middle walls of partition. It

might give almost blasphemous license to throw wide open to all men the way of immediate access to God. Jesus appeared to be usurping the right of divine forgiveness wholly apart from all the sacrificial requirements of the Law.

2. Jesus is despised and hated for his free association with sinners and common folk, with the loathed tax collectors of the Romans, and even with women of the street and other notorious characters. If this should continue, it might threaten all values and the sacred privileges of class, caste, race, rank, and institutional religion—almost everything in fact that seemed to make their life as the chosen people worth living. It might in time destroy all safeguards and throw open the way to one equal brotherhood. His universal principles were indeed full of dynamite, for here was the possibility of one classless society, one comradeship of all men, where there would be no special place for privileged Jew or cultured Greek, for circumcised or uncircumcised, baptized or unbaptized, white or colored, barbarian, Scythian, slave or free man. It might lead disastrously not only to spiritual equality but to social equality, to the recognition of one human family, one spiritual brotherhood under a common Father, where all would be conceived as being created spiritually equal before God.

3. Jesus was condemned for not fasting like the disciples of John and the Pharisees, for the utter absence of ascetic holiness and professional piety; in short for his shocking lack of religion, of correct opinion and of orthodox belief. Instead, he was simply natural, yet he was considered hopelessly secular, vulgar and commonplace. He was as joyous as at a wedding feast, "eating and drinking" until men said: "Here is a glutton and a drunkard, a friend of taxgatherers and sinners" (Matt. 11:19).

4. Worst of all, Mark records in two instances that Jesus was guilty of the capital offense of breaking the sacred Sabbath. He deliberately worked on God's day of rest, recorded in Genesis as established since the creation. He healed the sick and did his works of mercy, so that he seemed publicly to defy the Law of Moses, even justifying himself by saying that he was doing as David did, that he was free from all human bondage. He went so far as to say that man was not made for the Sabbath or any

other institution however holy, but that the Sabbath was made for man—with all other institutions, laws, means, methods, and traditions. Man, under God, was the master of his fate, never merely a means but an end. Man was of infinite worth, more sacred than the Temple or the Law, a son and not a slave.

Here was the inevitable clash between erudition and intuition; between legalistic bibliolatry and immediate spiritual vision. Jesus seemed to these good people to be an innovator and a destroyer; to defy the tradition of the elders, the Law of Moses on divorce, the Law of God on the Sabbath, the very holiest things in life. Instead, he was merely proclaiming boundless good news of the rule of God over men's lives, illustrating it by making sick folk well and broken lives whole. Yet he aroused a hornet's nest of opposition from all the vested interests of the day, from the rich, from literalists and legalists, fundamentalists and religionists, from racial and religious bigots, from nationalists, militarists, zealots and patriots. His opponents were often not the worst but the best people of the day. They built the tombs of the prophets in reverence, but stoned the contemporary messengers of God. They were prejudiced against all foreigners and heathen, and jealously hated a prophet in his own country.

Jesus' contemporaries were not sinners above all others but just like ourselves. Circumstances change but men are alike in every age. We begin to study Jesus' answer to some carping critic in some petty detail or alien circumstance only to find him speaking eternal truth for all time. Thus Jesus says to the sick of the palsy not only "Thy sins are forgiven," but "the Son of Man hath power on earth to forgive sins." That seemed blasphemously bold to legalists. When Jesus calls Matthew of the hated class of Roman tax collectors and dines with these publicans and sinners, his unanswerable reply to his critics is: "Those who are strong have no need of a doctor, but those who are ill: I have not come to call good men but sinners." Once said, his words enter forever into the folklore, the literature, the thought and speech and heart of the race. Jesus replies to his critics: "No one stitches a piece of undressed cloth on an old coat. . . . No one pours fresh wine into old wineskins, other-

wise the wine will burst the wineskins, and both wine and wineskins are ruined."

His gospel cannot be contained within the limits of Jewish
or any other legalism. It involves a new way of life, a new creation. Just as in studying the temptations we found that they
were perennial, typical of all human temptations, so in the case
of opposition to Jesus, the parties who oppose him and the principles on which their opposition is based are essentially the same
in every age and in our own day. Jesus' chief opponents in
Galilee were the Pharisees. They were the elite of Israel and,
apart from the godly common folk to which Jesus' family belonged, they were religiously the best people of the time. It is
because there is something of the Pharisee in every age and in
every one of us that it is important that we understand them.

According to the great Jewish historian, Josephus, there were
four principal Jewish parties in Palestine: the Sadducees, the
Pharisees, the ascetic communities of the Essenes, and the warlike Zealots. As they all faced the central Jewish problem of
their national survival under the hated Roman conquerors, each
believed that there was but one thing needful to solve the problem. The Zealots believed that if they, as a fanatical few, struck
with the sword to throw off the Roman yoke, the mighty
Jehovah would unsheath his omnipotent sword, fulfill his
promises and set them free. The religious, legalistic Pharisees
believed that if the nation would but keep the six hundred and
thirteen precepts of the sacred Law for a single week, from
one Sabbath to another, God would work a miracle, send the
promised Messiah, and deliver his people from the oppressor. The
worldly, wealthy and cynical Sadducees expected no miracle of
deliverance, but advocated a policy of appeasement and compromise to preserve their special privileges and profit under the
Roman system. The Essenes despaired of any solution for the
nation, but took refuge in flight and escape from life, to seek
their individual salvation in a life of ascetic monasticism. Each
of the four parties sought its own solution and each failed.[1]

[1] Because it is almost impossible to understand the life of Jesus and its
significance without a fuller knowledge of these four parties and of condi-

All were involved in the final fall of Jerusalem, the doom of Israel, and the dispersion of the Jews to the ends of the earth. We shall find Jesus working out his own solution for the problem of the nation and the individual and offering the only way of salvation. But, save for the chosen few, we shall find that this was rejected by all parties and by the nation as a whole. Finally Herod and Pilate, Pharisees and Sadducees, Jews and Gentiles— all who represent the sinful, self-centered human heart—turned against him to crucify him. And why? Not because he was a Galilean carpenter, not because of his blameless character, nor because they were amazed at his words of wisdom and his works of mercy, and not only because he challenged their privileges and prejudices, the Law, the Sabbath and the Temple, but *because he was from God*. God is the one reality in existence that many men will not face. For if God is Creator, Sovereign, Father, and Saviour, then the essence of sin is the self-centered life, and the duty of every man is to turn to the God-centered life. That is why many wish to get as far away from God as they can, in a far country of selfishness and sin, and why they must reject and oppose Christ if they are unwilling to accept him.

It would be a fruitful study to trace out the modern counterparts of the four causes of opposition to Jesus in his day. Jesus and his cause and the coming of the Kingdom of God are being as violently opposed today as in his own time. Who are the people, whether they resemble the Pharisees or the publicans and harlots, the elder brother or the prodigal in the parable, whether they count themselves good or bad, who oppose Jesus' way of life and the rule of God in their hearts today? What forces of evil in city, state, nation, and the world, and what parties in the ranks of organized religion, are opposing Jesus' way of life and the coming of God's Kingdom?

The life of Christ as the most moving, transforming story in the world, the greatest drama in history, has recently been retold by the brilliant writer of detective stories, Miss Dorothy L. Sayers,

---

tions in Palestine at the time of Christ, they are described at greater length in Appendix II on Historical Backgrounds of the Life of Jesus which should be read after this chapter.

acted as a cycle of plays in wartime England, and placed on the radio by the British Broadcasting Company. The plays show that Jesus was put to death in a society resembling in many respects our own, by people extraordinarily like ourselves and that if he were visibly to enter human life today as our eternal contemporary he would again meet with the same fate. We Gentiles treat Christ today—and God—just as the Jews treated Jesus nineteen centuries ago. Each age builds the tombs of its ancient prophets and heroes and crucifies its contemporary leaders. In ever-changing circumstances, the self-centered smugness, isolationism, greed, prejudice and spiritual blindness of each age are always similar.

Before leaving this chapter, let us note that if the enemies of Jesus were wrong, he was fundamentally right, and that his opponents were unconsciously bearing witness to his greatness and graciousness of character and the truth of his principles. John in the desert had a great reputation for ascetic holiness, but Jesus freely moved among men, eating and drinking with them. Though persecuted, no other was so joyous. He was like a bridegroom at a wedding feast and could say on the darkest night: "I have told you this that my joy may be within you, and your joy complete." Jesus had to explain to John's disciples why he and his followers were so joyful. When men complained that he was a friend of sinners and welcomed them to his fellowship, he showed that the work of winning the lost yielded the greatest gladness on earth, and brought joy even in heaven in the presence of the angels of God.

The sure source of his joy was the doing of God's will in the service of man. Therefore no one could take his joy from him or from his followers. They were not to exult that the demons were subject to them when their work was successful, nor to be discouraged at apparent failure, but always to rejoice that their names were written in heaven, that is, their source of happiness lay in their unbroken spiritual relation to God. Thus, independent of circumstances, in any and every environment, they could rejoice in the Lord always and learn to be content in whatsoever state they were. Jesus' thought of God was the most glad and confident and his religion was the most joyous on earth. Love, joy, and peace were the first fruits of his spirit. But they were his love, his joy, and his peace. His followers caught them from him. Because he possessed them, he could impart them. Those who lived with him became like him. Since the source of their joy was in God and his Kingdom, his followers were men who had discovered a great secret. They were like a man who has found a treasure hid in a field and in his joy sells all that he has and buys that field.

Jesus rejoiced in all the common things of life, but he always taught that God is better than man's best: "If for all your evil you know to give your children what is good *how much more* will your father give"— himself, his Holy Spirit, all good gifts to meet the every need of those who ask him. And Jesus' thought of God molded his own character. His joyousness was the sign of a radiant nature which permeated all life and overflowed in all familiar ways. The fascination of Jesus for his followers was such that they followed him everywhere, even to death. In time they caught his love of nature and of men, and all the world seemed new when seen through his eyes. "In his words the sparrow achieved its immortality and the lilies of the field blossomed eternally." They saw that Solomon in all his glory was not arrayed like one of these. The common flowers of the field became God's punctuation points to teach his followers to look for God's beauty everywhere.

The very opposition of his enemies becomes the occasion not of bitterness and defeat but of some of Jesus' greatest utterances, and of the finest triumphs of his character. When they accuse Jesus of being a destroyer, they only furnish him his great text for the Sermon on the Mount. And when, finally, these same enemies achieve his seeming defeat and compass his death, his Cross is made the occasion of life for the world. As he is perfected in suffering, in the alchemy of God he transmutes sin into salvation, death into life, shame into glory.

5

THE TEACHER AND PROPHET

CHRISTIANITY ENTERED THE WORLD NOT PRIMARILY AS A teaching but as a gospel; as glad tidings of that which God had done for man in Christ. The little company of the saved who were looking for the coming of the Kingdom at first had little interest in doctrine or ethics. But as problems of theology and morality soon arose, both within the community and in controversy with their opponents, they turned to Jesus' life and words as the standard and norm of Christian behavior. Though variously interpreted, these became the objective test and frame of reference for the subjective experience of the early disciples. They began to collect and preserve the Sayings of Jesus, probably about the middle of the first century.

Following the rapid sweep of their missionary effort, the teachings of Jesus were needed in their pastoral work for the instruction of converts. There was a growing personal interest in Jesus himself, and a treasuring of his words similar to the oracles of the Hebrew prophets. While the gospel remained the story of the passion and the resurrection, the teachings of Jesus were singularly adapted to provide an introduction and explanation of this gospel. The teachings also had apologetic value in the Gentile world and for the persecuted community of Palestinian Christians as a defense against the charge of uttering subversive doctrines. Henceforth there were two streams in the Christian tradition: preaching and teaching; the Passion and resurrection on the one hand, and the teachings of Jesus on the other. The two most certain facts were that Jesus had taught and that he had been crucified.

Jesus saw the heart of the Law and the prophets in the demands to love God and one's neighbor, and counted all else secondary, or in some cases contradictory, to these high commands. He gave little weight to the ceremonial, formal, or impersonal elements in the Hebrew tradition. He had come for the sin-sick, not the righteous. He companied with sinners, the people of the land who did not strictly keep the Law, and like them he ate with unwashed hands. But in repudiating the binding force of tradition and the whole legalistic system of Pharisaism, by substituting a strangely modern Protestant liberty of individual conscience and the great spiritual and ethical essentials as the heart of true religion, he was really threatening, undermining and challenging the force of the complete and awful Law of God. In this one aspect he seemed to be, however unwillingly, a destroyer. The Pharisees and Sadducees at once sensed this menace, and most of all that brilliant young Pharisee, the student of Gamaliel, Saul of Tarsus. He had made careful inquiry of the teaching and work of Jesus before he began to drag his followers to prison and death. Jesus, in stripping off all the ethnic restraints and cutting away a labyrinthine forest of ceremonial nonessentials, was not only fulfilling but ending Judaism. Logically the Pharisees were forced either to accept his radical and revoluntionary innovations or destroy him who would in the end destroy the bondage of the Law. For them and for Paul, it was a life and death matter.

In Jesus' day, many great leaders were giving their summary of the Law, as Hillel had done a generation before in his negative version of the Golden Rule. Thus Rabbi Simlai shows that six hundred and thirteen precepts were given to Moses on Mount Sinai; David reduced these to eleven essentials (Ps. 15:2-5); Isaiah to six (Isa. 33:15); Micah to three (Mic. 6:8); Amos to two (Amos 5:15); Habakkuk to the one principle of faith (Hab. 2:4). But none of these endangered the Law for all the rest of the six hundred and thirteen precepts were also binding. Jesus, however, dares deliberately to condemn Moses' easy provision for divorce. This and the Sermon on the Mount threatened the whole Law.

Jesus, like the prophets, and rabbis used parable, allegory, image, antithesis, comparison and poetic parallelism, and there are similarities to his doctrines throughout Judaism, yet his teaching was nevertheless creative and original. Jesus himself was new and unprecedented. "Love thy neighbor as thyself" is found in an unimpressive context in a half verse of the Old Testament, but it became for Jesus basic, and in its universal application, original. Each phrase he used seemed like a window and many of his sayings enable us to look into his own transparent soul, for they were unconsciously autobiographical.

Jesus is the most open yet the most mysterious personality in history. His followers loved him and would have died for him, yet they never lost their sense of awe in his presence. They felt they understood his simple stories of the lost sheep, the lost coin, and the lost son, yet they sensed a height and depth and reach in the inexhaustible truth he revealed concerning the nature of God and his Kingdom that was ever beyond them. And after well-nigh twenty centuries we have not yet overtaken him. His teaching seems simple and practical, appealing first to the heart and will but also to the mind. Jesus' life was his message; his acts are words and his words are acts. When he places before his quarreling disciples a little child as a model, they—and we—can never forget it. It is something done and said once for all for the human race.

Jesus' startling paradoxes sometimes stun and shock us, as when he says, "whosoever would save his life shall lose it," yet they come from the profoundest depths of human experience. His aphorisms, his bold figures of speech are pictorial, dramatic, unforgettable. His experience and his language seem strangely universal. He draws his images from the daily life of the countryside, the village, the city streets, the lake, the mountain, and the plain. He uses illustrations of the fisherman, the carpenter, the merchant; from the home and from public life, from peace and from war. The sower in his field, the fisherman and his net, the father whose children ask for food, the importunate man who wakes his neighbor at midnight, the shepherd who seeks his lost sheep, the woman who sweeps her house, children playing in the streets, unemployed workers waiting to be hired, the rich householder fearing thieves, the sparrow singing in the eaves—all these are simple, true and universal.

Jesus speaks chiefly to two groups: the multitude who seek to live by his teaching, and the inner group who must leave all to devote their whole time to the proclamation of the coming Kingdom. Jesus does not call all men to sell everything and give to the poor; but the rich young ruler, whose wealth was a stumbling block to him, was apparently called, vocationally, to leave everything as Peter and John had done, and join the itinerant group. The training of such a peripatetic school was the practice of Rabbinic circles in Jesus' day. When a disciple volunteers to join the sacrificial, traveling group which has left all to follow Jesus while he is a fugitive and outcast from Herod's territory, Jesus warns him that, with the Son of Man, he will not have where to lay his head. When Jesus calls another to join the inner group and he asks leave to attend his father's funeral, Jesus replies that in this crisis there is now no time for funerals but only for the urgent proclamation of the coming Messianic Kingdom (Luke 9:57-62). Only by knowing the temporal circumstances in the first century can we understand the timeless principles in his teaching.

Jesus' teaching was as much and as little systematic as life itself. Jesus speaks to some individual, in some temporal or local circumstance, with such penetrating spiritual insight, that he sees straight to the heart of God, the heart of man, and the heart of eternity. He appears to be speaking eternal truth applicable to all men, to all circumstances and to all time.

The word Father on Jesus' lips was something new for the world. Used in a different sense, the word can be found in numerous passages of the Old Testament, in Jewish writings, and in the non-Christian religions. The young Pharisee, Paul of Tarsus, found that Jesus' conception was utterly new: "You have received no slavish spirit that would make you relapse into fear; you have received the Spirit of sonship. And when we cry, 'Abba! Father!' it is this Spirit testifying along with our own spirit that we are children of God; and if children, heirs as well, heirs of God, heirs along with Christ" (Rom. 8:15-17).

In the Jewish home the word father stood primarily for authority, the one to whom obedience was due, and who should be imitated by the son. Both Jesus' life and teaching reveal man's one central obligation to love God with all his being. All else is derivative from this. We are to love our neighbor, not because of his intrinsic worth, or his character, or conduct, but we are to love him in God. We are to imitate God, and we are to love man because God loves him. And man is a brother, not because of his own worth, but because he is a child of the heavenly Father. In the later church he is the brother for whom Christ died. Only because of his standing before God do we later realize the intrinsic worth of the individual, the priceless meaning of personality, and the brotherhood of all men. Jesus' faith and ethics are all derivative from the one absolute of God as Father. We are to repent, which means the redirection of the whole life with a total change of mind, of character and of attitude, because of what God is. We are to view our neighbor henceforth as one loved by the infinite God. And we are to love both God and man and thus fulfill the whole Law, because God loves.

The Sermon on the Mount furnishes the best example of Jesus' authoritative teaching. It is not only the charter of the Kingdom of God, which is its theme; it is also the great summary of Christian ethics. Matthew sees its importance as the ordinance governing the Christian communities throughout the world when he gives it the first place in his Gospel among the discourses of Jesus. When Jesus abrogated and supplanted the Law, the Christian church needed rules of conduct for its own life. The group addressed is the Christian community the world over and for all time. We cannot in literal deeds perform the Sermon on the Mount, but we can be transformed by it as men have been in every age. It is not a command to do something, but to be something. It is not law but gospel. It embodies a new spirit, a new attitude, a total change of character, a reorientation to life.

Jesus' point of view is the pure and perfect will of God, not human ability. Literally to give to every beggar, to make no provision for the future, to "sell what you possess and give it away in alms," to part with your garments, to offer no resistance to any evil or evildoer would lead to social anarchy. But prophets and poets are often compelled to use such bold language and to appeal to the imagination and spiritual understanding of their hearers. It is only one of the paradoxes of history that the materialistic and warlike West accepted the oriental Jesus when his way of life, spiritually understood, was bound to disrupt and finally transform their society. The West felt the words of Jesus to be the divine will, however impossible they seemed to be for sinful man.

Jesus saw intuitively the law of God as a moral order written in the very structure of the universe and in the soul of man, to which men should conform in humble obedience and complete faith. A warped soul like Nietzsche, with no spiritual conception of the nature of humility and no experience of God, could see in Jesus' principles only a servile, "slave morality," and would replace the Beatitudes and the Sermon on the Mount by the lawlessness of the blond beast of his superman. He poured scorn not only on loving compassion but on liberty, justice, democracy and peace. We have seen what this transvaluation of all values and the inversion of the moral order means in our own day when applied to world conquest, and to what depths of misery and moral degradation it plunges the world. It gives a faint picture of what a rule of evil motivated by hate could be, just as Jesus' Sermon on the Mount envisages a Beloved Community, or rule of God on earth, realized through love. A portion of this Sermon we shall now study.

The Sermon on the Mount
Matt. 4:17, 23, 25; 5:1-7:29; Luke 6:20-49

From that day Jesus began to preach, saying, "Repent, the Reign of heaven is near." (Matt. 4:17.) Then he made a tour through the whole of Galilee teaching in their synagogues, preaching the gospel of the Reign, and healing all sickness and disease among the people (Matt. 4:23). He was followed by great crowds from Galilee and Decapolis and Jerusalem and Judaea and from across the Jordan. (Matt. 4:25.) So when he saw the crowds, he went up the hill and sat down; his disciples came up to him and opening his lips he began to teach them. He said:

"Blessed are those who feel poor in spirit!
the Realm of heaven is theirs.
Blessed are the mourners!
they will be consoled.
Blessed are *the humble*!
they *will inherit the earth*.
Blessed are those who hunger and thirst for goodness!
they will be satisfied.
Blessed are the merciful!
they will find mercy.
Blessed are the pure in heart!
they will see God.
Blessed are the peacemakers!
they will be ranked sons of God.
Blessed are those who have been persecuted for the sake
of goodness!
the Realm of heaven is theirs.

Blessed are you when men denounce you and persecute you and utter all manner of evil against you for my sake; rejoice and exult in it, for your reward is rich in heaven; that is how they persecuted the prophets before you. You are the salt of the earth. But if salt become insipid, what can make it salt again? After that it is fit for nothing, fit only to be flung outside and trodden under foot. You are the light of the world. A town on the top of a hill cannot be hidden. Nor do men light a lamp to put it under a bowl; they put it on a stand, and it shines for all in the house. So your light is to shine before men, that they may see the good you do and glorify your Father in heaven." (Matt. 5:1-16.)

THE SERMON ON THE MOUNT CLEARLY SHOWS STRUCTURE. TAKEN in its context the theme is the Kingdom of God and his righteousness. It may be divided as follows:

1. The character of the sons of the Kingdom and the conditions of entrance into the way that leads to it (Matt. 5:1-16).
2. The relation of the old Law to the spirit of the new Kingdom (Matt. 5:17-48).
   The fivefold fulfillment of love:
   Not only no murder but no anger;
   Not only no adultery but no thought or look of lust;
   Not only no breaking but no making of oaths;
   Not only no revenge but mercy;
   Not only no hatred but love even of enemies.
3. The new righteousness of the Kingdom: regarding alms-giving, prayer and fasting (Matt. 6:1-18).
4. The relation of the Kingdom to earthly treasure and worldly life (Matt. 6:19-34).
5. The relation of the sons of the Kingdom to their fellowmen and to God (Matt. 7:1-11).
6. Conclusion. The Golden Rule of conduct. Enter the way that leads to the Kingdom by utter obedience, by doing the will of the Father in heaven. Contrasts between true and false prophets; the house built on rock or on sand (Matt. 7:12-28).

Jesus, of course, taught no system of philosophy, theology, or ethics; fortunately he formulated no binding creed. Nevertheless there are certain fundamental convictions and guiding principles that constantly reappear in his teaching. The Greeks held to three absolute values or ultimate principles: the true, the good and the beautiful; and they were generally agreed upon four cardinal virtues: wisdom, courage, temperance and justice. For Jesus the ultimate values or foundation principles were not the three Hellenic abstractions, but rather the concrete and personal Hebraic realities of God as Father, and derivatively from this one absolute, man as brother, involving ultimately one universal brotherhood, and implying also the sacredness of human personality, the priceless worth, rights and responsibilities of each individual soul.

Based upon these ultimate realities, Jesus holds to no self-centered, self-attained Greek virtues but to four fundamental attitudes, or relationships between God and man: humility, faith, moral purity and love. Stated more explicitly these are: 1. Repentant humility, or complete, continuous, utter dependence upon God as Father; 2. As obverse and reverse, the opposite of humility is bold faith, or utter trust in the grace and goodness of God; 3. The single eye of the cleansed heart, the moral purity that can see the vision of a holy God and enter into fellowship with him; 4. As the completion of all, the bond of the perfect life, the mighty motivation of love as the full sharing of life with God and man, which is the spirit of his realm. This is always expressed in the two basic commands by which Jesus sums up the Law and the prophets, to love God with all the heart and one's neighbor as oneself.

We shall find these four attitudes and relationships appearing and reappearing in the Beatitudes, the Sermon on the Mount, throughout the teaching and life of Jesus, in all the New Testament, in the early church and throughout Christianity. There is no place for hard, self-centered Stoic virtues, or Pharisaic pride, in Jesus' way of life. Christ is the end of the Law and of man's own self-righteousness. These four attitudes in place of man's former "virtues," based on these three ultimate spiritual realities, make this the highest and most universal system of ethical monotheism known in the world.

Faith is not specifically mentioned in the Beatitudes, though it is implied throughout the Sermon on the Mount: "Oh ye of little faith!" The three Synoptic Gospels each devote more than a chapter to faith (Mark 4:35-41; Matt. 9:27-34; etc.). For Jesus, faith means the trust of one's whole being in utter dependence upon God. Psychologically analyzed, it combines a practical activity of the will, an attitude of the mind which produces achievement, and a movement of the affection toward personal attachment. It is implicit in both science and religion, in all true human or divine relations. It is emphatically not merely intellectual assent to a doctrine or creed; it is the opposite of blind credulity or superstition. It is opposed to fear, not to knowledge, and to sight, not to reality, for in both science and religion it is the pathway of experience to knowledge. Faith is not trying to believe something in spite of the evidence, it is daring to do something regardless of the consequences. It is an adventure in action in the conquest of life. Our modern doubt is not whether God is better than Jesus, but whether he is as good as Jesus.

Jesus is never in conscious opposition to the will of God and he stakes his whole life on the goodness of God in unwavering trust. If the inmost quality of reality is expressed in Jesus, then God is love. This is why we study the wonderful teaching of Jesus and this is why faith is the expression of the inmost quality of our being, and why it is the test of what we are, as well as the expression of confidence in the object of our trust. To use a modern figure of speech, it is the live wire that connects us with the mighty Niagara dynamos, that brings to individuals, homes, and cities all the light, heat, and power that they need. But for the Christian, our contact is not with an impersonal power but with a Being whose nature is love. As faith was the test of the first four disciples, and of the woman who touched Jesus' garments, we shall find that it is the final test of each one of us when we come to study not only the Jesus of history but the Christ of faith. That is why our experience and blessing are according to our faith, why Jesus in Nazareth could do no mighty work, and why if we have faith as a tiny grain of mustard seed and let it grow naturally, we can in the end, figuratively speaking, remove mountains of difficulty, of doubt, or of sin. That is why the very essence of Christianity on the human side is "faith working by love."

Jesus' true followers—those who maintain the attitudes and relationships of humility, faith, purity, and love—are the very salt of the earth, the savor and antiseptic of society. For without these attitudes and conditions of the happy life, if Christians become insipid they are "good for nothing," to themselves, to God or to their fellow men. Jesus' true followers are ever the light of the world, to shine and not be hid, the hope of humanity to show the way of life. What a light is to a dark home the Christian is to the world. Jesus' followers should be distinguishable; they are as a city set on a hill, living witnesses and examples of the power of God as his new creation. Or else they are betrayers of a sacred trust. For it is never a light thing to be a "Christ-one," a true follower of Jesus, a herald of the Kingdom.

Viewing the Sermon on the Mount as a whole, these three chapters are unique in all literature. After spending a total of nearly thirty years in Asia, forced to familiarity not only with the sacred books of the East but with the great ethnic religions in actual practice, the writer has found nothing comparable to this Sermon on the Mount. Contrasted with all moral systems, like Gautama's "eightfold path," where men through self-denial and discipline seek to reach a goal, Jesus begins with the goal, the very rule of God, as the gift of his free grace. One of Jesus' major texts is "I come not to destroy but to fulfill." Such fulfillment was possible, not for a Galilean carpenter, even though he were the best of men, but only for God's anointed Messiah in proclaiming and bringing in the rule of God. This is the theme of the Sermon, as the proclamation of the Kingdom.

THE OLD LAW AND THE NEW GOSPEL
Matt. 5:17-48; Luke 6:27-36

Never imagine I have come to destroy the Law or the prophets; I have not come to destroy but to fulfill. (Matt. 5:17). You have heard how the men of old were told, *"Murder not*: whoever murders shall come up for sentence, whoever maligns his brother shall come before the Sanhedrin, whoever curses his brother shall go to the fire of Gehenna." But I tell you, whoever is angry with his brother without cause will be sentenced by God. So if you remember, even when offering your gift at the altar, that your brother has any grievance against you, leave your gift at the very altar and go away; first be reconciled to your brother, then come back and offer your gift (Matt. 5:21-24). You have heard how it used to be said, *Do not commit adultery*. But I tell you, anyone who even looks with lust at a woman has committed adultery with her already in his heart (Matt. 5:27-28). It used to be said, *Whoever divorces his wife must give her a divorce-certificate*. But I tell you, anyone who divorces his wife for any reason except unchastity makes her an adulteress; and whoever marries a divorced woman commits adultery. Once again, you have heard how the men of old were told, *"You must not forswear yourself* but *discharge your vows to the Lord."* But I tell you, you must not swear any oath (Matt. 5:31-34). Let what you say be simply "yes" or "no"; whatever goes beyond that springs from evil. You have heard the saying, *An eye for an eye and a tooth for a tooth*. But I tell you, you are not to resist an injury (Matt. 5:37-39). You have heard the saying, *"You must love your neighbour* and hate your enemy." But I tell you, love your enemies and pray for those who persecute you, that you may be sons of your Father in heaven: he makes his sun rise on the evil and the good, and sends rain on the just and the unjust. For if you love only those who love you, what reward do you get for that? do not the very taxgatherers do as much? and if you only salute your friends, what is special about that? do

not the very pagans do as much? You must be perfect as your
heavenly Father is perfect (Matt. 5:43-48).

IN THIS REMARKABLE PASSAGE, WE REACH, PERHAPS, THE HIGH-
water mark of Christian ethics for all time: "You must be
perfect as your heavenly Father is perfect. You must be complete,
full-grown in love, all-encompassing in your affection, as is your
Father in heaven." Luke's version of this passage from the Sayings of Jesus is "Be ye merciful as your Father is merciful." The
imitation of God is a Jewish ideal. Jesus never condemns or
criticizes the Law or Moses as a whole, but he quotes Moses
against Moses. Jesus sees the Law as given on two levels: 1.
Under the perfect will of God man is utterly to love God and his
neighbor and to see marriage in the divine plan, as man and
wife whom God has joined together and who should not be
torn asunder by human divorce (Gen. 2:24). Before this perfect will of God all are under sin. 2. Jesus sees the relative will
of God expressed on a lower level to restrict the consequences
of man's sin. Because of the hardness of man's heart under sin,
Moses declared his social legislation which was to restrict the
fruits of sin as much as possible, saying in substance: "If you
do put your wife away give her a bill of divorcement, so that
she will not be homeless without economic status but can marry
again." The woman was cruelly handicapped and unjustly
treated throughout the ancient world and Moses was trying to
protect her. Jesus forbids the use of the relative law made in the
light of sin to provide a divine sanction for the general principle
of divorce, which had become scandalous under Hillel's liberal
interpretation. The perfect will of God prohibits all sin and in
the Genesis passage referred to above implies indissoluble
monogamy.

All of Jesus' five contrasts in the Sermon on the Mount between himself and "them of old time" recognize that the Law
was good in forbidding murder and adultery and in restricting
revenge and unlimited divorce. But Jesus goes deeper and farther,
tracing sin to the inward motive and attitude of men's self-centered lives, and lifting all life up to the view of the perfect will

of God. We shall find that *Jesus never legislates* though Matthew seems to imply that he did so. Regarding the Law, Jesus saw what Paul later explicated. He saw the heart of the Law in the divine will expressed in the great commandments and spiritual essentials, not as a body of burdensome prohibitory legislation. Jesus as well as Paul could have said: "He that loveth his neighbor hath fulfilled the Law." Love, for Jesus, was not a sentimental emotion but a positive, forthgoing ethical activity with its imperatives: do, go, sell, heal, cast out demons, show mercy, that you may be sons of your Father. We shall find later that love's logical climax is the unconditional surrender of one's life to God in the service of men. When the love of Christ constrains us, it can make Martin Luther say: "My soul is too glad and too great to be at heart the enemy of any man." And it can make us each the servant of all, and moves us to love even our enemies. It passes forever beyond the pagan standard of the ancient world as typified by Cyrus than whom "no one ever did more good to his friends and more harm to his enemies."

Henceforth we can conceive of no ideal character without the Christlike quality of forgiveness. Jesus' followers are bidden to forgive seventy times seven, four hundred and ninety times, that is, infinitely. It has taken slow centuries to work this principle of love in some small measure into our standards and statutes and the state's attitude to criminals. We are only beginning to learn that our object is not to punish but to redeem and to make new men. After twenty centuries the world is not yet able to rise to the moral height of Jesus' teaching. Thomas Jefferson while President of the United States, after subjecting the Gospels to the most rigid historical criticism possible in his time, wrote: "There never was a more pure and sublime system of morality delivered to man than is to be found in the four evangelists." During his Presidency, he compiled what is known as the "Jefferson Bible" of which he says it is "a document in proof that I am a real Christian." He pasted the teachings of Jesus in parallel columns in English, Greek, Latin, and French under the title "The Life and Morals of Jesus of Nazareth," reading for more than an hour every night "of something moral" before retiring. This is characteristic of the impression which the teachings of Christ have made on most of the finest minds throughout the centuries.

Jesus imposes no rigid precepts which are right in all circumstances. If I am his follower my duty is only to do the will of God as revealed in Jesus and interpreted by God's Spirit, just as Jesus interpreted the Law by his own spiritual insight, and just as Protestants are to interpret the whole Bible in the light of the New Testament, and all according to "the mind of Christ." Jesus offers no rewards and punishments for merit or demerit, for when we have done all, before the perfect love of God we remain unprofitable servants and our righteousness is as filthy rags. There is an inevitable result of blessing in doing the will of God, in the beatitude of being Godlike, but this is not offered as a reward of merit.

When Jesus laid down the revolutionary principle that nothing that went into the mouth could defile a man, but only that which came out of the mouth, thus "making all meats clean," he was practically canceling out the whole system of Mosaic ceremonial law and its binding taboos. He was cutting away at a stroke the whole principle of Jewish legalism, for the distinction between clean and unclean meats was the most important feature of Mosaic law considered as a code of ritual observances. The emancipation from the Law we thus owe to Jesus; its explanation we owe to Paul. Our religion is hence rightly called Christianity not Paulinism. It was Paul and the Pharisees who realized how radical and revolutionary Jesus really was.

Love in the ethic of Jesus is seen to be relevant to every human situation, for love was the human symbol of the moral nature of God. It was also the perfect standard before which Jesus demanded repentance. God, whose nature is unconditioned love, judges men by his very presence so that repentance becomes man's only final response. And repentance implies surrender, entering by faith into the Godlike life of love, that we may be sons of our Father. Behind all law lies the single ultimate duty of love. This is the one and only absolute obligation in Christianity. Separate precepts are obligatory in concrete circumstances *only*

when they express the duty of love. The context of the precept
not to resist evil but to turn the other cheek always forbids personal egotistic retaliation. But when resistance arises out of
concern for the lives of others dependent upon us, the injunc-
tion gives us no guidance. My clear duty is to love, but there is
no guarantee in Scripture or in human experience that if I do
turn the other cheek and feed my enemy, it will always succeed
and bring him to repentance, or that he will yield his life to
love. If a man does me a personal injury by striking me on the
cheek, my duty is clear, but if I see a bully beating a little child,
a man violating a helpless woman, or money-changers making
the house of God into a den of robbers, there is no precept that
tells me what to do. If the Good Samaritan had arrived while
the robbers were beating their victim, what would have been
his duty? Love will bid me do what is best for all concerned,
whether by giving positive aid to the injured, or by nonviolent
or forcible resistance to evil.

Jesus did not say, "If a man take the widow's cloak, let him
take the orphan's coat also." If I am to do unto others as I
would be done by, love will show me how to act. If I were the
child being beaten, or the woman being wronged, or the man
being robbed, or if I were the criminal or violator, or the money-
changers in the Temple, if I had any spiritual understanding
I would not want anyone merely to turn the other cheek to me
in the bondage of prosaic legalism or literalism. Some, like
Gandhi in our day, are undoubtedly called to be vocational
pacifists, but for most of us it is gratuitous and misleading to
identify love solely with nonviolent resistance, or any other
specific method or technique. The Sermon on the Mount gives
the Christian a principle of love as the spirit in which he is
always to act, but never a rigid precept for specific action in all
circumstances. It is only the legalist, the literalist, and the
absolutist who will so misunderstand it.

At this point we see Tolstoy led into error by making the
text "resist not him that is evil" into what he calls "*the new law*."
There can be but one sun, one center in a solar system. That
center for the Christian is love—to love God, our neighbor and

even our enemies. Unfortunately that center Tolstoy never found, for his demonic pride disrupted every friendship and almost every relationship of his life, even that of his own unhappy and quarrelsome home. All resistance to evil or evil men became for Tolstoy the one sin. A Tolstoyan under his "law" could not protect his own wife from a violator. All government service, all law courts, all police were sinful; even marriage was a "fall" to the sins of the flesh. This "law," contrary to the spirit and character of Jesus himself, led Tolstoy into philosophical anarchy. If this were rigidly applied, it would finally disrupt the state, the church, and all organized society. It frustrated Tolstoy's own unlovely character.

The rational basis of conduct seems to be found in experience interpreted by reason ("why do you not yourselves settle what is right?"). The basis of Christian conduct is experience, interpreted by reason, in the spirit of Christ. But what is the spirit of Christ? Is it Jesus dying upon the Cross, crying, "Father forgive them," or is it the same Jesus, motivated by the same love, driving the money-changers from the Temple in flaming moral indignation? We believe it is both; for God judges and he redeems; Christ judges and he redeems, in righteous love. The state must judge, and according to Paul, the earthly state is divinely authorized and organized upon a basis of force. While the state must organize man's secular life and wield power, the church must redeem and proclaim God's gospel of love. The Christian as a member of both state and church must live in two worlds. He must as a citizen render to Caesar the limited, qualified obedience to the state enjoined by Jesus, and as a child of the heavenly Father, he must render to God the absolute, unqualified obedience due to him.

We must remember that Christians always have differed on some of these questions. We have no record that Jesus ever told any centurion or army officer to throw away his weapons and leave the army. Why, if his teaching had been explicit, were some of Jesus' followers, including their leader, Simon himself, carrying swords on the last night? And what did he mean by telling each disciple to sell his cloak and buy a sword? Was it for self-protection? Certainly it was not for his protection, for the Saviour of the world could have no weapon used for him in his cause. That is a very different matter from the magistrate, or president, or policeman, or citizen of a state holding the sword "for the maintenance of order, constituted by God" (Rom. 13:1-9). St. Augustine and the majority of Christians for nineteen centuries have understood that devout believers should not resist *personal* injuries, but that the duty of the forcible protection of the state and the defense of their country was God's will for them. Undoubtedly some are called as "vocational pacifists," but the majority have always felt it to be their duty when their country was attacked to be its conscientious defenders rather than conscientious objectors. Some absolute pacifists and perfectionists, who practically make Gandhi a second Christ, seem to think there is some magic in nonviolent resistance. They believe that love expressed in nonviolence will so melt the heart of a militarist dictator that their only duty is to be meticulously "perfect," and that if they only love enough, God will so miraculously protect their country that there is no need for anyone to defend it. In the last draft in Britain, one in three hundred, and in New York State one in ten thousand, maintained the position of the conscientious objector.

Many sincere Christians, under Christ's command to love, have prayed daily during the war for the leaders of America, Britain, China and Soviet Russia, and, specifically, for their enemies, for every member of the great but misguided German nation and for all Japanese, determined that no shadow or poison of hatred shall darken their souls in this world agony. But with a clear conscience and without hatred they have felt that they could forcibly defend their country and civilization. In the light of the Sermon on the Mount, let us not judge one another any more, but strive to fulfill the law of love as each understands it in the best light that he has. All without exception, however, are called to be makers of peace and builders of a warless world. Someday, we shall do away with war as once we did away with slavery. In relation to both evils, the absolutist and the relativist, the idealist and the realist, will both doubtless have their part to play. As Professor Hocking well says: "The church must cherish and protect its pacifists, even while it recognizes that the fight is a good fight. Without their spirit, there can be no lasting peace." Harry Emerson Fosdick adds: "The fact is that Jesus is everlastingly right—not that mankind *ought to be* one family, but that mankind *is* one family, and never can be happy until that truth is recognized and acted upon."

The New Righteousness and the Old
Matt. 6:1-18; Luke 11:9-13

Take care not to practise your charity before men in order to be noticed; otherwise you get no reward from your Father in heaven. No, when you give alms, make no flourish of trumpets like the hypocrites in the synagogues and the streets, so as to win applause from men; I tell you truly, they do get their reward (Matt. 6:1-2). Also, when you pray, you must not be like the hypocrites, for they like to stand and pray in the synagogues and at the street-corners, so as to be seen by men; I tell you truly, they do get their reward (Matt. 6:5). Let this be how you pray:

'our Father in heaven,
   thy name be revered,
   thy Reign begin,
   thy will be done
      on earth as in heaven!
   give us to-day our bread for the morrow,
   and forgive us our debts
      as we ourselves have forgiven our debtors,
   and lead us not into temptation
   but deliver us from evil.' (Matt. 6:9-13.)

When you fast, do not look gloomy like the hypocrites, for they look woebegone to let men see they are fasting; I tell you truly, they do get their reward. No, when you are fasting, anoint your head and wash your face, so that your fast may be seen not by men but by your Father who is in secret, and your Father who sees what is secret will reward you (Matt. 6:16-18). So I tell you, ask and the gift will be yours, seek and you will find, knock and the door will open to you; for everyone who asks receives, the seeker finds, the door is opened to anyone who knocks. What father among you, if asked by his son for a loaf, will hand him a stone?—or, if asked for a fish, will hand him a serpent instead of a fish?— or, if asked for an egg, will he hand him a scorpion? Well, if for all your evil you know to give your children what is good,

how much more will your Father give the holy Sp
heaven to those who ask him? (Luke 11:9-13.)

A S JESUS HAS BEEN CONTRASTING THE OLD LAW ANE
gospel at six points, he now contrasts the old ׳גׅׅ׆ׅ׆ׅ׆ׅ׆׀׆ׅ׆ׅ׀׆ׅ׀׆ׅ׀ׅ׆ׅ׀ׅׅ٭eous-
ness, or piety, and the new in three antitheses. At all costs, his
followers are to avoid ostentation in their religion. Their whole
life is to be centered in, and related to, not men or self, but
God. This vital inward spiritual reality will exclude all exter-
nality, legalism, literalism, and formalism. Jesus takes the Pharisees' trinity of virtues—almsgiving, prayer, and fasting—and
relates each not to the praise of men, but to "your Father who
sees what is secret." Oliver Wendell Holmes said: "My religion
is summed up in the first two words of the Lord's prayer, 'Our
Father.' "

Here in the Lord's Prayer is what I most need to know of
God, of myself, and of my neighbor. The relation of God and man
is the relation of a father and child in the family. The child
partakes of the nature of the parent, it bears his image, it is
capable of communion with the father and of carrying on his
work. The Lord's Prayer is not quietistic; when I really pray
"Thy Kingdom come" I must co-operate as a fellow worker
with God, I must be about my Father's business, even though
I know that only God in his good pleasure can "give" us the
Kingdom in its full consummation. If I enter completely into
this relationship of simple trust and walk by faith, it banishes
all fear and worry from life.

The six petitions of the Lord's Prayer fall naturally into two
divisions; the first three are concerned with God: "Thy name,"
"thy Reign," "thy will"; the second three voice man's own needs:
our bread, our debts, our temptations. And this is the right order
in spiritual experience, for it suggests the whole philosophy not
only of prayer but of life. The first three petitions are concerned
with universal spiritual issues, the second three with individual
needs. The same God who is the Lord of history, marks the sparrow's fall and ministers to the daily needs of his children, both
material and spiritual. The central petition that sums up the

whole prayer is "Thy Kingdom come," that is in the future, in the final consummation, "the coming of the Kingdom of God in power." In this brief prayer of six sentences Jesus has compassed and embraced God and man, heaven and earth, the spiritual and the material; the past, the present and the future; time and eternity; the ideal and the real; man's duty to God and his fellows. All the essentials of life are summed up in a working prayer which ever teaches us to advance in the spiritual life; and it embodies a working creed of what we may believe about God, about human nature and destiny, about the meaning of life, about the means of grace and the hope of glory. The prayer is revealing and thoroughly characteristic of Jesus' life and teaching. It opens up to all mankind the possibilities of prayer as the very heart of religion, as religion in act. Thus in Jesus we touch the height and depth and breadth of universal religion.

We are unable to make here a complete study even of this brief Sermon on the Mount. But we must not omit its great summaries and conclusion:

> O men, how little you trust him! Seek God's Realm and his goodness, and all that will be yours over and above. Ask and the gift will be yours, seek and you will find, knock and the door will open to you. Whatever you would like men to do to you, do just the same to them; that is the meaning of the Law and the prophets. Enter by the narrow gate. Now, everyone who listens to these words of mine and acts upon them will be like a sensible man who built his house on rock.

Jesus makes a great summary of right relations to our fellow men in the Golden Rule. It has been accepted almost everywhere as a simple ideal of conduct. It shows not only Jesus' spiritual insight but his knowledge of the human heart and a wealth of natural wisdom which makes the self-love of our self-centered lives, which is common to all men, the practical standard of measurement of our duty to others. If we apply this to our attitude to the poor, the Negro, the weak brother, or the enemy, we have at hand this universal frame of reference, this convenient measuring rod. Here is a standard of conduct which betrays and exposes our rationalizations, our wishful thinking, our harsh dgments, and often shows us in Jesus' sight to be "hypocrites" play actors.

At the close of the Sermon, we have dramatically portrayed striking contrasts the two gates, two ways, two kinds of trees nd fruits, two kinds of prophets and of teachers; we have two ltimate foundations of life—rock or sand, obedience to the will f God or disobedience—and finally there are two destinies, salvaon or destruction. The standard of judgment is not profession ut practice: "By their fruits ye shall know them." Final enrance into the Kingdom is won not by calling Jesus, "Lord, ord," but by him who does the will of the Father in heaven. Iere is the acid test for every life and by it we must judge ourlves. The man who does the will of God is building his house pon the everlasting rock of God's truth. All else is shifting and. God has written his moral law in the structure of the unierse and of our own souls, just as he has written the law of ravity in the structure of the material universe. We may be ustained in our airplane so long as we keep the law but when e break or defy the law we crash. And we crash morally and piritually just as we wreck ourselves in the material world.

Jesus, at the logical conclusion of the Sermon on the Mount, aving placed the two ways before us, the way of the Kingdom r the rule of God, and the way of the self-centered life that leads p destruction, cries "Enter!" The road that leads to life is both arrow and close, and there are few (as yet) who are finding it. Vith simple, childlike confidence in our heavenly Father which esus begets in us, let us enter! For all things are now ready. The ternal reality of the Kingdom of God is ever at hand and is ven now before us. This is Jesus' way of life. Now is the accepted me. And as his disciples he bids us *Enter*!

In the light of Jesus' teaching, we must view the Kingdom of od in eternal perspective. We must ask not only what the rule f God meant to Jesus in the first century but what it means to s in the twentieth. We believe that the Kingdom of God should ean for us just what it meant for Jesus, an inward experience, ur daily task and our final goal. For us also it is both a present eality and a future consummation. One implication of the recognition of the Kingdom as both present and future is, as Reinhold Niebuhr shows, that history itself becomes an interim and Christ becomes its interpretive center. We rightly divide time as before and after Christ. The period after Christ is that between the disclosure of history's true meaning and its fulfilment. There is always a tension between the standard revealed by Jesus and man's sinful history. Jesus anticipated the growth of evil as well as good, "until the harvest." The injection of Jesus and of the Kingdom into history does not gradually transform it into something quite different. We pray "Thy Kingdom come," but history never becomes the Kingdom of God. God only can bring in the final consummation.

We can leave the future with calm confidence to God. And the follower of Jesus can place himself under the rule of God as a member of his Kingdom. The Christian can say with George Macdonald in his *Robert Falconer*: "This is a sane, wholesome, practical, working faith: first, that it is a man's business to do the will of God; second, that God takes on himself the special care of that man; and third, that therefore that man ought never to be afraid of anything." Jesus' cause to which he dedicated his life and to which he calls his followers is the Kingdom of God. For us this means the rule of righteousness in the personal life and social relationships of all mankind. This is the one thing which we are to seek—first, last and always. Is it not the supreme cause, the *summum bonum* of humanity?

Among his sixty-five parables, many of which show what the Kingdom of God resembles in some one aspect, Jesus says: "The Realm of heaven is like treasure hidden in a field; the man who finds it hides it, and in his delight goes and sells all he possesses and buys that field. Again, the Realm of heaven is like a trader in search of fine pearls; when he finds a single pearl of high price, he is off to sell all he possesses and buy it."

Here we have two parables like matchless pearls which show the inconceivable value of the Kingdom. Both bear directly on the missionary work and preaching of the disciples. Once a man sees the Kingdom of God as it really is, as the eternal spiritual reality, the *summum bonum*, all truth, goodness, beauty and happiness, he will leave all, sacrifice all to possess it. *For it costs all that a man has.* He cannot keep back part of the price. It cost Jesus a cross. Paul counted all things to be as refuse to possess it. We must be ready to cut off a hand, to pluck out our very eye, to forsake all that we have to enter or possess it.

One man finds it by chance as he is digging deeper in his field, while the merchant has long sought for just such a gem. One finds it as the object of his long search; the other is found by it. Both classes of discoverers are included in a volume like William James' *Varieties of Religious Experience.* When Tokichi Ishii, awaiting his death sentence in a Japanese prison stumbled accidentally upon the passage in the New Testament "Father, forgive them for they know not what they do," it pierced his heart like "a five inch nail." Scales fell from his eyes as he said: "Through this simple sentence I was led into the whole of Christianity."[1] Kagawa saw the whole of Christianity in the single passage "Blessed are the pure in heart for they shall see God."

Mr. H. G. Wells [2] says that from the day this Kingdom was preached, the world began to be different. He writes:

> This doctrine of the Kingdom of God, which was the main teaching of Jesus, and which plays so small a part in the Christian creeds, is certainly one of the most revolutionary doctrines that ever stirred and changed human thought. . . . For the doctrine of the Kingdom as Jesus seems to have preached it, was no less than a bold and uncompromising demand for a complete change and cleansing of the life of our struggling race, an utter cleansing, without and within. It was not merely a moral and social revolution that Jesus proclaimed . . . wherever and in what measure his Kingdom was set up in the hearts of men, the outer world would be in that measure revolutionized and made new. . . . To take him seriously was to enter upon a strange and alarming life, to abandon habits, to control instincts and impulses, to essay an incredible happiness. . . . Is it any wonder that to this day this Galilean is too much for our small hearts?

[1] *A Gentleman in Prison,* p. 76.
[2] H. G. Wells, *Outline of History,* pp. 572-599.

FINDING THE LOST

Luke 15:1-32

The taxgatherers and sinners were all approaching him to listen to him, but the Pharisees and the scribes complained, "He welcomes sinners and eats along with them!" So he told them this parable, "Which of you with a hundred sheep, if he loses one, does not leave the ninety-nine in the open field and go after the lost one till he finds it? When he finds it, he lays it on his shoulders with joy, and when he gets home he gathers his friends and neighbours: 'Rejoice with me,' he says to them, 'for I have found the sheep I lost.' So, I tell you, there will be joy in heaven over a single sinner who repents, more than over ninety-nine good people who do not need to repent. Or again, suppose a woman has ten shillings. If she loses one of them, does she not light a lamp and scour the house and search carefully till she finds it? And when she finds it, she gathers her women-friends and neighbours, saying, 'Rejoice with me, for I have found the shilling I lost.' So, I tell you, there is joy in the presence of the angels of God over a single sinner who repents." He also said: "There was a man who had two sons, and the younger said to his father, 'Father, give me the share of the property that falls to me' (Luke 15:1-13). He squandered his means in loose living (Luke 15:13) But when he came to his senses he said, 'How many hired men of my father have more than enough to eat, and here am I perishing of hunger! I will be up and off to my father, and I will say to him, "Father, I have sinned against heaven and before you; I don't deserve to be called your son any more; only make me like one of your hired men."' So he got up and went off to his father (Luke 15:17-20). But the father said to his servants, 'Quick, bring the best robe and put it on him, give him a ring for his hand and sandals for his feet, and bring the fatted calf, kill it, and let us eat and be merry; for my son here was dead and he has come to life, he was lost and he is found.' So they began to make merry. Now his elder son was out in the field . . . and he would not go in (Luke 15:22-25, 28). The father said to him, 'My son, you and I are always together, all I have is yours. We could not but make merry and rejoice, for your brother here was dead and he has come to life again, he was lost but he is found.'

WE MUST NOTE THE CONTEXT OF THESE PARABLES OF THE LOST sheep, the lost coin, and the lost son as revealing the worth of each soul in God's sight and of sinners in particular. Luke sets apart five chapters (15-19) to the gospel of the outcast—the three parables of the lost, the poor widow, the Pharisee and the publican, the story of Zacchaeus and the outcast taxgatherers. In all, Jesus reveals God's love for the unlovable and his will to love the loveless into loveliness. These parables are not primarily a defense of Jesus for keeping bad company, in the face of constant criticism for receiving sinners and eating with them, but a defense of God for his indomitable love for sinful men. The defense of Jesus, if any were needed, was that he wanted to be where God was and to be doing what his Father was doing. He was a friend of sinners precisely because God was so. For sheer artistry these stories are among the greatest in the world's literature. But, much more important, these parables reveal the mind of Jesus, as a friend of publicans and sinners, and the heart of God in his fundamental attitude toward men. If these parables are true then God is love. The stories are revolutionary in showing the nature of God, refuting some of the theologies of ancient Judaism and of all harsh and loveless Christian orthodoxies. The parables are so clear that they are themselves a commentary on the character of God and the teaching of Jesus. Yet they are as many-faceted as a fine-cut diamond.

In the first two parables, we have God seeking the lost; in the third he receives the repentant sinner who has been called home by his confidence in the Father's love and forgiveness. In speaking of the "lost," Jesus is not referring to final perdition. Anything is lost when it is away from the one to whom it belongs. These parables are not so much the story of a sheep, a coin, and a prodigal son, as they are of the Good Shepherd, one who is seeking a lost treasure, and of the prodigal's Father. The pathos of the story is not the necessary suffering of the prodigal feeding on husks, but the sorrow of the lonely father, long watching, wearily waiting and running breathless with joy to meet the wayward son. All parents who have tasted anything of the tragedy of life will know the meaning of these parables, as thoughtless, self-centered, inexperienced youth never can. These souls are lost to the divine fellowship and service, away from home and happiness, not in their proper place, nor fulfilling their true end of serving God and enjoying him forever.

No modern writer will feel the temerity of being adequate to write a criticism or commentary upon these matchless parables, "to gild refined gold, to paint the lily." He can only ask that they be read and reread from time to time as our experience deepens and opens our eyes to new aspects of truth. The sinners in the three parables are not only loose livers and disloyal tax-gatherers, but those too poor or careless to be religious and keep the Jewish law, as well as the loveless Pharisaic self-righteous who despise them, like the hardhearted elder brother. Yet none is beyond the pale of God's love, and none is forgotten. God does not merely love mankind in general, but one by one, each in his particular sin, or selfishness, or shortcoming.

THE SOCIAL TEACHING OF JESUS

Luke 10:25-37; Mark 12:28-34; Matt. 22:34-40

Now a jurist got up to tempt him. "Teacher," he said, "what am I to do to inherit life eternal?" He said to him, "What is written in the law? What do you read there?" He replied, *"You must love the Lord your God with your whole heart, with your whole soul, with your whole strength, and with your whole mind. Also your neighbour as yourself."* "A right answer!" said Jesus; *"do that and you will live."* Anxious to make an excuse for himself, however, he said to Jesus, "But who is my neighbour?" Jesus rejoined, "A man going down from Jerusalem to Jericho fell among robbers who stripped and belabored him and then went off leaving him half-dead. Now it so chanced that a priest was going down the same road, but on seeing him he went past on the opposite side. So did a Levite who came to the spot; he looked at him but passed on the opposite side (Luke 10-25-32). However a Samaritan traveller came to where he was and felt pity when he saw him; he went to him, bound his wounds up, pouring oil and wine into them, mounted him on his own steed, took him to an inn, and attended to him. Next morning he took out a couple of shillings and gave them to the innkeeper, saying, 'Attend to him, and if you are put to any extra expense I will refund you on my way back.' Which of these three men, in your opinion, proved a neighbour to the man who fell among the robbers?" He said, "The man who took pity on him." Jesus said to him, "Then go and do the same." (Luke 10:33-37.)

IN THIS PARABLE OF THE GOOD SAMARITAN AND IN SCORES OF OTHER passages, we see the inevitable social implications of Jesus' teaching: "Then go and do the same." His teaching is of course primarily individual and personal concerning the immediate relation of each soul to God, but the Kingdom and the family of God are inescapably social conceptions. In the light of Professor

H. J. Cadbury's *Peril of Modernizing Jesus*, we must take care not to read our own social thinking into Jesus' words. He rarely dealt with social institutions, or social motives, or problems. He approached social questions through the individual, saying, "make the tree good." His primary interest was not in making a better world, which he conceived to be God's task, but in fostering active goodness in men and women. He sought not the saving of society but to make a society of saviours; not to prevent robbery and injustice on the road to Jericho but to multiply good Samaritans; not to defend the rights of men but that all should be merciful like their heavenly Father. Jesus did not have a modern social outlook, yet he begets the attitude which develops into that outlook. And it is he who motivates our social vision and passion. "Jesus began"; we must continue and develop. He cast in the leaven which is still yeasting; he kindled a fire that has the potential of a conflagration to burn away dross.

The social implications of the gospel have been obscured, however, by several factors: (1) The early teaching of the speedy coming of Christ and the Kingdom left neither time nor responsibility to change the old social order that seemed to be doomed. (2) The early emphasis of the Fourth Gospel upon individual salvation as "eternal life" and the hope of a future heaven lost the mighty social hope of the coming Kingdom. (3) The over-emphasis of Protestantism since the Reformation upon a selfish, personal, possessive "salvation" that ignored or was blind to the social implications of Jesus' teaching. So far as we can recover the teaching and life of the historic Jesus, it will help us to grasp the full-orbed whole gospel of Christ. There was nothing selfish and exclusively individualistic in Christ's vision of the Kingdom of God as a redeemed society. Every advance toward the Kingdom not only involves a process of social education but a conflict with hostile social forces such as Jesus himself waged against the evils of his day. Jesus forces us to shift the emphasis from our selfish rugged individualism to the common good. He was the kind of a person who could make a noble leader say: "While there is a lower class, I am in it; while there is a criminal element, I am of it; while there is a soul in prison, I am not free."

Bishop Gore said: "Much that we are accustomed to hear called legitimate insistence upon the rights of property, the Old Testament would seem to call the robbery of God and grinding the faces of the poor." If evil is socialized, salvation must also be not only personalized but socialized. Organized groups and societies are needed to make the individual socially effective as a prospective citizen of the Kingdom of God. It should be the permanent social function of the church to proclaim the Kingdom and to be its human agency as well as to offer salvation to individuals. Wherever organized evil opposes the advance of God's rule, there is the social battle front. Instead of loving our neighbor as ourselves, contemporary Christians have often left the brother, for whom Christ died, in squalid slums, doomed him to the periodic hell of unemployment, and robbed him as truly as the rich robbed the poor in the days of Amos. It is not we as individuals but the economic system of monstrous injustice that we uphold which robs and crushes humanity, and we are responsible for that system. Christian people are often the chief supports of a system which means privilege for a few and monstrous injustice for many.

The great issue for decades following the war will be whether we are to provide justice for all, or special privilege and profit and power for the few—a few rich men and the class dependent upon them, and the relatively favored few of the white race. Economic injustice and race prejudice have been the flagrant sins of the Anglo-Saxon and Teutonic races. "The land of the free," boasting of its "free enterprise," has been the country of multi-millionaires and of pestilential slums. It has left ten million of its citizens in inexcusable illiteracy, many more than ten million in slums, urban and rural, and has left thirteen million Negroes segregated like untouchable outcasts, often impoverished, and denied equal justice at almost every point. Of sixty-one million babies born in the world last year, only seventeen millions, or less than one-third, belonged to the white race, and forty-four millions, or more than two-thirds, belonged to the colored races. If practically all Communists, as well as Moslems, Buddhists, Bahaists and members of several other religions, are free from any appreciable race prejudice, with its accompaniment of cruel injustice, are Anglo-Saxon and Teutonic Christians the ones most afflicted with this disease? Because intermarriage between any two individuals who come from communities widely separated in race, religion, or culture is normally unsuccessful and unhappy, are we, by our rationalization, to allow the fear of this for a few individuals to justify our persistent refusal to give equal justice, or equal rights, or equal education to the Negro race which we once enslaved and still segregate and rob? Race riots and race prejudice in both world wars have shown seams of weakness in our civilization which is basically unchristian.

Though the number has been greatly reduced in recent years, for many decades lynching has been the symptom of the deep-seated malady of race prejudice in certain states in America. We could place in evidence at this point a photograph of a lynching mob composed almost exclusively of members of the two principal churches and Sunday schools of the town where the lynching took place. In a debate in Soviet Russia on the subject of religion, the audience asked the speaker the connection between America's professed principle of Christian love and the practice of lynching. In a day when the "godless atheists" of Russia, with all their faults, seem almost as passionately concerned for social justice as was the prophet Amos, and are seeking to realize equal racial brotherhood in a classless society of unbroken comradeship, many of the professed followers of Jesus seem to be the greatest opponents of equal justice for the poor and of the equal racial brotherhood of all. His own followers seem to be the chief problem of Christ today as the leaders of his own people, the Pharisees, were in his time.

Almost the whole Sermon on the Mount is for Jesus' followers in the materialistic Western world "a hard saying." But who is right, he or we? Are we to admit that "this Galilean is too much for our small hearts?" To take Jesus seriously is indeed to enter upon a strange and alarming life, to abandon habits, to control instincts and impulses, to essay a difficult adventure which involves an incredible happiness. Here is one whose teaching implies the abolition of both slavery and war. We were willing legally to abolish chattel slavery and to outlaw war "as an instrument of national policy." We have done both—on paper. But, as a master race, we are not yet willing to abandon the exploitation and economic enslavement of another people, nor the economic injustice that results from our predatory social order of "free enterprise," which in practice means freedom for the wolves but not for the sheep. In plain language we are not ready to stop enslaving the Negro economically, nor to cease robbing the poor, as in the days of Amos, though our injustice is more monstrous today than in the time of Amos twenty-six centuries ago. Let God be found true though every man be a liar. Before the flaming eyes of love and wrath that drove the money-changers from the temple and before him who uttered the parable of the Good Samaritan, shall we admit that Jesus as prophet and teacher is right and follow him? Or, shall we turn back, each one to his own stubborn, selfish and sinful way, or merely call him "Lord, Lord" as nominal Christians? At least let us not be Pharisaic hypocrites.

Let us note also that we cannot separate the individual and social implications of Jesus' teaching; we cannot divorce what God has joined together in one whole gospel. There were two inseparable commands to love God and our neighbor. We cannot wrong our fellow men and say, in the words of Jesus, "corban," it is a gift to God. We cannot be contented with our own selfish "salvation" in some future heaven and turn hard hearts toward our needy fellow men under our modern systems of capitalism, imperialism and human exploitation. When a child which was claimed by two women was brought before King Solomon so that he might decide who was the real mother, he bade his soldiers cut it in two and give half to each mother. Had his command been carried out there would have been not two children, nor even two half-children, but two fragments of putrefying flesh. When men thus rend and tear asunder Christs' organic gospel, trying to divide it into two fragments, personal and social, they have not two gospels, nor even two half-gospels, but two half-truths, the one selfish and therefore sinful, the other shallow and impotent. Each by itself, if it excludes the other, is not real religion at all, but pseudo-religion. And we are left with an impotent and divided church in an anarchic world—a world, and a church, of rich and poor, possessors and dispossessed, owners and owned, in an intensifying class conflict drifting toward industrial warfare and ever the holocaust of another world war, which threatens our "Christian" civilization.

Even in the few brief passages from Jesus' teaching that we have been able to study with our limitations of space, we have surely found that Jesus is the supreme prophet and teacher of all mankind. It was he who revealed the will of God in life, word, and deed. The rule of God in the hearts of men that Jesus actually did found was not *a* religion, new and separate, but religion itself. He gathers up into his conception of God and man the highest known values of life in the swift, piercing insight of his own experience. If the pure in heart could see God, he, above all men, had the undimmed vision of the Almighty and Eternal. His is the religion of the human heart in its simplest and fullest form. Paul finds love the greatest thing in the world, but "We love because he first loved us." How knew this man "never having learned"; how could he with unerring instinct always pierce to the heart of spiritual reality and see the essential even if it contradicted all tradition, all custom and all authority? Surely "never man so spake."

6

The Great Question: Who Say Ye That I Am?

Mark 8:27-38; Matt. 16:13-20; Luke 9:18-21

Then Jesus and his disciples set off for the villages of Caesarea
Philippi. On the road he inquired of his disciples, "Who
do people say I am?" "John the Baptist," they told him,
"though some say Elijah, and others say you are one of the
prophets." So he inquired of them, "And who do you say
I am?" Peter replied, "You are the Christ." Then he forbade them to tell anyone about him. And he proceeded to
teach them that the Son of man had to endure great suffering, to be rejected by the elders and the high priests and
the scribes, to be killed, and after three days to rise again; he
spoke of this quite freely. Peter took him and began to re-
prove him for it, but he turned on him and noticing his
disciples reproved Peter, telling him, "Get behind me, you
Satan! Your outlook is not God's but man's." Then he called
the whole company to him with his disciples and said to
them, "If anyone wishes to follow me, let him deny himself,
take up his cross, and so follow me; for whoever wants to
save his life will lose it, and whoever loses his life for my
sake and the gospel's will save it. What profit is it for a man
to gain the whole world and to forfeit his soul? What could
a man offer as an equivalent for his soul? Whoever is
ashamed of me and my words in this disloyal and sinful generation, the Son of man will be ashamed of him when he
comes in the glory of his Father with the holy angels.

A RAPID READING OF MARK'S GOSPEL WILL SHOW THAT JESUS'
searching question "Who do you say I am" marks the climax
of this earliest Christian record. This question is a watershed
dividing the Gospel into two approximately equal parts; it is the
crucial question which makes history. Mark's original text is:
"The beginning of the good news of Jesus, *the Christ*." As an
introduction, Mark shows that John's baptism of repentance

prepares the nation for its Messiah, while Jesus' baptism, when he is anointed by the Spirit, and his temptations clarify his call to the Messianic office. His proclamation of the good news that God's reign is *near*, introduces the call of the first four disciples to prepare them to proclaim with him the approach of the Kingdom. From Capernaum, Jesus goes through the cities of Galilee proclaiming the Kingdom, which is attested by his mighty works of healing and the making whole of the sick and the demented. Jesus' ministry provokes the growing opposition of the religious leaders in defense of the threatened infallible Law and this opposition steadily develops to the inevitable end. Seeing that the leaders and the nation as a whole are refusing to repent and receive him, Jesus withdraws and prepares the Twelve to proclaim the coming Kingdom. Now at last they are ready for the supreme test question, the question of destiny: *Who am I?*

After his teaching and the Sermon on the Mount, we might have expected that the ultimate question would be concerned with the nature of God, or the coming Kingdom, or of man's supreme duty as the test of discipleship, or of the great commandments which summarize the Law and the prophets. For these had been Jesus' themes until this moment. Now the supreme issue is his Messiahship. And once this is settled and this key question is answered, Mark's Gospel moves swiftly and logically to its climax with but few digressions. The transfiguration is the preparation "for his decease which he was about to accomplish," a victory he has to achieve, for "he *must* go through with his death and departure at Jerusalem" (Luke 9:31). Then there follows the explanation that John is Elijah the forerunner of the Messiah. There is the repeated foretelling of his Messianic death to the blinded disciples. There is the girding up of his loins for the last journey toward his awful fate; the pathetic "triumphal entry," the last conflicts with the leaders over the implications of his claims, the thirteenth chapter concerning the last things and his triumphant return, the Passover and the Lord's Supper, Gethsemane and Golgotha, and all the vivid details of the Passion which the writers of all four Gospels obviously feel are the last divine acts of the drama of salvation.

For Mark, the Synoptics, and the early Christians, the story is one consistent whole, pregnant with Messianic meaning. The writers all endeavor to show God's way of saving man through Jesus as the Messiah—a crucified Messiah who becomes the world's Saviour. If the above represents the outline of Mark's thought, the focal, crucial question of all is *"Who am I?"* Let us remember that the issue was not what honor they would do to Jesus. The answer to this question will reveal the disciples' conception of the nature of God, of the Kingdom or rule of God, of the way of salvation and the duty of man. And the question is equally searching and significant for us today.

Matthew, who copies almost all of Mark, tells the same story of redemption, but with added emphasis upon the teaching of Jesus and of his fulfillment of prophecy, but he leads up, as does Luke, to the same great climax "Who do the crowds say I am" and then "Who do you say that I am?" According to the first three Gospels, some think Jesus is John the Baptist returned, some Elijah, others Jeremiah, or "one of the ancient prophets risen again," but, significantly, none suggest that he is the Messiah. For Jesus had not spoken publicly of the secret of his vocation, nor had the humble aspect of his appearance suggested the conquering Deliverer of Israel.

Caesarea Philippi was in the far pagan north under the shadow of Mount Hermon, within the territory of Philip. Jesus' test question was perhaps asked after the menace to his life in Galilee by Herod Antipas. Not in Judea or Galilee, but in pagan Caesarea, far from the Temple, the synagogues, the priests, the scribes and Pharisees of proud Jerusalem, in this outcast semi-Gentile territory was this first confession made which was to be the foundation of the universal church. With fierce opposition growing and events closing in about him, Jesus feels he must know if these weak men are ready for the momentous confession which was to become the basis of their immediate mission, of the Christian church, and of their making of history. If none born of woman was greater than John, Jesus must now stand alone as the final messenger of God to Israel, the Anointed One through whom the Reign of God is to come. This was why the Kingdom was at last at hand *in him*. His recent journeys for retirement with his disciples in the region of Tyre and Sidon, in the Ten Cities and the northern borders of Hermon, almost banished and outlawed by the Jewish leaders, perhaps indicate a period of suspense in Jesus' mind in which he was pondering the nature of his mission and its issue, as well as his feeling that the crisis had arrived in the life of the disciples upon whom he must soon solely depend. This marks the turning point of his mission, his ministry and his message. Have the Twelve by their own spiritual insight recognized him as the Messiah, and what manner of Messiah is he? The one essential test for them is personal devotion to him *as Messiah*.

Characteristically, Peter, the first to discern his Messiahship, the first to witness his resurrection, the natural and spiritual leader of the Twelve, answers: *"You are the Christ!"* To call him "the Son of the Living God" or a hundred other titles could add nothing to this momentous confession. Jesus' heart leaps within him as he hears at last for the first time from human lips the antiphonal response to the heavenly voice heard within at his baptism. Jesus now says, in substance: "You are a man blessed of God, Simon, for it was my Father in heaven, not flesh and blood, that revealed this to you. *Now* I can tell you, Rock is your name and on this rock of your faith and confession I will build for eternity and the gates of Hades and all the powers of evil shall never prevail against this spiritual kingdom." It is the striking contrast between the Jewish and the Christian conception of the Messiah which forms the climax of the Synoptic Gospels.

Matthew now adds what was probably a Jewish-Christian tradition from the Jewish circle of "the Petrine party" of Antioch where Peter was held in peculiar esteem (Matt. 16:18-20; I Cor. 1:12). It cannot be regarded as a genuine utterance of Jesus. The word "church" is used in the Gospels only here and in Matthew (18:17); but here it is in accordance with a much later usage of the whole world-wide church with its smaller congregations, known only in the later period of the Acts and when Matthew wrote his Gospel. Jesus was always proclaiming the coming Kingdom, not a church which Paul and the apostles later established. This passage in Matthew is not mentioned by the Church Fathers of the entire second century. The earliest documents which accorded spiritual authority to all the Twelve never gave Peter such an absolute and unique status. At Antioch Paul resisted Peter "to the face, because he stood condemned." Unstable Simon was not as yet rocklike in character; rather the rock is his confession of faith. This Jewish tradition became the main proof-text for the Roman Catholic doctrine of the Papacy, and the claims of the see of Rome were based upon it, as the historic representative of Peter through the ages. Parts of this passage cannot bear close scrutiny; but against the spiritual edifice that Christ founded, the powers of Hades have never prevailed, even during the Dark Ages or the intellectual revolution of the Renaissance.

These later passages of the Synoptic Gospels are obviously colored by the experience and faith of the early church, which are read back into the account of Jesus. Jesus was doubtless convinced both of his own doom and of the final triumph of God and of his Kingdom. But this is recorded by the Evangelists in terms of the Crucifixion and resurrection which seemed crystal clear and indisputable to the early church, but would have been unintelligible to the disciples at this period. They were startled and surprised by the resurrection and were not expecting it as they would have been if these clear prophecies had been made in these explicit terms. So also the Great Commission with which Matthew summarizes his Gospel, with its trinitarian baptism, is in the language and experience of the later church and not of the Kingdom which Jesus always proclaimed.

This does not mean, of course, that the early church and the gospel of Christ preached by Paul were wrong. It means that our quest at this point is the recovery, in so far as possible, of the historic Jesus, and not the interpretation of the later church, its sacraments and its rudimentary theology: "This is doubtless a case in which the original prediction of Jesus has been conformed to the later events in which it was fulfilled." It is our conviction, however, that the final, crucial question of the historic Jesus for his disciples was "Who am I?" And also that Peter and the Synoptic Gospels give the correct answer: "Thou art the Christ." It is therefore from this moment that the portrait of Jesus who is to become the eternal Christ, begins to appear in clear outline. In the second half of the Synoptic Gospels, from the time of this destiny-determining question, the light falls more and more upon Jesus as destined to be the Messiah and the Son of Man in the sense of Daniel (7:13-14).

Jesus, apparently, also sees the prophets' vision of the ever-lasting Kingdom which is to be bestowed on the saints of the Most High in the person of the "Son of Man." He here finds language in which to predict his own redeeming and expiatory work (Mark 8:38; 9:1; 13:26; 14:61-62). Here he begins to combine three differing and seemingly contradictory streams of prophecy: the final consummation of the coming Kingdom and of the Messiah, the Son of Man in Daniel, and the Suffering Servant of Isaiah (52:12-53:12). In Jesus' time, the Servant was probably not identified with the Messiah, for passages which speak of the humiliation of the Servant are interpreted of the people of Israel, while only those which speak of the glory of the Servant are referred to the Messiah. The Messianic woes or pangs are appointed not for the glorious Messiah but for the inhabitants of the earth during the great tribulation. It is in the light of this background that we must realize the stunning shock to Simon and the Twelve when Jesus says that the glorious Messiah himself must be spat upon and be crucified!

Cicero says that the very name of the cross should not be thought of, seen, or heard in good Roman society. But this cold Roman could have no conception of the horror with which a devout Jew would resent the insulting statement that the glorious Deliverer of Israel, eagerly awaited through centuries of captivity and gloom, would finally be rejected by all Jewish religious leaders and crucified by his own people at the hands of the hated, pagan Roman governor. Here is the final paradox of history, the great overturning and humiliation, the transvaluation of all values.

As soon as Peter makes his epoch-making confession of Jesus

as the Messiah, then and only then are the long-prepared disciples ready for the final, shocking truth. Jesus strictly forbids them to tell anyone the Messianic secret. He does not decline the Messianic title, but the false expectations of the people that had pressed upon him from the time of his temptations. Yes, he was indeed the Messiah, but a Messiah who *must* suffer, must be despised and rejected of men. As truly as God must ultimately reign and rule, so truly God himself must suffer in his great representative. This Messiah, who was also Son and Saviour, must reveal the very heart of God which was love. This love was dimly foreshadowed in the tragedy of Hosea's broken home and faithfulness to his unfaithful wife, in the history of Jeremiah's lifelong crucifixion, in the figure of the Suffering Servant who was despised and rejected of men, who was wounded for our transgressions and bruised for our iniquities, who was numbered with the transgressors and bare the sin of many. But all these and other prophecies were fulfilled and realized only in Jesus. The remnant is finally reduced to One.

Jesus now takes to himself definitely the office of the Man through whom the Kingdom is to come, the Son of Man who is to redeem his people, the Suffering Servant who is to bear their iniquities, the Lamb of God who must be slain. From now on, we shall find that the future and supernatural aspect of the Reign of God and of the Messiah assume clearer form in the record.

Jesus now announces to Peter and to all that the Son of Man has to endure great suffering, must be rejected by the elders, high priests, and scribes and be killed. Every agonizing detail is etched upon his consciousness. But he shows that this eternal truth which is the very heart of the gospel, not only applies to himself, as the Christ, but to every prospective follower of his throughout the centuries:

> If anyone wishes to come after me, let him deny himself, take up his cross day after day, and so (as a cross bearer) follow me; for whoever wants to save his life will lose it, and whoever loses his life for my sake, he will save it. What profit will it be for a man to gain the whole world and lose or for-

feit himself? For whoever is ashamed of me and my words, of him will the Son of man be ashamed when he comes in his glory and in the glory of the Father.

The doctrine of the Cross for the true disciple was the very gospel which was to be proclaimed to all the world. Therefore Jesus "spake the saying openly." It could only be finally understood in the light of the Crucifixion and the resurrection which Paul, having fully experienced, was to explain and proclaim.

The wooden cross for Jesus meant perfect obedience to the Father's will. It was not from Judas, or Pilate, or the high priest, or from the multitude, but "the cup which my Father hath given me." So the Cross for Jesus' followers means loyalty to Christ and his principles in every wooden circumstance or human situation. The essence of the Christian life is not found in self-realization, nor in negative self-renunciation which is but a means, but in self-consecration to the divine will which Jesus exemplified. Here we touch the deepest depths, the most characteristic vital heart-center of Christianity. Its symbol is rightly the Cross. This is the epitome not only of the life of Jesus, but of all true Christian life. "If *anyone* wishes to come after me." There is no other way for him or for any true follower of his. "*Whoever* wants to save his life shall lose it." As Jesus sternly sets his face to go up to Jerusalem to claim the city for God, he calls his followers to abandon everything for God's Kingdom which is surely coming. And the Kingdom is henceforth unescapably bound up with Jesus himself: "Whoever is ashamed of me; of him will the Son of man be ashamed." The natural man must protest against a cross for Jesus or for himself, as Simon Peter did, or Simon of Cyrene, compelled to carry Jesus' cross, but who became the father of two early Christians (Mark 15:21-22). When Peter reproves his Master, Jesus sees the recrudescence of his original temptation to be a successful Messiah, and says in the Aramaic idiom "Get back, get away, you are a hindrance and a temptation to me with your human viewpoint, which is contrary to God's."

7

THE CRISIS IN JERUSALEM

Mark 10:32—Mark 13:37; Luke 18:31—Luke 22:38; Matt. 20:17
—Matt. 25:46

They were on the way up to Jerusalem, Jesus walking in front of them; the disciples were in dismay and the company who followed were afraid. So once again he took the twelve aside and proceeded to tell them what was going to happen to himself (Mark 10:32). James and John, the sons of Zebedaeus, came up to him saying, "Teacher, we want you to do whatever we ask you" (Mark 10:35). So Jesus called them and said (Mark 10-41), "Whoever wants to be great among you must be your servant, and whoever of you wants to be first must be the slave of all; for the Son of man himself has not come to be served but to serve, and to give his life as a ransom for many" (Mark 10:44-45). And when he saw the city, as he approached, he wept over it, saying, "Would that you too knew even to-day on what your peace depends! But no, it is hidden from you! A time is coming for you when your enemies will throw up ramparts round you and encircle you and besiege you on every side and raze you and your children within you to the ground, leaving not one stone upon another within you—and all because you would not understand when God was visiting you." Then he went into the temple and proceeded to drive out those who were selling. "It is written," he told them, "my house shall be a house of prayer, but you have made it a den of robbers."

ALREADY DRIVEN FROM HEROD'S TERRITORY WHERE HIS LIFE WAS in danger—"for Herod purposes to kill thee"—Jesus now sets his face to go up to the citadel and seat of the enemy; for no prophet can perish out of Jerusalem. Already the shadow of Gethsemane and Golgotha are upon him and he goes with open eyes to meet his fate. Mark gives us a vivid picture of Jesus, alone now in his mental agony, striding on ahead, the awe-stricken disciples behind, and still farther in the rear a group of terrified adherents. No wonder they were all afraid, for the journey meant certain death. The shepherd would be struck down and the sheep scattered. With this "shuddering awe" upon Jesus, he wishes to be alone, and his followers, sensitive to this unwonted mood, feel the impending doom which is to engulf them all. Three times he warns the disciples of the nation's rejection of their Messiah (Mark 8:31; 9:30-32; 10:33-34). Jesus, as the nation's one last hope, is to be mocked, spat upon, scourged and put to death as a criminal. Is this to be the climax of Jewish history after two thousands years of preparation of the chosen people for their Messiah and Saviour?

Yet Jesus' fate in Jerusalem is to be the means by which he is to be invested with Messianic glory in the purpose of God. The Twelve had been afraid to ask the meaning of the mystery of his death, for they had been disputing as to which of them was to be the greatest in the coming Kingdom (Mark 9:30-37). Jesus shows that the test of greatness is in humble service, to be the servant of all. Placing a little child in their midst and taking him in his arms, as Mark twice notices, Jesus shows for all time the beauty of the childlike spirit. A child is not consciously humble; he is utterly unself-conscious, he is helpless, yet dependent; trustful, teachable, confident, entering with fresh wonder the ever-new experiences of life. And with this example before them, the disciples must start their lives over again from the beginning in this new spirit. Only the childlike in spirit, who turn and become as little children, can enter the Kingdom of Heaven and become great in it. Service and humility are the marks of true greatness. Jesus not only shows repeatedly that humility is the doorway of entrance and the condition of every advance in the Kingdom, but he shows forever the standard of true greatness and the infinite value of the little child.

The journey to Jerusalem and Jesus' every act and word in the city of the Great King is Messianic. Jesus is going up, through whatever tragedy, to possess the Kingdom. James and John, "sons of thunder," who in flaming anger would have called down fire from heaven on a Samaritan village that withstood them (Luke 9:54) and had just been disputing who was to be the greatest in the Kingdom, now press forward to ask for the first places of honor and authority in the new age. Jesus is amazed at their blindness. Can they drink his cup of suffering? Can they be immersed in the baptism of martyrdom which he is about to endure? Self-confident, like Peter shortly after, they declare they are competent. Yes, says Jesus, they shall indeed share his fate. James was soon put to death by Herod Agrippa in 44 A.D. (Acts 12:2) and Papias is quoted as saying that "John the divine and his brother James were slain by the Jews." When the ten burn with jealous anger at this sin of pride which all of them shared, Jesus declares again and unforgettably the standard of true greatness in the Kingdom which he had repeatedly described from the time of the Beatitudes and the Great Sermon: to be a servant, a bondslave of all, and finally, like their Master, to give their own lives in uttermost sacrifice. As pride is man's primal sin, repentant humility is always Jesus' first Beatitude. It is the little wicket gate where Bunyan's Christian enters the way that leads to the foot of the Cross. There the burden of sin rolls away and he goes on his way "glad and lightsome with a merry heart."

It is not surprising that from now on every act and word of the Master, and in contrast those of the blind self-seeking disciples, is seen in the light of the Cross. We can now hardly separate the original words of the Master and the afterthoughts of the disciples and the Evangelists. A ransom "for many" points back to the great chapter of the Suffering Servant—despised and rejected of men, a man of sorrows and acquainted with grief, bearing our griefs and carrying our sorrows, wounded for our transgressions and bruised for our iniquities, brought as a lamb to the slaughter and stricken for the transgression of his people, he bears the sin of "many." The idea of a "ransom" was a price paid to secure benefits for another, especially life and liberty. We must not try to read back into this word fully developed theories of the Atonement. Jesus' death, like his life, was all one unbroken and perfect piece of service and self-sacrifice for his followers; though they were only to understand this after the shame and agony of his death and the triumph of his resurrection. Nothing could thereafter prevent the disciples and Evangelists from reading the supreme sacrifice of his love into every appropriate prophecy of the Old Testament and almost every word and act of his life. Henceforth, all was understood, and rightly understood, only in the light of the Cross. But Golgotha cast its dark shadow long before the light of Calvary broke upon them.

The "triumphal entry" was dramatic with pathos. Mark represents Jesus' entry into the holy city as "the coming of Zion's King." Jesus apparently sees himself, and the Evangelists certainly feel him to be, consciously fulfilling prophecy:

> Rejoice indeed O maiden Sion,
>   Shout aloud, dear Jerusalem.
> Here comes your King,
>   triumphant and victorious,
>   riding humbly on an ass, . . .
> His words make peace for nations,
>   his sway extends from sea to sea,
>   from the Euphrates to the ends of the earth . . . .
> He shall set his feet on the mount of Olives . . . .
> The Lord will come suddenly to his temple . . . .
> Do you take this house, my very own house,
>   for a robber's cave? [1]

The disciples looking back see their Lord, who had emptied himself and taken upon him the form of a servant, no longer on foot but mounted and surrounded by rejoicing and expectant multitudes, who spread their garments beneath his feet as for a royal conqueror, shouting hosannas (or God save the King) for the expected restoration of David's throne, and crying "Blessed is the Kingdom that cometh." Yet their Lord is meek and lowly, riding upon a humble ass, a peaceful monarch, "just and having salvation." The Evangelist believes the event was designed by Jesus for his Messianic purpose. Schweitzer thinks the episode had Messianic significance in the mind of Jesus himself, but that the crowds looked upon him as Elijah the forerunner of the Messiah. For Jesus is as yet a veiled Messiah; his secret is still undisclosed. Yet wild rumors are astir, the authorities are alarmed, and the

[1] Moffatt's translation. Zech. 9:9, 10; 14:4. Mal. 3:1; and Jer. 7:11.

Messiahship, true or false, is the issue at his trial; though to the pagan Pilate, he will be made intelligible not as a religious Messiah but only as a "King of the Jews." Even the multitudes who at best only think of a political Messianism are not ready for a spiritual revolution which would change men's hearts and prepare them for God's rule. All misunderstand him. All his followers will forsake him and flee, and the rulers and religious leaders will put him to death.

Every detail is now etched upon the memory of the disciples. While the first thirty years of Jesus' life are passed over almost in silence, the events of the Passion Week cover, roughly speaking, a third of all of Mark's and Matthew's and a fourth of Luke's Gospels. All four Evangelists seem to feel that there is deep, pregnant meaning in this unfathomable, superhuman tragedy; from first to last it is a solemn mystery of God.

Jesus had chosen the Passover at which to make his supreme attempt and finally challenge the nation. If, as the Fourth Evangelist maintains, the death of Jesus occurred on the Preparation of the Passover, then Jesus was crucified on the fourteenth of the Jewish month Nisan.[2] If John is right as to the date, we may follow Mark's narrative of the crucial week as follows: Jesus enters Jerusalem on Monday, the tenth of Nisan (Mark 11:11); on Tuesday he cleanses the Temple (11:15-18); on Wednesday come the controversies in the Temple and the discourse concerning the future (11:20 ff.); on Thursday occurs his final appearance in the Temple; he arraigns the scribes and Pharisees, and partakes of the last meal with his disciples. This is followed by the agony, the arrest, and the trial before the Sanhedrin (14:12-72).

[2] According to Mark and Luke, the Last Supper appears to have coincided with the Paschal meal. Most scholars hold that John is right here (John 19:14; Mark 14:12; Luke 22:7). The Jewish high priest, even though the trial was irregular and unjust, would try to get it over before the holy Passover. The room for the Last Supper had been prepared for the Passover. Everything is ready except the lamb. Perhaps Jesus, aware of Judas' treachery, does not wait for the lamb but sits down on Thursday evening with the disciples. Jesus had been accustomed to observe the weekly *kiddush* ceremony with his disciples where a solemn thanksgiving was pronounced over a cup of wine at the conclusion of a meal. He now shares with them the Last Supper.

On Friday the final trial before Pilate takes place, followed by the Crucifixion (Mark 15).

On his arrival in Jerusalem, Jesus "looked round about at everything; but as it was late, he went away with the twelve to Bethany." The next morning as his first symbolic act, "entering the temple he proceeded to drive out those who were buying and selling inside the temple; he upset the tables of the money-changers and the stalls of those who sold doves. . . . This came to the ears of the scribes and high priests, and they tried to get him put to death, for they were afraid of him."

Jesus has come to the Temple to challenge the hostile forces arrayed against him where they are most strongly entrenched. In the vast outer court, twelve hundred feet in length by six hundred in width, the Temple fair, or oriental bazaar, is in full swing with its lively trafficking and profiteering in the lucrative trade in which the priests were financially interested. Wine, corn, oil, and incense were for sale, with cattle and doves for the sacrifices, while bankers were busy exchanging foreign money into Greek and Roman equivalents, or into the half shekel for the Temple tax. Similar scenes are observable at Mecca today and in the noisy temples of Asia. Suddenly there is an uproar and a prophetic voice rings through the great throng: "It is written my house shall be called a house of prayer for all nations but you have made it a den of robbers." Jesus dares to challenge the whole "system" in this Holy of Holies of Israel's religion. Before his burning moral indignation there is no intervention by the Temple guard. By this bold challenge of the authorities in a public affront to the Jewish religion which centered in the Temple, probably as a Messianic act, Jesus did what the Scriptures had foretold that the Messiah would do (Isa. 56:7; Jer. 7:11; Mal. 3:1-3; Zech. 14:21). He had come to cast fire upon the earth and this was the means by which he would "acomplish his decease in Jerusalem" (Luke 9:31). Perhaps he was seeking to take the Kingdom by force and to give his life in order to compel its advent. From this moment all his opponents are united in trying swiftly to destroy him. His challenge had been not to Rome as the chief enemy, but in the citadel and center of religion, and that the highest yet known on earth.

Jesus replies to the authorities by his parable of the wicked husbandman (Matt. 21:33-46; Luke 20:9-19). Here the owner of the vineyard, sending servant after servant to be rejected, finally sends his "beloved son" whom they kill. But Jesus warns his people that the vineyard will be taken from the wicked usurpers and given to others, and that the stone which the builders reject will become the chief cornerstone. Jesus repeatedly warns of the destruction of Jerusalem in these last appeals to the conscience of Israel. And soon Simon Peter is to interpret these warnings and to charge the Sanhedrin with the murder of their Messiah (Acts 2:23; 3:14; 4:10-11; 5:29-31).

The Pharisees and Herodians in order to catch him, now ask the difficult question whether it is lawful to pay the tribute money or head tax to Caesar. If Jesus answers that it is lawful, presumably he will lose all popularity with the multitude, for Judas of Galilee's popular battle cry "No tribute to the Romans" had been in the air ever since 6 A.D. If Jesus says it is unlawful, he becomes a dangerous revolutionary whom they can ask Pilate to eliminate. When Jesus asks for a denarius he expresses no opinion as to the theoretical rightfulness or wrongfulness of Caesar's rule, but shows that since they themselves were receiving his money and keeping his coins in circulation, they were already acknowledging his rule and answering their own question.

When Mark wrote his Gospel he saw that Jesus' words could be read in the light of Paul's recognition of the divine authority of government (Rom. 13:1-8), and thus defend Christianity from the charge of disloyalty to the state. Jesus' words have been of enormous influence historically. As Lord Acton showed, they 'gave to the civil power, under the protection of the conscience, a sacredness it had never enjoyed and bounds it had never acknowledged: and they were the repudiation of absolutism and the inauguration of freedom." This brief sentence is but typical of the way in which the whole life and teaching of Jesus have entered into every phase of Christian culture and civilization,

their standards and ideals, their laws and institutions—the ver
warp and woof of the life of "Christendom."

No sooner are the Pharisees and Herodians for the momen
routed than the Sadducees try to entrap Jesus by a catch ques
tion regarding the resurrection. These conservative ecclesiastic
had a horror of fanaticism, and of popular movements or re
ligious enthusiasm; they counted themselves rational modernist
who believed in no supernatural resurrection. This was a recen
belief in Judaism whose vogue dated from the period of Mac
cabean martyrdoms of the last two centuries. The Sadducee
bring forward one of their stock arguments to prove that th
Law could have contemplated no such resurrection in view o
its provisions for remarriage (Deut. 25:5-10). Jesus replies tha
they neither understand the Scriptures which they quote, no
the power of God whose resources are not confined to the nar
row limits of the materialistic Sadducean imagination. The pur
pose of marriage on its physical side is to continue the race in
a world subjected to the prevalence of death. When death i
abolished, physical marriage and birth will also be abolished
Those who attain to the resurrection will be in this respect a
the angels in heaven. And Jesus adds the argument from Exodu
(3:6) where God is represented as still the God of the ancien
patriarchs, despite the fact of their decease. This argument fo
life after death Mark wished to record for his Roman readers
He shows that Jesus' spiritual view of the resurrection is similar
to Paul's (I Cor. 15) in answer to contemporary crudely mate
rialistic conceptions.

There now follows Jesus' final discourse about the events of
the future (Mark 13:1-37; Matt. 24:1-25; Luke 21:5-38). Mark
shows that the occasion of the discourse was the disciples' ques
tion of when the destruction of the Temple, which Jesus had
prophesied, would take place. But Matthew, having copied
Mark's question "When shall these things be," adds his own
eschatological question: "and what shall be the sign of thy com
ing and of the end of the world," supposing, apparently, that the
destruction of Jerusalem, the second coming of Christ and the
end of the age, or world, were all to take place almost immedi-

ately. Herod's Temple, begun about 70 B.C., was still unfinished and was justly accounted one of the wonders of the world. It was impressive in grandeur, built of pure white marble, its eastern front covered with plates of gold which threw back the rays of the rising sun for miles around. Yet Jesus is convinced, like Micah and Jeremiah of old, that the Temple and the holy city are doomed (Mic. 3:12; Jer. 26:6, 18). Such a prophecy seemed blasphemous, for the Temple signified the visible presence of the Deity; yet the city and the Temple were utterly destroyed by fire by Titus in 70 A.D.

The practical object of Jesus' discourse was not to satisfy morbid curiosity but to warn against false messiahs and multiplying prophecies of the end. From the time of the Maccabees to Bar Cocheba's claim to be the Messiah in 132 A.D., there was a Messianic background to almost every popular movement that swept over turbulent Palestine. This morbid interest in the comfort of apocalyptic prophecy has not been confined to the Jews but has been prevalent throughout history, especially in times of catastrophe and world war. Here is a typical pronouncement: "Our earth is degenerate in these latter days. There are signs that the world is speedily coming to an end. Children no longer obey their parents. Every man wants to write a book. The end of the world is evidently approaching."

The writer saw this written prophecy, not uttered during the first or second World War, but inscribed upon an old Assyrian tablet now in the museum at Constantinople. Its approximate date is estimated as 2800 B.C., or long before the time of Abraham. In the light of this and multiplied similar evidence, it is well to remember that men have been making these prophecies and eagerly believing them for more than 4,700 years.

We would do well to take to heart the sane words of warning of Jesus not to be credulous over millennial hopes, but to remember that the most certain authentic words in this last discourse are:

Take care that no one misleads you (Mark 13:6). When you hear of wars and rumours of war do not be alarmed (Mark 13:7). If anyone tells you "Look, here is the Christ, or Look, there he is" do not believe it (Mark 13:21). No one knows anything of that day or hour, not even the angels in heaven, not even the Son, but only the Father (Mark 13:22). It is not for you to know the course and periods of time that the Father has fixed by his own authority (Acts 1:7).

Another thing that should place us on our guard is the warning, "Let the *reader* note this" (Mark 13:14; Matt. 24:15). Most scholars think that Mark's ultimate source here was a written document called "The Little Apocalypse," an oracle circulated among the Christians in Judea shortly before the siege of Jerusalem and which actually led them, according to the testimony of Eusebius, "in obedience to an oracle vouchsafed to the leaders there by revelation," to flee from the doomed city and escape across the mountains of Gilead to the little city of Pella, where the church remained in safety during the terrible Roman war in Palestine. The "reader" indicates not the student of the book of Daniel concerning "the abomination of desolation" (the small altar of Zeus which Antiochus Epiphanes placed upon the great altar of sacrifice about 168 B.C.), but the reader of this Christian oracle. "Let them that are in Judea flee" shows that the prophecy was designed originally not for Mark's readers in Rome, but for the people of Judea to whom this small apocalypse was addressed. Mark's purpose was to show Christ as having foreseen the course of future events, both the calamities which were to fall upon the church and upon the world.

All the Synoptic writers were looking for the coming End of the Age. Jesus was the Messiah declared to be the Son of God with power by the resurrection, destined to come again in glory (Mark 8:38), and a host of Gentile converts were "to wait for the coming of his Son from heaven" (I Thess. 1:9-10). As the years passed, the cry went up, "O Lord how long?" Tacitus in his *Histories*, after referring to the wars, portents and calamities of the time, says that, "Never has it been proved by such terrible disasters to Rome or such clear evidence that the gods were concerned not with our safety but with vengeance on our sins." There was a similar outlook in the Jewish, Greco-Roman,

Persian and ancient oriental world. As the days lengthened and Christ did not come quickly, Christians began to insert explanations and preliminary conditions, or to reinterpret the parables, such as "the gospel must first be preached to all nations." The impatient ones were corrected when "they imagined God's Reign would *instantly* come into view" (Luke 19:11). But the readers of Matthew, especially, were sorely tried when they read that the end of the world will come, the stars will fall from heaven, the Son of Man will come on the clouds and gather the elect from the four quarters of heaven, before this generation shall pass away, so that some standing there should witness the great consummation (Matt. 24:29-34). Simple integrity demands that we must recognize that *some* one made a mistake. It was the Fourth Gospel which corrected all this by pointing out that Christ had come already, once for all, that the believer individually was even now a partaker of eternal life, that the coming of the Spirit, and the certainty of the many mansions in the world beyond were the essential fulfillment, not of apocalyptic dreams, but of the sane and sure promises that Jesus had made when on earth. So tactfully that it is not realized, John corrects Matthew, Mark, and Luke and defends Jesus against his early disciples and reporters.

At the close of Jesus' arraignment of the rulers in Jerusalem, he utters the heartbreaking cry over the doomed city:

I will send you prophets, wise men, and scribes, some of whom you will kill and crucify, some of whom you will flog in your synagogues and persecute from town to town; it is that on you may fall the punishment for all the just blood shed on earth from the blood of Abel the just down to the blood of Zechariah the son of Barachiah, whom you murdered between the sanctuary and the altar. I tell you truly, it will all come upon this generation. O Jerusalem, Jerusalem! slaying the prophets and stoning those who have been sent to you! How often I would fain have gathered your children as a fowl gathers her brood under her wings! But you would not have it! See, your House is left to you, desolate. For I tell you, you will never see me again till you say, Blessed be he who comes in the Lord's name.

Jesus' teaching was too popular and too provocative for the rulers to allow it to continue. The cleansing of the Temple was his final symbolic act and meant his death warrant. The high-priestly clan in Jerusalem must now make common cause with the scribes, Pharisees, Herodians, and all his enemies to have him speedily put to death. The high priest at the time was Joseph Caiaphas (18-36 A.D.), but his father-in-law, Annas (6-15 A.D.), was still alive and was the real head of the priesthood. Five of his sons and sons-in-law had held the high priesthood during his lifetime, and had their palace in Jerusalem where the council was held which decided on the death of Jesus.

We shall probably never understand Judas and his motive for betraying his Master. It could hardly have been merely the base love of money, later attributed to him. Jesus would not have chosen that kind of a man. If Judas was from Judea and all the other apostles were Galileans, he may have become alienated from them; or the word for Iscariot may have been *Sicarius*, meaning a left-wing Zealot, and Judas may have hoped to force Jesus' hand in order to make him declare his Messiahship and assert his power. It is also not clear whether Judas betrayed the place where Jesus could be found, or the Messianic secret that Jesus did indeed claim to be the Messiah, which would provide them with the evidence needful for a capital charge. If Judas had never dreamed that his betrayal would lead to the Crucifixion, it may have driven him in remorse to "repent" and hang himself as Matthew relates. "The Field of Blood," according to Matthew, was so called because purchased with Judas' blood money, while Peter in the Acts ascribes the name to the blood of Judas which was poured upon it. Matthew sees in the event the fulfillment of a prophecy in Zechariah (11:13) which he wrongly ascribes to Jeremiah (Matt. 27:3-10; Acts 1:16-19).

Jesus would have gathered his people into the Kingdom of God which he had come to proclaim, but it was already evident, especially after the hatred and plotting against his life that followed upon his cleansing of the Temple, that the leaders and the people as a whole, would repudiate him, put their Messiah to death and thus reject God who sent him. This could only end in the destruction of Jerusalem and the Temple, and the dispersion of his people to the ends of the earth, as Jesus had repeatedly warned them. The Cross was to represent his final earthly failure and the beginning of his divine success. Jesus finally declares they shall never see him again until the great consummation.

8

THE CRUCIFIXION AND ITS MEANING

Mark 14:12—Mark 15:39; Matt. 26:17—Matt. 27:56; Luke 22:7
—Luke 23:49

And as they were eating he took a loaf and after the blessing he broke and gave it to them, saying, "Take this, it means my body." He also took a cup and after thanking God he gave it to them, and they all drank of it; he said to them, "This means my *covenant-blood* which is shed for many; truly I tell you, I will never drink the produce of the vine again till the day I drink it new within the Realm of God." (Mark 14:22-25.) Then they came to a place called Gethsemane, and he told his disciples, "Sit here while I pray." (Mark 14:32.) "Abba, Father," he said, "Thou canst do anything. Take this cup away from me. Yet, not what I will but what thou wilt." (Mark 14:36.) Immediately morning came, the high priests held a consultation with the elders and scribes and all the Sanhedrin, and after binding Jesus they led him off and handed him over to Pilate (Mark 15:1). They forced Simon a Cyrenian who was passing on his way from the country (the father of Alexander and Rufus) to carry his cross, and they led him to the place called Golgotha (which means the place of a skull) (Mark 15:21-23). Then they crucified him and *distributed his clothes among themselves, drawing lots for them* to decide each man's share. It was nine in the morning when they crucified him. The inscription bearing his charge was: THE KING OF THE JEWS. They also crucified two robbers along with him, one at his right and one at his left. Those who passed by scoffed at him, nodding at him in derision and calling, "Ha! You were to destroy the temple and build it in three days! Come down from the cross and save yourself!" So, too, the high priests made fun of him to themselves with the scribes; "he saved others," they said, "but he cannot save himself! Let 'the Christ,' 'the king of Israel' come down now from the cross! Let us see that and we will believe!" Those who were crucified with him also denounced him. When twelve o'clock came, darkness covered

the whole land till three o'clock, and at three o'clock Jesus
gave a loud cry, *"Elôi, Elôi, lema sabachthanei"* (which
means, My God, my God, why forsake me?) (Mark 15:24-
34). One man ran off, soaked a sponge in vinegar, and put
it on the end of a stick to give him a drink, saying, "Come
on, let us see if Elijah does come to take him down!" But
Jesus gave a loud cry and expired (Mark 15:36).

JESUS SPENDS THE LAST NIGHT WITH HIS DISCIPLES IN THE SHADOW
of the Cross. He knows already of the plotting of the leaders
and of the treachery of Judas. He has sent in advance to prepare the room for the last solemn meal saying: "With desire I
have desired to eat the passover with you before I suffer." In studying the conflicting accounts of the Last Supper, we must dis-
tinguish between the meaning of the meal which was intended at
the time, and the meaning which the church believed it discovered
subsequently in its own faith and experience under the guidance of the Spirit. The Roman Church, for which Mark was
writing, was chiefly concerned in the foresight of Jesus regarding his betrayer, and the institution of the eucharist (Thanksgiving) or Lord's Supper. Mark wishes his Roman readers to
understand that the last meal was the Passover[1] and that Jesus
was instituting a permanent sacrament. Dr. Klausner holds that
Jesus and his disciples celebrated the Passover on Thursday
the thirteenth of Nisan, and that during the ensuing night before
Friday, they had to celebrate the Passover meal. All was done

[1] As we have seen, according to John (19:31), the death of Jesus occurred
on the Preparation of the Passover, on Nisan 14; and on the Sabbath. In
that case, Jesus came suddenly on Thursday evening to eat the last meal
which had been planned for Friday. Following the rule of the Sadducees, the
lambs may have been slaughtered on Thursday evening and "our Lord and
his disciples ate their Passover the same night, though without the customary
unleavened bread." We may thus believe that the Fourth Evangelist is
correct that Jesus was crucified on the day preceding the first day of the
Passover, and also that the Synoptics are right that the Supper was the
Passover meal put back by twenty-four hours because on that year the feast
commenced on the Sabbath. The four Evangelists are following two different
traditions: Mark, Matthew and Paul follow one tradition, and Luke (22:15-19)
the other. The former see the Last Supper as a new covenant in the sacrificial
blood of Christ, while Luke's original version views it as chiefly eschatological
in the light of the coming Kingdom. The early church accepted both views.

in secret for fear of his persecutors, for the same reason that compelled Jesus to lodge outside the city during the week.[2]

As St. Paul's account of the Supper is our earliest written record and as it has influenced Luke and probably the other Evangelists, we must read it carefully, for Paul weighs every word:

> I passed on to you what I received from the Lord himself, namely, that on the night he was betrayed the Lord Jesus took a loaf, and after thanking God he broke it, saying, "This means my body broken for you; do this in memory of me." In the same way he took the cup after supper, saying: "This cup means the new covenant ratified by my blood; as often as you drink it, do it in memory of me." For as often as you eat this loaf and drink this cup, you proclaim the Lord's death until he comes.

When Paul says he has received it "from the Lord" he probably means through the apostles. He says that the Lord's Supper was instituted by Jesus on the night of his betrayal; that he blessed the loaf as his body "broken for you"; that his followers were to do this in remembrance of him; that the cup after supper signified a new covenant "in my blood" (Jer. 31:31-34); and that the eucharist is given an apocalyptic significance of the Messianic banquet to "proclaim the Lord's death until he comes" (I Cor. 11:23-27).

Thus Paul alone makes the Lord's Supper a Christian institution. For both Paul and Mark it is dramatic and symbolical but neither miraculous, magical, nor an expiatory sacrifice. The making or renewal of any divine covenant among Semitic people was with blood, as was the first covenant by Moses (Exod. 24:6-8), and the sacrifice of the Paschal lamb at the time of the exodus when the meal was eaten standing and in haste as the Lord's Passover (Exod. 12:11).

Mark, followed by Matthew and Luke, has preserved for us

[2] Dr. Joseph Klausner's *Jesus of Nazareth*, p. 326, published by The Macmillan Company. If Jesus was crucified on Nisan 14, in one of the cycle of years in which Nisan 14 fell on a Friday (26-36 A.D.), it would indicate 30 A.D. as the probable date of his death.

the memories of Peter who was nearest to Jesus during the last hours:

> Then they came to a place called Gethsemane, and he told his disciples, "Sit here while I pray." But he took Peter and James and John along with him; and as he began to feel appalled and agitated, he said to them, "*My heart is sad*, sad even to death; stay here and watch." Then he went forward a little and fell to the earth, praying that the hour might pass away from him, if possible. "Abba, Father," he said, "Thou canst do anything. Take this cup away from me. Yet, not what I will but what thou wilt."

Gethsemane helps us to see at least a little of what was in this cup of fate for Jesus, in the deeper meaning of the Cross. We are not here viewing merely the death of an individual martyr. A thousand thousand heroes had died in battle or in the flames of martyrdom courageously, or with stoic calm. But Jesus throughout his life felt himself to be in some unique way the representative of Israel and the representative of God. He had called the nation to repentance as God's Messiah. When the rulers began to oppose and reject him, he had concentrated upon the Twelve who might carry on his work and proclaim the coming of the Kingdom of God. Everything was now at stake, the fate of his followers, of Israel and of the world. And all fail him: "They *all* left him and fled;" all forsook, or denied, all crucified him. Of the chosen Twelve, for whom he had hoped and prayed and striven, and who were quarrelling to the last as to who should be the greatest, one, the leader and boldest of them all, went out to deny him with cursing and swearing, one to betray him for thirty pieces of silver, "the price of a male slave," and the rest to desert him.

The beloved nation that he would have gathered into the Kingdom of God, as a hen gathers her brood under her wings, is now to reject him—the scribes, Pharisees, Sadducees, Herod and the Herodians, Zealots, and all the rulers gathered in the official Sanhedrin are to condemn their Messiah to death. He is to be betrayed and handed over to the Gentiles, and Pilate, the official representative of conquering Rome, the ruler of

the world, is to scourge and crucify him, as though the representatives of all humanity were to have a part in the guilt of his
death. Finally even the multitude of the common people join
in condemning him, a similar multitude to that which had first
followed him in Galilee when he had come as the friend of
sinners to seek and to save the lost. If we take the record as it
stands, when asked by Pilate, "What am I to do with Jesus?"
they all said, "Have him crucified." And after Pilate had washed
his hands they demanded the release of the violent revolutionary
Barabbas, and the crucifixion of the Prince of Peace who had
been hailed with hosannas one short week before.

There was something significant in the thrice-repeated "all"
in connection with the Crucifixion: Jews and Gentiles, the
Sanhedrin, Herod and the Roman Governor, the rulers and
the masses—there was something broadly human in this universal event. Whether they were yet conscious of it or not, all
had sinned, all were guilty, and in the future all men would
in time feel convicted before the Cross if, awakened, they came
within the range of its moral meaning. It was both universal
in its scope and personal in its focus. At the memory of this
Cross men in distant lands and far-off centuries would feel, as
before no other event in history, in the presence of one "who
loved *me* and gave himself up for *me*."

To realize what was in Jesus' cup of fate and something of
the significance of his death, we may both compare and contrast
the last hours of Jesus and of Socrates as the two most moving
and significant records of death that we have in history. If we
compare Plato's *Phaedo* with the account of the Passion in the
four Gospels, we see that the story of the last hours and of the
last words of both are recorded by their friends in touching
detail. Both were innocent. Of Socrates it was truly said that
he was "a man, the best of all of his time, the most wise and
just." Both Socrates and Jesus went to their deaths voluntarily,
refusing to seek escape when unjustly condemned by their rulers.
Both died devoted to a high ideal. The death of each was the
result of his own revolutionary life and teaching. And both
confidently expected to live after death.

But the contrasts are more striking than the similarities. In Socrates we witness the death of an isolated individual, cheerful, calm, courageous, and, compared to Jesus, almost irresponsible, so far as a sense of the sin of others is concerned. He is not dying consciously for his nation, for humanity, for God or the Kingdom of God. The cup of hemlock was a paralyzing poison which was almost painlessly to end his own life; not to make guilty his nation and humanity. Stoically, he sums up his philosophy, repeating his belief in the true, the beautiful and the good, and in the four virtues of wisdom, fortitude, temperance, and justice. He tries nobly to prove philosophically the immortality of the soul, and affirms his belief in the various gods, swearing "by Jupiter" and asking that his vow of a cock be paid to Aesculapius, the god of medicine. And he has a dim sense of one God over all, and of the soul which goes to "the invisible world, to the presence of a good and wise God, whither if God will, my soul also must shortly go." Simmias, his friend, pathetically adds that, taking the best of human reasonings, they must each embark on this human philosophy "as one who risks himself on a raft, so to sail through life, unless one could be carried more safely and with less risk, on a surer conveyance or some divine reason"—some sure Word of God such as Jesus reveals.

Jesus on the other hand, standing at the climax of two thousand years of ethical monotheism, knows that he is in the immediate presence of God as Father, whose Kingdom he has proclaimed and whose absolute will he has sought to do as no other that ever lived. He is the only one who could be accounted by his fellow men sinless, in the uttermost devotion of his perfect sacrifice in life and death. Yet Jesus feels in some inexplicable way that he is to be a crucified Messiah, a Suffering Servant who is to bear iniquity, a Son of Man, representative man, whose vicarious sacrifice in the purpose of God may have meaning for both God and man.

Jesus seems to feel, in some mysterious way that Socrates and other men did not, the crushing burden of human sin, of his nation and of humanity: "He fell into an agony and prayed with greater intensity, his sweat dropping to the ground like clots of blood" (Luke 22:44).

"With bitter cries and tears, he offered prayers and supplications to him who was able to save him from death . . . and learned by all he suffered how to obey." (Heb. 5:7-8.) Finally, Jesus has a consciousness of being a Saviour, believing that whoever will confess him before men, him will his Father confess, and whoever shall be ashamed of him, of him will God himself, who has sent him, be ashamed. As no other, his consciousness seems to be identified at once with the holy God and with sinful man. Surely it is with no fear of mere physical suffering and of death that he agonizes. It is rather before the horror of sin, man's sin that inevitably separates from God, sin that means death. And Jesus must bear it all: the crucifixion of Israel's Messiah, the seemingly final failure of the chosen people, the rejection of God, the sin of man as man, the sense of a whole world's guilt and agony channeled into a single heart.

Throughout the Supper, the agony in the garden, and the trial, there are interwoven the two strands of divine exaltation and human sadness. Despite his utter spiritual loneliness, Jesus' sympathy and compassion for the disciples never fails: for Peter who was denying him, for Judas who was betraying him, and for all who were failing him in that hour; yet he says with generous appreciation, "Ye have continued with me in my trials." The hymn they sang at the Supper was probably one of the Hallel Psalms (115-118) which were sung at the Passover celebration. When Judas betrays him with a kiss—which was the customary method of saluting a rabbi—the rabble from the rulers with swords and staves seize him and drag him away.

According to the combined accounts, Jesus underwent four judicial trials: before Annas, Caiaphas the high priest (who officiated from 18 to 36 A.D.), Herod Antipas, and Pilate, who alone could condemn him to death. According to John, Jesus had a preliminary examination before Annas, who probably occupied the same palace with Caiaphas, his father-in-law. All found it difficult to discover a charge on which the witnesses could agree, for under Jewish law, a capital conviction was impossible unless the testimony of at least two witnesses was in agreement. During the trial, after Peter thrice denied him, the Lord turned and looked upon him—a look that broke Peter's heart.

The tradition in the early church that it was the Sanhedrin which in the first place found Jesus guilty of death, had perhaps arisen out of the controversy between the early church and Judaism. Naturally the church sought, as far as possible, to absolve the Roman power with which they desired to be on friendly terms and, as throughout history, they unconsciously sought to make a scapegoat of the Jews. The Gospels seem eager to make the Jews say, "His blood be on us and on our children," and equally anxious to make the notoriously cruel Pilate strive to release Jesus. Many human opinions are unconsciously due to wishful thinking and to prejudice and this seems evident in these accounts.

This anti-Semitism, with the long persecution of the Jews, usually by Christians, is one explanation of the "mystery" of why the Jews as a nation never accepted Jesus as their Messiah, and why Christianity as a whole has been a Gentile and not a Jewish religion. If Jesus Christ both convicts of sin and saves from it, it should lead us to search our hearts to see if there be in us any of this deadly taint. Across the centuries this race prejudice has been fanned to flames from time to time, in the medieval persecution of the Jews which hounded them from country to country throughout Europe, which reappeared in Czarist Russia in pogroms often fomented by the priests, and which manifested itself in Germany till it reached its climax in the wholesale robbery and slaughter of the Jews under Hitler. This race prejudice has been one of the most degrading things in human history. The two races habitually marked for suffering seem to have been the Jew and, in recent centuries, the Negro. It is noteworthy that all the great cardinal sins of humanity seem to be revealed and judged before Jesus, in his teaching, his life and his death.

It may have been that the section of the Sanhedrin which was hurriedly called together was not the full council of seventy-one members, which was the Supreme Court of Judaism, but the quorum, or lesser Sanhedrin of twenty-three members, which could be easily assembled and might be more amenable to the wishes of Annas and Caiaphas. Their object was probably not to give Jesus a fair or formal trial, but to see how they could most quickly and quietly do away with him. A claim to be the Messiah was not an offense punishable by death according to Jewish law, but the rulers were not so much concerned with the *Jewish* aspect of his offense, as they were of so proving his Messianic pretensions that it would render Jesus guilty of breaking the *Roman* law of sedition against Caesar. Such a demand as they made for Jesus' own confession was expressly forbidden by the doctors of the Law, and if these examinations were trials, they were at many points completely illegal.

The real trial, of course, was before Pilate. Jesus was eventually put to death on the sentence of Pilate, presumably on the technical charge of treason against the Roman imperial authority, a crime which could be regarded as implicit in the claim of Messiahship, if interpreted in a political sense. It is probably true that the indictment was correctly formulated as "alleging that he is a king, Messiah," but to say that he forbade tribute to Caesar was known to be shamelessly false. Apart from legal technicalities, the real cause of the death of Jesus was the attitude of the leaders of the Jewish people. There was an absolute conflict and contradiction between Jesus' mission and message and the leaders' interpretation of the Law and the prophets; between his way of life and theirs. According to Mark's account, it was difficult to convict him; even the charge of destroying the Temple could not be established. The high priest goes to the heart of the matter, however, when the witnesses fail to agree and he raises the question of Jesus' Messiahship, carefully avoiding the holy name of Jehovah, or God, as the Evangelists do in Jesus' reply: " 'Are you the Christ the Son of the Blessed?' Jesus said: 'I am. And what is more you will all see the Son of man seated at the right hand of the Power, and coming with the clouds of heaven.' Then the high priest tore his clothes and cried, 'What more evidence do we want? You have heard the

blasphemy for yourselves' . . . . They condemned him, all of
them, to the doom of death." Jesus' reply here—as in his other
statements—seems to indicate that (Dan. 7:13-14) he has found
the prophecy of his Messiahship, not under the title of the Son
of David, but the Son of Man.

Six mockings of Jesus are noted: by the high priest's servants, Herod and his soldiers, the soldiers of the Roman garrison,
the general public, the priests and scribes who rail at him upon
the Cross with the cruel taunt: "He saved others; himself he
cannot save. He trusteth on God; let him deliver him now;" and
the robbers also that were crucified with him "cast upon him
the same reproach." His crown of thorns is the cruel imitation
of the laurel wreath worn by a Roman emperor, which they
place upon his brow. Apparently Jesus was physically unable to
bear the cross; they "bring him" or carry him in a state of
physical collapse after the scourging, commandee'ing one Simon,
a member of the Jewish dispersion from Cyrene west of Alexandria in North Africa. A centurion was in charge of the four
Roman soldiers who were Jesus' executioners. But throughout,
Jesus is not dealing with the soldiers who drive the nails, nor
with Judas, nor Pilate, nor the high priests: "The cup which
my Father hath given me shall I not drink it?" Thus for all time
he sets an example for his followers as to how they are to accept
their cross of suffering and all life as their portion in the provi-
dence of God.

Dr. Joseph Klausner, as a Hebrew, gives valuable testimony
to the Jews' conception of the Messiahship and of the Crucifixion:

In the first and second centuries of the Christian era, belief in the earthly kingdom of the Messiah was very strong. . . .
The Jews expected the Messiah at any time. Every day there
arose false Messiahs, visionary patriots, stout-hearted but
feeble-handed, who passed away like a shadow, once the Romans or the Herodians had made an end of them and their
deeds. . . . In the older *Talmudic* literature, we find an
ambiguous attitude toward the Messianic promises: there
is a certain wariness as touching the persons of the Messiahs,
but a deep and enthusiastic belief in the Messianic hope

itself. . . . Jesus from the moment of his baptism, looked upon himself as the Messiah.

Concerning the Crucifixion, Dr. Klausner says:

> Scourging always preceded crucifixion: so Josephus twice informs us. This was a horrible punishment, reducing the naked body to strips of raw flesh, and inflamed and bleeding weals. And when afterwards the victim's hands were nailed to the crosspiece and his feet tied (or nailed) to the base of the beam, leaving the sufferer unable to drive away the gnats and flies which settled on his naked body and on his wounds, and unable to abstain from publicly fulfilling natural needs—nothing could have been more horrible and appalling. None but the Romans, whose cruelty surpassed that of ravening beasts, could have made choice of this revolting means of death.[1]

Jesus is offered myrrhed wine as a merciful anesthetic in his agony, but he refuses it. The two robbers crucified with him may well have been Zealot revolutionaries. The inscription on the Cross is noted in all four Gospels, but it is given with slight differences in four ways. That the crucified Messiah, however, was none the less the King of the Jews is five times reiterated by Mark in this chapter. Jesus was crucified at the third hour, or 9:00 A.M., and hung upon the Cross for some six hours before he died. Golgotha was outside the city wall at the time of the Crucifixion ("outside the gate," Heb. 13:12). According to the Synoptics, the veil of the Temple, the inner veil which separated the Holy Place from the Holy of Holies, was rent in twain. According to the symbolism of the book of Hebrews (6:19; 9:3; 10:20), the veil of sin which has hitherto separated man from God was removed, so that all men now possess a living way of immediate access to God.

Mark notes the cry, "My God, my God why hast thou forsaken me." Luke omits it, perhaps because it might be interpreted as an utterance of despair, and the words were softened in texts of Mark current in Italy, Gaul, and Carthage. But Mark

[1] Joseph Klausner, *Jesus of Nazareth*, pp. 350, 402, published by The Macmillan Company, New York.

may not have understood it as a cry of despair and early Christians may have considered that the sin of man made him feel forsaken. The loud cry may have been interpreted from Psalm 22, which in a strange way dominates all the Passion, and may have been reflected back into the account of it. Many saw in the words the fulfillment of prophecy derived from this Messianic Psalm which is not as a whole one of despair, for the sufferer is confident of the love and protection of the God of all holiness, even unto death. Dr. T. R. Glover says: "Strange to think that is the cry of the feeling of Jesus. One is almost tempted to say that there, as in a supreme instance, is measured the distance between feeling and fact. So he felt; and yet mankind has been of another mind, that there, more than in all else that he was or did, there was God."

As given by the four Evangelists, the seven words from the Cross were: "Father forgive them; they know not what they do"; "Woman behold thy son"; "Today thou shalt be with me in Paradise"; "My God, My God why hast thou forsaken me?" "I thirst"; "It is finished"; "Father into thy hands I commend my spirit."

THE MEANING OF THE CROSS

If this were merely a life of the historic Jesus, it would end with the cry, "It is finished," but if this is a life of Christ, it must go beyond the historic events to their meaning. By accident the late Dr. F. C. Burkitt of Cambridge found in a foreign land a remarkable story "of how the Son of God, victorious over death, was ascending through the regions of heaven to His glorious Father, and, as He passed along, one of the highest Angels ventured to accost Him and to say, 'My Lord, the great Design, the inauguration of Thy Kingdom on the earth, is it all finished? And Jesus said, 'It is finished!' The Angel said, 'My Lord, I have heard nothing: dare I ask what Thou hast done?' Jesus replied, 'I was known as the child of respectable working folk, I lived unnoticed for some thirty years, then I came forward for a few months and talked with

men and women of all sorts, and I think some of those who
listened will be influenced all their lives, some fishermen, some
petty tradesmen, some women good and bad. And in the end
enemies had Me executed.' 'My Lord, my Lord,' exclaimed the
Angel in horror, 'was there no other way?' 'No,' said Jesus,
'*there was no other way.*'[2]

Before entering upon difficult controversial subjects upon
which men always have differed, and always will, we must remind ourselves that we have found in every chapter of this life
of Jesus four differing records and that there never has been
one agreed-upon orthodox position in Judaism or Christianity
concerning the nature of God, or his coming Kingdom, the Messiah, or the person or work of Christ, but many varying points
of view.

Fortunately for us the disciples were united in love in a great
spiritual experience and mission, while doctrine was only rudimentary, or still in a free, fluid state, not crystallized in any creed.
There were fundamental differences between Paul and Peter,
Paul and James, between the Synoptics and John, and between
Jewish and Gentile Christians. For nineteen centuries there has
been a left and a right wing of theological opinion, liberal and
conservative, and at times radical and reactionary. It may help
us to observe, with Luther, that God begins very gently in the
Scriptures with Jesus as a man, and leads us on gradually to
Christ as Lord, and finally up to God. As Luther says, "We must
begin from below, and after that come upwards." He holds that
apocryphal stories of Jesus' miraculous youth were "mere folly":
"He ate, drank, slept and waked; was weary, sad, joyous; wept,
laughed; was hungry, thirsty, cold; sweated, talked, worked,
prayed." He was no almighty man; and yet, in Luther's view, he
was not mere man, for only God could atone for human sin.

The meaning of the Cross depends upon the significance of
the Person who hung upon it. At every point the person and
work of Jesus are interrelated. What he was determined what
he did, and what he did was a revelation of what he was. We have

[2] Quoted by permission from J. Warschauer's *Historical Life of Christ,*
p. xii, published by The Macmillan Company, New York.

no record of a life, work, and teaching that were in such perfect harmony. Our whole study leads us to the conclusion that Jesus was truly and always man, subject to our human limitations, yet that in some unique way, "God was in Christ."

But whatever the divine source of Jesus' life, from first to last he remained truly man "tempted in all points like as we are." From his disciples in the first century to the present he always remains our brother and our friend: "O, thou great Friend to all the sons of men." The emphasis has shifted from that of Horace Bushnell, eighty years ago, where he maintained in his *Character of Jesus* that his life was such that it "forbids his possible classification with men." We would rather believe that it was God's highest glory that compels his classification with us as truly man.[3]

Though differing in thought and language, and still believing that Jesus was a mystery, our first records and all the early Christians and New Testament writers regarded Jesus as the Messiah, and believed that his death was of deep significance. They could confine his meaning to no one name or title, and they almost burst the bounds of language and seek to bend it to new uses in describing in manifold metaphors his person and his work. They find him in turn rabbi, teacher, prophet; leader, exemplar, victor; Messiah, Immanuel, Lord, Master, Saviour, Son of Man and Son of God. Jesus' early self-designation as Son of Man was not an obvious declaration of his Messiahship but proved suggestive in leading his disciples to seek to determine who he really was. When the nation was not ready to receive him and the rulers became growingly hostile, his chief work was in training the disciples to understand his con-

[3] The modern temper is far removed from the elaborate development of the Greek metaphysical view maintained in the Council of Chalcedon in 451: "One and the same Christ, Son, Lord, only begotten, acknowledged in two natures, without confusion, without change, without division, without separation; the distinction of the natures being by no means taken away because of the union, but rather the property of each nature being preserved and concurring in one person." We desire no such dogmatic certainty when we humbly believe that he was always truly man, but that God was in him revealing himself and redeeming mankind.

ception of Messiahship and his proclamation of the Kingdom of God.

Jesus' supreme self-designation was described by the one word "Son." But this implied the correlative of Father, and finally led to the revelation of his innermost self-consciousness in the great words recorded in one of the earliest Sayings of Jesus:

> All has been handed over to me by my Father: and no one knows the Son except the Father—nor does anyone know the Father except the Son, and he to whom the Son chooses to reveal him. Come to me, all who are labouring and burdened, and I will refresh you. Take my yoke upon you and learn from me, for I am gentle and humble in heart, and you will find your souls refreshed; my yoke is kindly and my burden light.

Between Jesus and God all is common. After his baptism this unshared Sonship is always for him the supreme reality. He speaks with immediate authority from God, he forgives sin, he repeatedly proclaims himself the touchstone of destiny for humanity—"Everyone who will acknowledge me before men, I will acknowledge him before my Father in heaven."

During his lifetime, the message of the disciples is confined to the proclamation of the Kingdom, but immediately after the resurrection, which had created a new world of experience and expectation for the disciples, their one message, which has taken the place of Jesus' gospel of God and his Kingdom, is *Christ, crucified and risen*: "Jesus the Nazarene, a man accredited to you by God through miracles, wonders, and signs which God performed by him among you . . . this Jesus . . . you got wicked men to nail to the cross and murder (Acts 2:22-24). This Jesus God raised, as we can all bear witness (Acts 2:32). God has made him both Lord and Christ, this very Jesus whom you have crucified" (Acts 2:36). Only after the resurrection was he the fully manifested Messiah, the crucified, risen and conquering Jesus Christ. Before this his Messiahship was a veiled mystery. Jesus' message was theocentric, that of Paul and the New Testament writers and apostles was Christocentric. Judaism was theocentric and Jesus remained a Jew; Christianity became Christocentric.

The word atonement is used in two senses as a reconciliation, to bring about at-one-ment, or as a reparation made for wrong. The modern mind finds itself more in sympathy with the realistic Hebrews, with their sense of history, than with the speculative, philosophic Greeks. Later speculation maintained the monstrous theory that God played a trick on the devil by confronting him with the divine in the shape of a man, by "baiting the hook with Christ." It also held the cumbersome, artificial theory of two natures in Christ, who was both God and man, unconditioned and conditioned; and that man had to be saved not so much from his sin as from his finiteness in metaphysical terms, by making man partaker of God's own immortal life.

In some strange and unaccountable manner, God and man meet in Jesus. Jesus reminds us of our kinship to our Creator. If man was made in the image of God, if he has the capacity for sonship and is only separated from communion with God by his sin, then the function of Jesus must have been to call a prodigal humanity home to its heavenly Father.

Jesus Christ reveals God, not only as he had always been accepted as Creator, but also as Redeemer, one God, always governed by one holy purpose. Christ thus connects creation and redemption, for all history is creation groaning to be redeemed. God's costly redemption only reveals his original purpose of love in creation. It was not only a Creator but a Father who, in the agelong process of evolution—inorganic, organic and spiritual— was giving himself to the uttermost throughout the whole universe, in the patient and costly process culminating in the production of human personalities, made in the image of God and restored to that image through Christ. Though man *discovers* the divine only gradually, from the God of "wrath" conceived in the awful storm cloud above Sinai, to the God of grace in the darkness above Calvary, yet God in the whole costly process of creating must have been moved by such self-giving as Jesus shows in his love of man. Throughout the whole process there is the unseen push of God's creative purpose and the unrealized pull of his redemptive love. The whole living universe partakes of God's life; it is a sharing of his life, and must all be, could we but see the end, a revelation of his love. Thus all life is sacramental.

We see God's costly self-limitation in man's freedom and man's sin. As the meaning of the acorn is seen only in the oak, so the purpose of God, the meaning and end of history, and the potentialities of man are all revealed, and only fully revealed, in Jesus Christ. In him we see both the alpha and omega, the beginning and the end; one God, Creator and Redeemer, the same yesterday, today and forever. If this world is the serious business of God, if the whole sweep of inorganic, organic and spiritual evolution is the revelation of the outgoing of God's very being, then my life has meaning, and my sin, as rebellion against God, is a betrayal of Christ's life and purpose. The scars of man's sin are upon the whole creation and its blight upon all man's tragic life. Throughout the whole costly process, God, if he be God, *must* bear man's sin, for he alone can. In no atom of the creation, in no man, no prophet or saint, is the full purpose of God or his character as holy love finally revealed save in Christ Jesus. He only completely reveals God, convicts man of his sin and saves him from it.

Who then is this man? Who is this dying upon a criminal's cross between two thieves? How am I to think of this man without whom the truth of God, the character of God, the significance of the universe and the meaning of history become something less than they are? How am I to interpret this man without whom I cannot think of God at his full value—all powerful, all wise, all loving; Creator, Redeemer, immanent and indwelling Spirit—and whose highest designation is "the God and Father of our Lord Jesus Christ?"

If God was in man to the utmost, then God must seek to be in every man to the utmost possible, and we must see finally in Jesus the culminating of an agelong divine process. We believe that Jesus was not the utmost achievement of man, but the final achievement of God and the chief means of God's achievement for man. In Jesus we see the purpose of God, the goodness of God incarnate in human weakness, and the final destiny of man. Jesus is so high and holy, and yet so native to our own spirit, that we criticize the Power behind nature from his standpoint. As Dr. A. T. Cadoux says:

> The outgoing and self-giving of God in creation has in Calvary its culmination, its interpretation, and its fulfilment. . . . For if the universe is the outgoing of God, then Jesus, in whom that outgoing finds its focus and redemption, can never be left out of any commerce with God in thought or act. Only in Jesus are we assured that God has the sort of goodness that completely commands us.[4]

If there hung upon that Cross of Golgotha only a dead Galilean carpenter, betrayed by a mistaken Messianic dream, then God himself is infinitely less than Jesus declared, and all reality, the whole universe, and all the tragic history of humanity are infinitely less than would be implied by the faith of all early Christians in "the God and Father of our Lord Jesus Christ." If we have such a God as Jesus revealed, we have everything—all things are ours. If we have not, spiritually we have relatively nothing. The gnat that flits in the sunshine, the worm that crawls in the dust, the smug, clever animal, man, that has his brief bitter day and ceases to be in a dying universe, all would have something no doubt. But, we repeat again, everything is at stake in Christ. It is not a question of the theological exaltation of Jesus. We may oppose and speak against him and it will be forgiven us. God himself is the issue. And ultimately God is to us all or nothing. We either have, potentially, "the fullness of the blessing of Christ," or a life without God and without hope in the world. We have no desire, with this seemingly stern "either or" alternative, to preclude the nontheistic humanist, or the sacrificial, atheistic Communist, for we believe that God and the truth of things are better than our halting faith and that doubting men will yet discover, in this short span of life or beyond it, the undreamed fullness that is in Christ. If Jesus is the final revelation of God in human life, then he is the link not only between God and man, but between God as Creator and God as Father, the living link between the Incarnation and the Atonement. Thus

---

[4] A. T. Cadoux, *A New Orthodoxy of Jesus and Personality*, pp. 167, 175. We are indebted to Dr. Cadoux in this section.

Jesus is the final revelation of the nature of God to man and also the means of winning man back to God, of restoring the lost image of God in man, "thus making the at-one-ment."

We may take any one, or all, or none of Paul's score of metaphors to describe or explain the meaning of the death of Jesus: redemption, bought with a price; propitiation, mercy seat, mediation, reconciliation, salvation, or atonement. Or we may not have any theory or understanding of the death of Jesus. The ultimate question is, what had God to do with this event. Was Jesus' death the act of a hero, or martyr, or pious carpenter, a man deluded with a Messianic dream, or falsely accused of such by his enemies—or, was he so the agent of God, chosen, anointed, possessed, and accepted as Son of God and Saviour of man, that in the Cross we are brought face to face with God himself?

Always God could freely forgive sin, as a loving parent can forgive his repentant child, without any transaction or legal process: "Who forgiveth all thine iniquities; who healeth all thy diseases; who redeemeth thy life from destruction." From the first, Jesus could say with authority, "Thy sins are forgiven thee." But, whether man knew it or not, it was always costly forgiveness. Only the loving father knows the agony of the prodigal's sin, and shame, and absence. In more than metaphor, he suffers daily, in a sense he "dies daily," until the son returns. If God is Father and if God is love, he must "die daily" in suffering sympathy—to use boldly an anthropomorphism—while "the whole creation groaneth and travaileth in pain together until now." The lonely father and the lost prodigal must both suffer. Now if a Son was sent to call a prodigal humanity home to God, if in fact Jesus' death, when understood, did move men to a complete change of mind and heart, to return home with the confession "Father I have sinned," then—wholly apart from our understanding, or appreciation, or subjective feeling—the Cross of Calvary has infinite meaning. Here is the act of God, the word of God, the gift and good news of God. This is the gospel of God.

Seen in isolation as a mere human event, the crucifixion of Jesus was the worst crime and the chief evil of all history, but if taken as a providential part of the whole scheme of things, "in the predestined course of God's deliberate purpose" (Acts 2:23), it can be made, and has been made, man's supreme good. If even that event and that evil can be completely transmuted and transfigured, then presumably any evil can be borne by love, vicarious and victorious. The world may then be a better world with a greater sum total of good for eternity than if evil, sin and suffering had never occurred. The fact that in the end, when rightly understood, the Cross makes such an increasingly universal appeal, has made it seem to believers as not primarily an isolated act of man, but the act of God and man, or God in man.

Do we believe that Jesus died for himself alone? Or, was his death unto God, for man and for me? If the former, we are left with the memory of a Galilean carpenter who is dead. If our answer is the latter, we are known of God, loved by God, found by God, with the good news which reveals to us the meaning of the Crucifixion, the meaning of life, the meaning of history. We also can cry with the great warrior of old: "The life I now live in the flesh I live by faith in the Son of God who loved *me* and gave himself up *for me*." This to Christian faith is the meaning of the Crucifixion.

9

THE RESURRECTION AND ITS CONSEQUENCES

Mark 16:1-8; Matt. 28:1-10; Luke 24:1-53; I Cor. 15:3-8

First and foremost, I passed on to you what I had myself received, namely, that Christ died for our sins as the scriptures had said, that he was buried, that he rose on the third day as the scriptures had said, and that he was seen by Cephas, then by the twelve; after that, he was seen by over five hundred brothers all at once, the majority of whom survive to this day, though some have died; after that, he was seen by James, then by all the apostles, and finally he was seen by myself (I Cor. 15:3-8). See, here is the place where the Lord lay. Now make haste, go to his disciples and tell them he has risen from the dead and that he precedes you to Galilee; you shall see him there (Matt. 28:6-7). He said to them, "O foolish men, with hearts so slow to believe, after all the prophets have declared! Had not the Christ to suffer thus and so enter his glory?" (Luke 24:25-26). They said to one another, "Did not our hearts glow within us when he was talking to us on the road, opening up the scriptures for us?" (Luke 24:32.)

WE COME NOW TO THE CHAPTER WHICH PRESENTS THE GREATEST difficulty to the modern mind, for if factual it is the least natural and most supernatural of all the events in the record. At this point also, the narrative is most fragmentary and conflicting. There is at least no collusion on the part of the writers nor effort to reconcile the four differing accounts. Though our four Evangelists and the early disciples differed widely as to their interpretation of the events, they were all equally certain of three points: Jesus' disciples had known him in the flesh and had heard and remembered his teaching; they were sure that he died by crucifixion, as the Roman punishment of a criminal; and they were all equally certain that he was alive again, risen from the dead as the living Christ or Messiah. With each chapter we have become more certain that the Synoptic Gospels were correct in their agreement that Jesus' central message had been his proclamation of the Kingdom of God, and that the modern rationalists and humanists were wrong in their theory that Jesus was primarily a teacher who went about doing good, proclaiming the fatherhood of God and the brotherhood of man. Regardless of times and seasons, either Jesus' proclamation of the rule of God was true or it was not. And in this chapter we must either mourn the memory of a dead Galilean carpenter, well-meaning but fundamentally mistaken, or we must face the reality of the living Christ. We unhesitatingly choose the latter alternative. We believe as firmly in the truth of the living Christ as in the fact of the historic Jesus.

There are four independent witnesses to the fact of the resurrection: 1. The Christian church was founded on faith in the Messiahship of Jesus and belief in the fact of the risen Christ. Before its birth, Christianity had been buried in the tomb with Jesus and would never have come into existence had it not been for the indubitable faith of all the early disciples in the resurrection. 2. The evidence furnished by the observance of the first day of the week instead of the Jewish Sabbath, which was the holy of holies of the Mosaic law. Because they believed Jesus had risen on the first day of the week, and had manifested himself on that day and on succeeding first days instead of on the Sabbaths, this became their weekly day of worship for the next nineteen centuries; 3. The very existence of the New Testament is a monument to the fact of the resurrection without which there would have been no occasion to write a single Gospel or Epistle; 4. The existence and perpetuation of the primitive rite of the breaking of bread, the Lord's Supper, or the Communion of the body and blood of Christ, not as mourning for a dead Jesus, but as a eucharist, or thanksgiving, for a living Saviour, has stood for nineteen centuries as a triumphant witness to "the sure and certain hope of a glorious resurrection": "For as often as you eat this loaf and drink this cup, you proclaim the Lord's death until he come." Thus these four institutions—the church, the Lord's Day, the New Testament, and the eucharist, constitute a fourfold chord not easily broken, of testimony to the universal primitive Christian belief in the resurrection of Jesus.[1]

There is an overwhelming weight of evidence for the *fact* of the resurrection, though not for its exact *mode* or detail. The earliest and most detailed account is by the Apostle Paul (I Cor. 15:1f.) written about 54 A.D., within twenty-five years of the event, and recording the appearance of Christ at Paul's conversion on the Damascus road which took place within ten years of the Crucifixion. We have a mutilated form of Mark's Gospel ending abruptly with the words "for they were afraid of . . ." The unmutilated form, however, evidently contained a record of appearances of the risen Christ, for his rising from the dead is predicted by Jesus at least five times in the earlier portion of this Gospel. Matthew records two appearances at the sepulcher and in Galilee; Luke three, at Emmaus, to Peter and "to the eleven," all in or near Jerusalem; the Fourth Gospel records three appearances, to Mary Magdalene, to the ten apostles, with Thomas absent, to the eleven with Thomas present, and in the epilogue to five disciples by the Sea of Galilee. And, finally, outside the Gospels, three appearances are recorded: to Stephen, to Paul on the Damascus road, and to the Apocalyptic Seer on the Isle of Patmos (Rev. 1:9-19). Fragmentary as these accounts are, it must be remembered that this spiritual fact underlies the whole New Testament, which is "radiant with the light of the resurrection."

Luke has probably truly recorded the mood of Jesus' followers after his death in the account of the two travelers to Emmaus: "Our own hope was that he would be the redeemer of Israel; but he is dead!" After they recognized him at the familiar evening meal which Jesus was wont to have with his disciples, they cried: "Did not our heart glow within us when he was talking to us on the road, opening up the scriptures for us?"

We note that nowhere is the attempt made to describe what

---

[1] I am obviously indebted here to *The Mission and Message of Jesus* by Major, Manson, and Wright, E. P. Dutton & Company, New York, pp. 211-214. On the whole I have found this the most valuable modern commentary that we possess on all four Gospels.

took place at the resurrection, but only to narrate its aftereffects and historic consequences. Paul, writing to the Corinthians says that Jesus appeared to him, and to six groups of disciples as official witnesses, presumably in the same way that he appeared to Paul. The apostle is not interested even in mentioning an empty tomb, nor in what happened to the physical body of Jesus, who now had the reality of a glorified "spiritual body." Paul means by "spiritual" what is controlled by spirit, a body no longer an impediment to the spirit or clog upon it, but its pure and unhindered expression. In this spiritual body Jesus had been seen by Cephas, by James, the brother of Jesus, by the Twelve who knew him best, "then by all the apostles," and by over five hundred Christian brothers "all at once," the majority of whom were still alive and witnesses to the fact of the resurrection when Paul wrote.

It may possibly be significant that these five hundred believed he had appeared to them all at one time, though it does not say that they were all in one place as the Twelve had been. They could have been scattered, as far away from Jerusalem as Paul was upon the Damascus road, or they could have been together like the Twelve. For about "forty days," following the Crucifixion, after they had been dismayed and their hope shattered by his loss, when they were in a highly sensitive mood, this convincing and overwhelming evidence was vouchsafed to them. For some cause there had been a total transformation of the minds of the Twelve and of the five hundred within a period of a few weeks. These despairing men from the depths of mental gloom had somehow all become confident, radiant, courageous, indomitably ready to face the Jewish nation and the pagan Gentile world with their contagious good news. One and all ascribed this total transformation to the fact that they had repeatedly seen their Lord, that he had been "declared to be the Son of God with power by the resurrection from the dead," and that they were in living contact with him. Easter had rent the air as with a trumpet.

The stubborn disbelief in the resurrection on the part of the early disciples had to be overcome by repeated appearances to many disciples. But much more important than these objective appearances was their overwhelming new spiritual experience, both as individuals and as a new glowing fellowship. They had found in Jesus, not a figure of a bygone age, but one who ever seemed to say, "Lo, I am with you alway, even unto the end," and they had found him "Immanuel, God with us." The resurrection was the affirmation that things seen are temporal and things unseen are eternal. It gave validity to the existence of a whole spiritual world. The deepest conviction of the fact of the living Christ was not conveyed by a story, nor by a book, neither by the tradition of an empty tomb, nor by visions, nor even by the testimony of eyewitnesses who had seen him. *The most convincing evidence of the resurrection was the new power in life and death that the world saw in changed men.* Something had transformed the fickle Simon into the rocklike Peter. He who had cursed and sworn that he did not know Jesus, was now charging all Israel and its leaders with the guilt of crucifying their long-awaited Messiah. This blundering fisherman had become a world apostle. The same power was manifest in suddenly changing the bigoted young Pharisee, Saul of Tarsus, the most ruthless persecutor of the church, into the Christlike Paul, who not only wrote but incarnated in his own character the greatest hymn to love ever written.

The religious thought of the early church regarding Jesus had two foci: belief in the Messiah and belief in the resurrection. The first was born of the impression which Jesus made on them, and found expression in Peter's confession at Caesarea Philippi, though this was shaken for the moment by the Crucifixion. If Jesus' death had been the end, it would have destroyed the faith of the disciples and Christianity would never have been born. The only impregnable doctrine is history. The reality of the experience of Peter, James, John, the hundred and twenty and the five hundred, of the continued existence of Jesus belongs to history. The Christian church of the centuries, against which the gates of hell shall not prevail, was not built upon an illusion or a lie, but upon a spiritual fact of experience, both objective and subjective. Peter says on the day of Pentecost: "This Jesus

God raised . . . Uplifted then by God's right hand . . . God hath made him both Lord and Christ (i.e. the Messiah), this very Jesus whom you have crucified." This would seem to imply that at the time of Peter's earlier confession, God had destined Jesus to fulfill the Messianic mission, though he was still the hidden Messiah not yet invested with power and glory. The risen Christ—"this very Jesus"—is now the transcendent Messiah, awaited as the Saviour and who pours forth on the disciples "what you now see and hear." The resurrection was thus to his own followers the final seal and sign of the full Messiahship.

The disciples saw Jesus because for them he was living. Henceforth he was their head and they were his earthly body, awaiting the final consummation of the Kingdom of God. They had seen him "after three days," or after a short interval. The resurrection is the living link which unites the story of the earthly Jesus (which has now become only an episode in the drama of redemption), with the Christianity of the living Christ. The followers of Jesus are no longer a heretical Jewish sect but the first-born of a great brotherhood of a new world religion. Christianity was not the religion of Jesus, but of the worshipers of Jesus. The personality of the Master linked together the good news of the Kingdom proclaimed in Galilee and the primitive church. These fierce, bigoted, monotheistic Jews, who would rather die than burn incense in the worship of Caesar, had not themselves deified the man that had been their companion in Galilee. They believed they had witnessed the act of God both in the Crucifixion and the resurrection. It was the latter that now made them sure of the significance of Jesus, of the Messiah, of the meaning of Calvary, of God himself as henceforth the Father of the Lord Jesus, and of the certainty of the consummation of his coming Kingdom. *It was not the memory of a Galilean carpenter, but the resurrection and the living Christ which made Jesus the chief regenerative power in the world's history.* Something had happened which had entirely changed not only the character of this group of blundering and timid men, but had potentially changed the whole history of the world. The men who had fled at his arrest within a few weeks were rejoicing to be beaten and imprisoned. They now ran to meet death unafraid, for death had become a conquered foe.

Peter, Paul, and "this new race of men" challenged their hearers to make the venture for themselves of coming into contact with this transforming power, and presence, and Person. Tertullian (c. 150-c. 222 A.D.), a pagan lawyer, proud of his Stoic learning, as he saw Christians martyred in the amphitheater and witnessed their victory over the universal fear of death, and their transformed lives, writes: "Every man who witnesses this great endurance, is struck with some misgiving. He is set on fire to look into it to find the cause of it. When he has learned the truth, at once he follows it himself." Tertullian was only one link in a continuous chain of living witnesses, unbroken across the centuries, who could testify to the living Christ in the church militant below, and the Christ of faith in the church triumphant above.

It was the life and death of Christians that compelled attention, the reborn slaves with their newness of life in Roman households, and scholars like Tertullian and Augustine, who formed an unbroken succession of living witnesses. As Dr. Glover shows, they not only outthought the classical pagans about them, they outlived them and they out-died them. That which differentiated them from the pagan world was Christ, crucified and risen. Just when, as Plutarch says, men were "in anguish and fear lest Delphi should lose its glory of three thousand years," just when the world of classical pagan culture and religion was breaking down after centuries of trial in Greece and Rome, this "new race" of men who derived their spiritual energy from a risen Christ, was coming to its own. And today a great host that no man can number can testify to their faith in Christ as a living Saviour. They need and ask no evidence of an empty tomb, and no objective appearance of a Christ who has been revealed *in* them, as truly as in Paul.

The day of Pentecost, which closed the initial phase of the history of the early disciples, inaugurated a new epoch in the long life of the church on earth. A great multitude throughout the centuries since, men like St. Augustine, St. Francis, Luther,

Wesley and a host of saints, solitaries, missionaries, and martyrs, men of both mystical and rationalistic types, were as sure that they were in immediate, vital relation to the living Christ as were Peter, Paul, James and the five hundred who believed that they had seen him alive. Peter, with the eleven, could say: "This Jesus God raised, as we can all bear witness. Uplifted then by God's right hand and receiving from the Father the long-promised Holy Spirit, *he* has poured on us what you now *see* and *hear* . . . God had made him both Lord and Christ, this very Jesus whom you have crucified."

The central Christian doctrines of Christ crucified and risen are consonant with the truth of the God and Father of Jesus and of his coming Kingdom. Thus there is an unbroken chain of life and of evidence from Jesus of Nazareth, his experience of God as Father, the reality of the Kingdom, the Crucifixion, the resurrection, the manifestation of the living Christ, and the outpouring of the Spirit upon all flesh willing to receive him, from Pentecost to the present. Because of Christ, risen and living, vital Christians believe that they already are partakers of immortality and have "the power of an endless life"; I am come that they might have vitality and might overflow with it."

The whole life of the Apostle Paul, the significance of the entire book of the Acts of the apostles, the founding of the Christian church, and the birth of Christianity as a world religion, all turn upon a single fact. That fact is the resurrection of the living Christ.[2] Christianity is either supernatural or it is "guilty of misrepresenting God," as Paul said. A pale humanism founded on a beautiful myth has only a slight advantage over the high religion of the Stoics, the imitation of Socrates which was once popular in Greece, the noble "eightfold path" of Gautama Buddha, or the heroic sacrifice of the devout but mistaken Communist. As Shirley Jackson Case says: "Peter's confidence that he had seen Jesus alive again after his crucifixion is one of the best attested facts in ancient history."

Paul presses the inescapable significance of the resurrection as

[2] The author has here rewritten several paragraphs from his *Maker of Men,* pp. 110-119.

either fantasy or fact, myth or spiritual reality: "How can some of you say that there is no such thing as a resurrection of the dead? If Christ was not raised there is nothing in our message, there is nothing in our faith either, and we are found guilty of misrepresenting God . . . If we have centered our hopes on Christ in this life, and that is all, we are the most pitiable people in the world." Therefore, Paul concludes, so differently from the groping hopes of Socrates and Plato, with the first shout of a triumphant humanity over its long-dreaded foe: "Where, Death, is your victory? Where, Death, is your sting? Thank God! He gives us victory through our Lord, Jesus Christ."

Every book in the New Testament confirms or implies Paul's view of the resurrection, especially the Acts. The twelfth apostle is chosen to take the place of Judas "as a witness to his resurrection." At Pentecost they were all filled with the Spirit from the risen Christ. Peter's first sermon, and those that follow, witness to the resurrection as the chief apostolic evidence that Jesus was the Messiah. The resurrection was the issue before the Sanhedrin. The conversion of Saul on the Damascus road centered in the resurrection vision, the light, and the voice, "I am Jesus whom you are persecuting." The temporary outward visions and appearances only confirmed the more important continued power of Christ over the minds and consciences of men in daily experience.

As Albert Schweitzer says: "The truth is, it is not Jesus as historically known, but Jesus as spiritually arisen within men who is significant for our time and can help it . . . Jesus as a concrete historical personality remains a stranger to our time, but his spirit is known in its simplicity and its influence is direct." [3] Professor Bacon maintained that the gospel was that God was in Christ reconciling the world unto himself and raising him from the dead; it was good news, not good advice, and Christianity began not at the birth, or the baptism, or in the life and teaching of Jesus, but in the resurrection.

While for Jesus' contemporaries, all turned upon the resurrection, for the Christian believer today the central ground of faith

[3] *The Quest of the Historical Jesus*, pp. 396, 399.

in immortality is in the nature of God and Christ himself, his character, his teaching, his death, his resurrection, and his indwelling life. The realistic Jew of the later centuries looked for the resurrection of the body, while the idealistic Greek believed in the immortality of the soul. The Christian doctrine is prevailingly one not of natural immortality but of resurrection as an act and gift of God who of his bounty bestows on individuals an immortality which is not theirs by nature. Christianity holds that Jesus begat in us "the power of an endless life." Because he lives we shall live also.

But let us face the stark alternative to this view of life after death. Let us suppose that Jesus and all the early Christians were mistaken. Then with him, Peter, Paul, the apostles, prophets, martyrs, and missionaries of all the centuries, and the seven hundred million professing Christians living today, have been deluded by this false hope. If Jesus is dead, then the universe with him ultimately is doomed to death. Then we are all denizens, not of Augustine's eternal City of God, but of mortal humanity's "city of dreadful night."

If we are to die as the animals die, not one of us is actually saved from sin. We believed we were forgiven or "justified," but this was all a doctrinal fiction and an opiate if there is no personal survival beyond the grave; no God, no freedom, and no immortality such as Kant postulated. Then we are not "foreordained to be conformed to the image of his Son."

A dead Christ would mean not only the spiritual death of the individual, but also in time of the race. Then the whole cumulative process of agelong evolution has been and will be, spiritually, largely in vain. And, on this hypothesis, most miserable of all was the tragic fate of this dead carpenter. Beautiful, of course, brave and poetic in considering the lilies and the birds, having no care nor fear, for his Father in heaven would care for all and give men eternal life. Beautiful—but false if not true. Then with Dean Church we would have to believe that we had been following "the memory of an obscure Syrian devotee, poor and miserable and ruined, floated up by accident, by the chances of an age of Oriental fanaticism, no one can tell how, to the summit and control of all these forces which shape the world." Then, as Bertrand Russell holds, "on man and all his race the slow, sure doom falls pitiless and dark." Then, "if Christ be not risen from the dead," we face the ultimate end of a dying universe and an impotent, or nonexistent, or defeated God.

We may say with George Matheson:

> Son of Man, whenever I doubt of life, I think of Thee. Nothing is so impossible as that Thou shouldst be dead. I can imagine the hills to dissolve in vapor and the stars to melt in smoke, and the rivers to empty themselves in sheer exhaustion; but I feel no limit in Thee. Thou never growest old to me. Last century is old, last year is an obsolete fashion, but Thou art not obsolete. Thou art abreast of all the centuries. I have never come up with Thee, modern as I am.

As to the incompleteness of life at death and the conviction that the fulfillment of life lies in personal immortality beyond the grave, scores of writers have agreed with Victor Hugo, who wrote:

> I feel immortality within myself. The nearer I approach to the end the more plainly I hear round me the immortal symphonies of the world to come . . . For half a century I have been writing my thoughts in prose and verse; but I feel I have not said one-thousandth part of what is in me.

Emerson wrote: "The blazing evidence of immortality is our dissatisfaction with any other solution."

We may summarize the grounds for our belief in personal immortality as follows:

1. Because of the testimony of science to a rational and trustworthy world where all legitimate human desires may be met. If, as science testifies, even matter and energy are indestructible, how can the most priceless thing upon this planet, human personality, achieved after millions of years of evolution, be lightly destroyed?

2. Because of the testimony of religion not only in nineteen hundred years of Christianity, but in five thousand years of the religions of Egypt and other lands. For a hundred thousand years, men have buried their dead in the hope of a life beyond

3. Because of the testimony of Jesus whose life and teaching were based on the assurance of eternal life. Nineteen centuries of Christian progress have rested upon the faith and reality of the living Christ.

4. Because of the character of God as Father. Ultimately our hope of a life beyond is grounded in God himself. If there is an eternal, infinite, all-powerful and good God, if there is a living, loving Father, then the future life seems to be assured.

5. Because of the testimony of Christian experience here and now. He that believeth, already "hath eternal life." "For I know whom I have trusted and I am sure that he is able to guard what I have entrusted to him for that Day."

Faith in a future life is progressively verified by an expanding spiritual experience in the present. Faith in immortality, instead of being a demonstration of logic, is a spiritual achievement. He who knows the inward, moral miracle of victorious life overcoming temptation, surmounting the limitations of time and space, and the buffetings of sorrow and separation, who can with Paul triumph in his troubles, has already taken hold on the spiritual and the eternal.

To the devout Christian, simple faith is enough. It may seem to him not only gratuitous but even impious to press beyond faith and seek scientific evidence for his beliefs. The faith of Socrates and Plato and the above five reasons for belief in immortality, however, all rest upon faith, hope, love, or the argument from analogy. There is one field where cumulative scientific evidence, that someday might amount to proof, is possible. It is to be feared, however, that this evidence is in an area so emotionally charged with prejudice that even to mention it will excite the violent resentment of some. But it is a field of experience that was well known to the Apostle Paul and has been to some others ever since his day. We are not urging the enviable man of simple faith, or the prejudiced or bigoted, to consider any scientific evidence for personal immortality. But the writer asks pardon for speaking in the first person to add his own testimony at this point to his belief in immortality, as based not only upon faith and experience but also upon scientific evidence. I can now state another reason for my own belief in personal survival in the life beyond death, but *only* for those who need and crave such evidence.

6. For the last six years I can add firsthand testimony derived from scientific psychic evidence of the survival of individual personality. This experience has been so repeated, so convincing, and satisfying to me personally, that I now have the same evidence in principle for the existence of the seven members of my family who are in the spiritual world, that I have for the four members of my immediate family still on earth. Once life after death was for me solely a matter of faith. Now it is faith plus the direct evidence of experience. Six years ago, a deeply spiritual Quaker friend felt a spiritual "concern" for me and wrote offering to put me in touch with direct evidence for personal survival. He not only did so but over a course of years I was able to find scientific evidence of a whole spiritual world of reality in the "unobstructed" or invisible universe. I desire at the outset, however, as a word of caution, to point out that at best (and it is often far from its best) this whole subject of psychic investigation is in a "twilight zone," and that there are not only severe limitations but positive dangers connected with it. I would strongly advise the local minister or layman not to dabble in the psychic field. For the same reason I would advise him not to try to make an independent scientific investigation in the field of electricity, radio, X rays, or explosives. He has neither the time, the equipment, nor the ability to make such a study.

I do not of course ask any man to take my word at second hand as to the possible value of any scientific evidence I have received. I offer no apology, however, for making this investigation. I have had the advantage of frequent travel over America, Europe, and Asia, which has brought me in contact with a number of psychically gifted persons of proven integrity of character; an advantage which the average local man cannot have. The fact of personal survival after death, however, has been confirmed in my own experience by psychic evidence so continuous and convincing that for myself I need ask no more. But

I shall keep this minor matter in its place, and that place is not central. To do the will of God on earth now is much more important for us than the thought of a future heaven. Here where it is hard is where we must learn to do God's will. Frankly I am not prematurely interested in "Jerusalem the Golden." In a time of war, however, with millions "dying," or rather passing through the portal which we call "death," I cannot forbear to give my own testimony as to our evidence for personal immortality. As it would take a volume the size of this to state it in scientific form, I must here confine myself to the bare statement of fact that I personally have received such evidence.

CHRIST IN THE CHURCH

Beginning with a hundred and twenty in a large upper room in Jerusalem, and increased by some three thousand converted on the day of Pentecost, and rapidly thereafter, the church had grown and extended its mission over Palestine, Syria, Asia Minor, the Roman Empire, and the world. Luke describes the wonderful experience of the day of Pentecost, seven weeks after the Passover at which Jesus had died. Beneath all the symbolism of fire and wind, Luke wishes us to see the counterpart of the giving of the Law on Mount Sinai. He wishes us to understand that the church was already in existence, as the new-born child has long been living, previous to the day of its birth.

The picture of the early community gathered in the name of Jesus is a beautiful one:

The believers all kept together; they shared all they had with one another, they would sell their possessions and goods and distribute the proceeds among all, as anyone might be in need. Day after day they resorted with one accord to the temple and broke bread together in their own homes; they ate with a glad and simple heart, praising God and looked on with favour by all the people. Meantime the Lord added the saved daily to their number (Acts 2:44-47). Now there was but one heart and soul among the multitude of the believers; not one of them considered anything his personal property, they shared all they had with one another. There was not a needy person among them, for those who owned land or houses would sell them and bring the proceeds of the sale, laying the money before the feet of the apostles; it was then distributed according to each individual's need (Acts 4:32-35).

The glimpse we catch of the early church in the second century in the Epistle to Diognetus is almost as beautiful as that in the Acts:

Christians are not differentiated from the rest of mankind either by country, language, or customs . . . . Every foreign land is their fatherland, and every fatherland is foreign. They marry like all other men and beget children, but they do not expose their offspring. They share a common table, but not a common bed. They are in the flesh, but do not live according to the flesh. They abide on earth, but live as citizens of heaven. They obey the established laws, and in their own lives they surpass the laws. They love all men and are persecuted by all. They are unrecognized, and yet they are condemned. They are put to death, and they have an increase of life. They are poor, yet they bestow riches on many. They suffer the want of all things, and they superabound in all things. They endure in dignities, and they are glorified in their indignities. They are slandered, and they are justified. They are abused, and they bless. They are scoffed at and they show reverence. While they perform good deeds they are punished as evil-doers. When punished they rejoice as attaining unto life. They are warred against as aliens by the Jews and are persecuted by the Greeks, yet those who hate them are unable to state the cause of their hatred. In brief, what the soul is to the body Christians are to the world.

As one who has been privileged to travel almost constantly among the stations of the world mission of the Christian church for the greater part of the last fifty years, the writer desires to add his testimony to that of John R. Mott, Robert Speer, Henry Van Dusen, and J. H. Oldham—to mention only a few—that he has moved among thousands of humble Christians, wise or simple, in many lands, who share today the same spiritual experience, in principle, as the early Christians recorded above in the first and second centuries.

The church was the community of the Kingdom living for the

higher order of that spiritual world and already subject to its law. Jesus had proclaimed the Kingdom and created a brotherhood which should live for it and inherit it when it came. He had left it a task, without specific directions or organization for its achievement. The church was at first an otherworldly society but soon it had to realize that it was to live for centuries on earth. Christians later recognized that they had a dual citizenship to maintain. They had to organize the church under competent officials, funds had to be administered, books must be kept, charity distributed and the church cleansed of deadly heresies which threatened its very life. The Apostle Paul, as the first Christian statesman, organized the churches. Many of the larger denominations in the world today may lay claim to being derived from the original apostolic community.

Many of the most enlightened Christians of later generations could not become "solitaries" like the Essenes or monks, but gradually began to play their part as responsible citizens in the state. Christianity could not, like Judaism, become a national religion. Jesus' far-reaching answer to their catch question, "Render to Caesar the things that are Caesar's, and to God the things that are God's," had forever shown the dual relation of the Christian to two worlds. Christians were to render submission to the state "for conscience's sake," but to acknowledge absolute and unqualified obedience only to God (Rom. 13:1-10). Always they "must obey God rather than men." The church existed for the Kingdom of God and the state for the present world. To each the citizen of both worlds must render his duties.

There was ever something volcanic in the fiery heart of the Christian religion. Lessing might say that "Christianity has been practised for eighteen centuries, but the religion of Jesus has never been tried." This was a half-truth in a sense, but the measure of failure was not always because of the rationalizations of the theologians, nor because of the unfaithfulness of the church. The religion of Jesus could not be literally put into practice except in the light of the coming Kingdom, for "with men this is impossible." Yet Jesus' way of life as an ideal, as in no other religion, is written in the hearts of all men.

To conclude this chapter on spiritual resurrection and its consequences, faith in the resurrection of Jesus has far-reaching results for his followers. The conviction of personal immortality not only gives hope and assurance but perspective to life. Those who share the life of the risen Christ have received a Kingdom which cannot be shaken. Eternity becomes even more important than time. One need no longer be impatient for quick, visible results. The petty ego surely should be less clamant for self-expression and for earthly recognition when it is sure of its destiny. And one has a larger hope for all men. It is not maintained that immortality proves the universalists' faith. But no materialist can demonstrate that death ends all, and no dogmatist can prove that spiritual opportunity ends with this life. There can be no appeal to fear and there need be no unethical belief in eternal punishment which would be more immoral than Hitler's Gestapo. If there were no spark of life and one were a "dead soul" the complete oblivion of annihilation would be no injustice. But if there is the least germ of life, or capacity for truth, the least potentiality of repentance or for spiritual achievement in one who passes through the portal we miscall "death," surely he will be given opportunity by a God of grace and love who is not confined to a life span that is often "nasty, brutish and short."

No one should hold the utterly unscriptural, unethical and irrational belief that life and its development are almost confined to two crucial moments: one at a miraculous new birth, and the other at the miracle of death when all saints are supposed by some to be, as it were, mechanically clapped into a mold and perfected, "to live happily ever after" in a monotonous, standardized heaven. Rather, the imperfect but growing soul will surely pass through the portal of life into the more spacious and favorable environment beyond, which is doubtless under the same fundamental spiritual laws that obtain throughout God's visible universe. We believe that there are "many mansions" there, many spheres or planes of being and that the spiritual world is as vast and various as the seemingly infinite material universe. We suspect that the world beyond will not be utterly strange, nor totally dissimilar to the best of this world, but will be without the deformities and scars occasioned by selfish sin. We shall not be strangers or orphans there, for there will be one connecting link in "this same Jesus," through his resurrection. And there will be those whom we "have loved long since, and lost awhile."

There will still be the same God and Father of our Lord Jesus Christ who will be the same yesterday today and forever. There will be the Kingdom of God, the very Kingdom that Jesus proclaimed, where his will shall be done. There will still be truth, beauty and goodness; still humility, faith, purity and love. But all life will surely be raised to a higher power, perhaps with new and undreamed dimensions added, and perchance new and other worlds beyond our ken, "above the smoke and stir of this dim spot that men call earth." There will still be personalities, made in the image of their Creator, capable of fellowship with God, in an ever-growing and infinitely wider brotherhood. And though differing, as one star from another in glory, we know the image that we shall bear when we are conformed to type, "in his likeness," in the fullness of the stature of Christ. The new spiritual body will doubtless be a more perfect instrument than "this body of death," as much so as mind is above matter, or spirit above flesh.

Too sure to ask for signs and wonders, and with little interest in speculation, we nevertheless assert our *credo*: We have in Christ the sure and certain hope of a blessed resurrection, in the power of an endless life. For Christ died for our sins and rose again. "Christ did rise . . . he was the first . . . for by man came also resurrection from the dead (I Cor. 15:20-21). For he must reign until all his foes *are put under* his *feet*. (Death is the last foe to be put down.) For *God has put everything under his feet* (I Cor. 15:25-27) so that God may be everything to everyone" (I Cor. 15:28).

10

THE GOSPEL OF PAUL

IN THIS CHAPTER WE ARE NOT LEAVING CHRIST TO STUDY PAUL; we are studying Christ in Paul. Jesus had lived a unique life in Palestine; but what did that prove? Could he save and change men? We take Paul as the first example of the *Gesta Christi*; he is a triumph of Christ. As we cannot know the historic Jesus apart from the Synoptic Gospels, so we cannot fully understand Christianity apart from Paul, its chief interpreter. The best way to understand Paul is to read and then reread his epistles in chronological order at a sitting. He says himself: "You don't have to read between the lines of my letters; you can understand them" (II Cor. 1:13). That is literally true for all who, like his Corinthian converts, recognize that such things have to be spiritually understood, in experience. Paul himself could have said with Plotinus: "Yonder is the true object of our love, which it is possible to grasp and to live with and truly to possess, since no envelope of flesh separates us from it. *He who has seen it knows what I mean.*" Paul would have us "*know* the love of Christ," which can be realized only by those who increasingly possess it, in a personal communion which leads in time to inner likeness to Christ himself.

Paul's ten principal Epistles, written chiefly between 50 and 62 A.D., do not constitute a Fifth Gospel but the First Gospel, written a decade or more before Mark. Since most will not take the time to read all the Epistles, let the student take the five that give the heart of Paul's message—Galatians, I and II Corinthians, Romans and Philippians. In four of these brief, burning letters, Paul pours out his very soul, and then states more ponderously to the Romans a reasoned outline of his position. In Philippians (3:4-10) and Galatians (1:13-24) in a few bold strokes Paul gives his early autobiography: A chosen member of the chosen race of Israel, of the fighting tribe of Benjamin, the tribe which produced the nation's first fighting king, Paul's namesake, Saul, and their greatest spiritual warrior, Saul of Tarsus; a Hebrew of Hebrews, a Pharisee of Pharisees, and the most zealous persecutor of the pernicious sect of the Nazarenes. In mid-career, on the road to Damascus, the book of Acts thrice states that Paul met the risen Christ in a heavenly vision which struck him to the earth and left him stunned and physically blind. With his whole life seemingly blasted, with all that he had counted truth appearing false, and his self-righteousness worse than filthy rags, Paul goes away to the solitude of Arabia to think out the implications of this event which was not only to transform Paul, but to affect the Roman Empire and to change history. He then returns to Damascus and later to his home city of Tarsus, to testify that Jesus is indeed the Jewish Messiah.

After three turbulent years, he went up to Jerusalem where he became acquainted with Peter and James the brother of Jesus, and then labored in Syria and the Near East. For the first twelve years or more he had worked chiefly among Jews until his experience at Antioch in Pisidia when, upon their rejection of the gospel, he cried: "Here we turn to the Gentiles" (Acts 13:46). As the apostle to the Gentiles, he was now used as God's instrument to free and transform a persecuted Jewish sect into a world-conquering religion. His four great missionary journeys carried him over the Roman world "from Jerusalem right round to Illyricum" (east of Italy). To the last he had his eye on Spain and the Pillars of Hercules, which were then considered the ends of the earth.

As practical as any Roman, with a genius for organization, Paul founded his churches throughout the Roman Empire. Driven from Thessalonica after three weeks, he founded there a church which after nineteen centuries is flourishing today in modern Salonica. Spiritually, Paul outthought and outlived the Greeks. As Plato proposed the chief problems for philosophy for all time, so Paul, though no philosopher or systematic theologian, out of his deep spiritual experience raised the major problems of theology, and threw light on their solution. Augustine, Thomas Aquinas, Luther, Calvin, Zwingli, and Wesley all founded their systems on this unsystematic man. He threw off, like sparks from an anvil, thoughts and metaphors that would kindle theological and philosophical conflagrations for centuries to come. As bold as Amos, yet with the vicarious love of the Suffering Servant of the great Prophet of the Exile, this persecuted man cried at last: "But no boasting for me, none, except in the cross of our Lord Jesus Christ, by which the world has been crucified to me and I crucified to the world (Gal. 6:14). For I bear branded on my body the owner's stamp of the Lord Jesus." (Gal. 6:17).

Concerning Paul's conversion, we are more interested in the fact than in theories regarding it. Psychologists may always differ as to how far it was a violent, subjective, psychological upheaval from repressed complexes, and how far his vision was as objective as it seemed to him. The fact remains that it almost instantly transformed his entire life, and was probably the most important event in the history of the Christian church. Paul says in substance: "I saw the risen Lord." But if God was in Christ, and Jesus was a crucified Messiah, then this involved the overturning of his entire life and system, a transvaluation of all values, a revolution in Paul's conception of God, of man, and of destiny. Either the Law was true and he that was "hung on a tree" was accursed, or, if Christ crucified was indeed the Messiah, then the Law, which had pronounced him accursed, was set aside and Christ had brought to an end this enslaving instrument. If Christ was the center of Paul's new world, he and his followers had passed from the religion of a Book to the religion of a Person. As the personal piety of Jesus as a Jew was theocentric, Christianity as a world religion now became Christocentric. It had passed from Law to love, from Moses to Christ, from the Old Covenant to the New, from an exclusive nationalism to a universal world religion. "The task of Paul and others is, as Dr. Cairns says, 'rethinking everything in terms of the resurrection.'"

It is significant that from the nature of his own experience, Paul must start, as many Christians in the later centuries, not with the birth in Bethlehem, nor the baptism, nor the earthly life of Jesus, but with the risen Christ. He is indissolubly united with Christ. He sees one Body, with Head and members. But, to follow this physical figure of speech, Christ is not only the directing Head, unifying and co-ordinating all the members, he is also the throbbing heart-center, pulsing the cleansing and energizing lifeblood through arteries and veins to every member of the entire body. Ideally and potentially, Christ is in us in every thought, motive, and act. He is influencing us, enabling us to work out our salvation because he is working within us, "in his goodwill enabling us to will and achieve it." In the "first, fine careless rapture" of Christianity, there were powerful churches all over the Roman world, in Asia, Europe, and North Africa, before a single Gospel had been written, before Paul's letters had been circulated,[1] and before there was a single church building in existence. With no book, no building, and no creed, Christians had only the great essentials of prayer, worship, sacrificial service, membership in a living witnessing church, and unbroken fellowship with their living Head.

The scenery, the art, architecture, and culture of Tarsus and Athens were noble, but Paul never sees or mentions them. He does not consider the lilies or the birds; he sees only *men*, marred but made in the image of God and capable of being restored to that image, in conformity to type. And what is this type? It is not the vague vision of some unknown heavenly being. It is always "this same Jesus." We have been diverted by the mistranslation of that passage about not knowing Christ after the flesh, where Paul actually says: "I estimate no one by what is external; even though I once estimated Christ by what is external (as a Jewish Messiah, of the seed of David), I no longer estimate him thus. There is a new creation." (II Cor. 5:16.)

[1] Paul's surviving letters were collected, edited and reissued only after 90 A.D. Half a century later they were incorporated into the Canon of the New Testament. Clement, writing to the Corinthians about 95 A.D., tells them to "take up the Epistle of the blessed Paul the Apostle." Second Peter, written long after 100 A.D., speaks of Paul writing in "all his letters" (now available for readers) of things hard to be understood, which may be twisted like "the rest of the Scriptures." It was only long after Peter had died, that Paul's Epistles were counted Scriptures.

If one will reread the Epistles of Paul with this in mind, he will be surprised to find the weight Paul gives to the life and teachings of the historic Jesus. Paul himself would doubtless have emphasized this more had not the Judaizers constantly thrown in his face the charge that he could not be an apostle for he had never even seen Jesus. Paul sees the character of the risen Christ as exactly that of Jesus, and "the mind of Christ" is the mind of Jesus. A close study will show that Paul's teaching reproduces much of the Sermon on the Mount. He even quotes from the Sayings of Jesus, the lost document Q, which Matthew and Luke partly reproduce.[2]

The Christ whom Paul describes as the ideal for Christlikeness always has the character of Jesus of the Gospels. When we are told that his simple converts are to copy him as he copies Christ (for most of them had never seen Jesus, they had no Bible, and could not read), it is just the traits of Jesus that he emphasizes in self-denying lowliness of mind, in love, sacrifice and suffering. Paul completely exemplifies the four attitudes taught by Jesus: humility, faith, purity and love. Harnack has pointed out the wide influence which the words gentleness, consideration, and lowliness of mind had during the first three centuries in Christian literature. These were the weapons with which the new religion began the conquest of the Roman world. Harnack thinks Paul's appeal to these characteristics of Christ imply his knowledge of the Sayings of Jesus, whether in oral or written form (as in II Cor. 10:1; Matt. 11:29). From some source Paul knew Jesus' life, his character, his mind and spirit.

It is no accident that we can study the character of Jesus and the mind of Christ almost equally well in the first three Gospels or in Paul's Epistles, for in both it is "the same Jesus." And we must also recognize that, whereas Jesus in the flesh failed to win the rulers or the Jewish nation, and was not able to transform

---

[2] For married people Paul says his instructions are the Lord's, not his own, that a wife is not to separate from her husband (I Cor. 7:10; Matt. 5:32; Luke 16:18). He quotes Jesus' instruction to the Twelve that the laborer is worthy of his hire (I Cor. 9:13; Matt. 10:10; Luke 10:7). He says that Christians are to judge themselves that they may not be judged (I Cor. 11:31; Matt. 7:1; Luke 6:37).

even the Twelve upon whom he concentrated his attention at the end, the living Christ, through Paul and the apostles after Pentecost was able to do far "greater works than these." The living Christ by his mighty works in the transformation of character built Christendom out of the falling Roman Empire and from the vitality of the barbarous European tribes. And out of an ever-imperfect Church Militant he is building the Church Triumphant.

We must clearly recognize the difference between Jesus' gospel, as the good news of God, and Paul's gospel of Christ. We found Jesus' message in the Synoptic Gospels in the two foci of God as Father and the coming Kingdom or rule of God. Paul's good news also has two foci, Christ crucified and risen. When Paul came to Corinth, humiliated after his relative failure in the cynical smugness of Athens, which was proud of its worldly wisdom, he determined to know nothing but Christ (as risen and living) and him crucified. When he closes his first great letter to the Corinthians he reminds them that this was always his gospel (I Cor. 1:21-24; 15:1-8): that Christ died for our sins, that he rose on the third day and was seen by a multitude of believers, and last of all by Paul himself. As God under the symbol of Adam, through the process of biological evolution, created man, who sinned and marred the divine image in which he was created, so Christ risen, as a life-giving Spirit, as the second Adam, became the creative source of a new race of men; "We all mirror *the glory of the Lord* with face unveiled, and we are being transformed into the same likeness as himself, passing from one glory to another." (II Cor. 3:18.)

The Galatians had been converted by faith in Christ alone and had begun bearing all the Christlike fruits of the Spirit such as "love, joy, and peace." Then the Judaizers, jealous for the Law of Moses and their exclusive Jewish privileges, bewitched Paul's converts by telling them that all Christians must be circumcised and keep the whole Law of Moses in order to be saved, or at least perfected. Paul knew from his own bitter experience that there was no good news in this but the slavery of death. Neither Paul, Peter, nor any other man had been able to keep the whole Law and save himself by good works. For if righteousness were obtainable by keeping the Law, then Christ died for nought. Blazing with moral indignation against this enslaving falsehood, Paul cleared the air and decided this controversial point. Few controversies in all history have ever been so settled, once for all, as by his Galatian letter. No man is, or ever has been, justified and perfected by his own works under the Law. By the free gift of God's grace in Christ, by simple trust in him, a man's sins are forgiven, he is accepted as God's son, and God, through Christ, by his Spirit, begins the patient work of slowly transforming him into the likeness of Christ. The believer is justified, or counted righteous, even before the long, painful process of making him actually so. Thus, from the first, he is not a slave earning his way by good works, but always a radiant son.

In a single verse he is able to sum up to the Galatians his whole experience and his whole gospel: "I have been crucified with Christ, and it is no longer I who live, Christ lives in me; the life I now live in the flesh I live by faith in the Son of God who loved me and gave himself up for me." (Gal. 2:20.) That is, through his living union with Christ, Paul counts his old sinful self as nailed to that Cross on Calvary, and by faith he reckons himself dead to sin, to self, and to the world. The old Saul of Tarsus is counted dead with Jesus on that Cross. As God's new creation, Paul can now say: "Christ lives in me, as God once lived in Jesus in Nazareth. The life I now live in this weak and weary body, I live simply by faith, that is by utter trust in the Son of God, motivated and moved by his love, who not only died for all, but loved *me* and gave himself up for *me*." And all this is no fiction or mere figure of speech. Faith makes it a fact. By their fruits ye shall know them.

As Paul can thus sum up his whole life in a sentence which states his relation to Christ, so as an evangelist he can state the whole gospel in a word to every man: "Confess with your mouth that 'Jesus is Lord,' believe in your heart that God raised him from the dead, and you will be saved." All life is focused in the present moment; now is the accepted time. Paul could have said with Emerson: "Now is the nick of time in matters that reach into eternity." There was grave danger in a later emphasis upon the death of Christ as a mechanical "transaction," in seeking to be saved by a shibboleth, or by a formula, or by correct intellectual belief in an orthodox creed. But the moment the sinner repents, believes, and genuinely accepts Christ, he is united to Christ. He is "in Christ" and Christ is in him.[3] He is not only like a member of a physical body, controlled and supplied with life by heart and head; he is one with Christ, a member of his spiritual body.

The fullness of Christ the Head is now at the disposal of every member. If we ask what is the content of that fullness, it is this same Jesus who loves me now and gives himself to me continuously, to the full measure of my need, as I am able to receive him. To believe in Christ crucified means that I am not only forgiven, but that I must always think of the Father and of the Son as loving me as much as when Jesus died upon Calvary. And, as in Jesus' parable, I can constantly recall the words of the father to the elder son: "My son, you and I are always together; all I have is yours." It is the same love that was in the Father who so loved that he gave his Son, the same love that was in Jesus who so loved that he gave himself, the same love that was in Paul for lost Onesimus and for the brother for whom Christ died, and exactly the same self-giving, costly, sacrificial love that must be communicated to us and reproduced in us. This is what it means to be a Christian.

And to what end are we followers of Christ? Not that we should save our individual selfish souls by belief in a mechanical transaction, or by believing in God as "punishing an innocent victim" so that we may spend eternity in a selfish future heaven

---

[3] Paul uses "in Christ" and "in the Lord" 164 times as the characteristic expression of his religious experience. He also uses "Christ in me" which means the exalted Christ living in Paul by his Spirit. He means more than if he were speaking of being in the air that he breathes. It is the relation of two persons who have become one, in spiritual union. It is closer than when man and wife become one flesh. It is "closer than breathing, nearer than hands and feet." It is unfortunate to describe this as Paul's "Christ mysticism." It can never be intellectually rationalized but it can be spiritually known by the childlike in spirit.

of bliss. We are saved to serve. Every true Christian is a Christ-one called to repeat the life of Jesus in all its spiritual essentials—in humility, faith, purity, and love. Especially in love which means self-giving in the full sharing of life, with God and with men. This is Paul's gospel of Christ crucified and risen. It is infinitely more than the first disciples could have dreamed when Jesus said, "Come and follow me." It is more even than the gospel or good news of God which Jesus proclaimed.

And this is Christianity! To think that Paul "perverted it," that "we must get back of this religion *about* Jesus to the simple religion *of* Jesus," to the humanist conception of a benevolent teacher who went about doing good, is pathetic. It is a superficial, threadbare half-gospel. It means to misunderstand Paul, to fail to comprehend Jesus, and to fall short of the fullness of Christ. Paul as Jesus' greatest follower, with more than the burden of an Atlas upon his shoulders and the sufferings of a Prometheus, the man most like his Master in his character, life, teaching and sacrificial death, counts himself but the bondslave of Christ. As the best of men he helps us to understand that Jesus was infinitely more than the best of men; more than any "man of genius."

It is "this same Jesus" that Paul seeks to have reproduced in all his true followers, for "all you who were baptized into Christ have taken on the character of Christ." From all the divine fullness in Christ the Head, the believer may even now draw, according to his need and the measure of his faith. For "all belongs to you"—all truth and all true teachers, the world, life and death, as a conquered foe; the present and the future—"all belongs to you; and you belong to Christ, and Christ to God." Over and over again, Paul exhorts us to reproduce the same spirit of love that was in Jesus, our pattern. Love is not a luxurious emotion but we are to understand it as it was incarnated in Jesus and to give our lives in the service of God and man as he did. The paean of Paul's great hymn to love in the thirteenth chapter of I Corinthians is but a picture of the life of Jesus. We are to understand love by Jesus rather than Jesus by love. And as in love, so in sacrifice and suffering, Jesus' lot was to be the portion of his followers. They were to suffer as he suffered, and to die as he died. And this was their chief glory. In the words of F. W. H. Myers, Paul felt: "Desperate tides of the whole great world's anguish forced through the channels of a single heart."

Paul's own thorn in the flesh was the classic example of suffering for the Christian: "It is enough for you to have my grace; it is in weakness that my power is fully felt . . . for I am strong just when I am weak." Yet it is only in connection with his sufferings that he dares to say boldly: "You had all the miracles that mark an apostle done for you, fully and patiently—miracles, wonders, and deeds of power." The true Christian is one who knows in his own spiritual experience the death and resurrection of Christ by dying with him and rising with him. All is summed up in Paul's aspiration for himself and his fellow-Christians: "I would know him in the power of his resurrection and the fellowship of his sufferings, with my nature transformed to die as he died, to see if I too can attain the resurrection from the dead." All true believers are henceforth one; there is no division or segregation between Jew or Greek, bond or free, black or white, male or female, all are one in Christ, and only in him.

Many are thankful that Paul was not a philosopher and that he had little interest in speculation. He simply tries to describe his own spiritual experience in order to help his followers live as Jesus lived, but he never forms a system or endeavors to crystallize his beliefs into a creed. Like his Master he was not orthodox. His practical letters are the work of a profound but quite unsystematic theologian, who cares little for theology as an abstract study, but everything for Christian living and experience. Seventeen epistles of the New Testament open with the invocation "grace and peace"; in thirteen of these, most of which Paul writes, all gifts come from "God our Father and the Lord Jesus Christ." We find in Paul both a Binitarian and a Trinitarian strain of thought.[4] He never feels obliged to speculate about

[4] In II Cor. 13:14, we have "the blessing of the Lord Jesus Christ, the love of God, and the communion of the Holy Spirit." Twenty-two New Testament formulas are Binitarian and one is Trinitarian.

the Trinity, which he never mentions; he never seeks to define the relation of Father, Son, and Spirit. He keeps his feet on the solid ground of experience. Instead of formal epistles he dictated his simple letters when weary with the toil of tentmaking or beset with the harrowing problems of some local church.

Professor Frank Porter, of Yale, has given us a deeply spiritual understanding of *The Mind of Christ in Paul*. He contrasts Paul, who habitually exalts Christ by terms which stress his identification with his followers at every point—in suffering, life, death and resurrection—with later Christians who think they exalt Christ by removing him forever from us, soaring away above the clouds amid a whole hierarchy of beings in the mediation of the Virgin, saints and angels. Professor Porter gives a suggestive parable from Wagner's interpretation of the legend of Lohengrin. Elsa is warned by her divine-human lover not to ask whence he came, what his name, and what his nature. Doubting, however, Elsa still asks her questions because she does not fully trust him. Lohengrin answers, but cannot escape the inevitable consequences of separation from her because of her unbelief. Christians often press the same metaphysical questions concerning Christ, which betray their doubts. They will not trust the love which the vision of him has brought them with its experience of joy and freedom and moral strength. Many of the later metaphysical creeds regarding persons, nature and substance, leave out Jesus altogether and his character and teaching. They often serve only to separate him from us by seeming exaltation. Blessed are they who have not seen, nor philosophically understood, nor scientifically proved, but have believed and know that they have received the fullness of the blessing from God the Father and the Lord Jesus Christ.

Paul seldom speaks of Christ as pre-existent and even then not speculatively. If he tells how the Divine One "emptied himself," it is not that we may metaphysically understand him but that we may learn his lesson of humility.[5] As a Jewish monotheist,

---

[5] Paul quotes an old Stoic creed fulfilled in Christ (I Cor. 8:6) as the Stoic Marcus Aurelius thus addressed nature: "From thee are all things, in thee are all things, unto thee are all things" (See Rom. 11:36 and Phil.

Paul has a strong aversion to the Greek *logos*. In his favorite Christology, all that is ascribed to Christ may be shared by the Christian; this is Christ's glory as it is ours.

Perhaps we can now see why Paul's gospel of Christ could so appeal to men and sweep the Roman Empire. The world had been prepared for the Christian gospel by Jewish monotheism, Greek culture, Roman government, and the oriental mystery religions, or pagan redemption cults of the Mediterranean. The Jewish religion, which was the highest that the world had known, seemed to Gentiles nationalistic, exclusive, and bigoted. The pagan religion of Greece was bankrupt and its superstitions and corrupt polytheisms were neither rational, moral nor spiritual. Rome had gained the world but lost its own soul. Its cold emperor worship, whether of Augustus or Nero, could only offer a stone in place of bread. The oriental mystery religions had sprung from primitive nature worship, which celebrated the rebirth of spring after the death of winter, through their "dead and resuscitated" mythical gods. There was Greek Orphism which had influenced Plato; the Persian worship of Mithras which was once a powerful competitor of Christianity; the Egyptian cult of Isis, Serapis and Osiris, and other oriental cults, some of which promised a "new birth," a Lord's Supper of feeding on the body and blood of the god, and union with the deity. But many of these were so rife with superstition, mythology, astrology, magic, idolatry and immorality, that they could not fully satisfy heart-hungry men in a world that had now grown old.

If we analyze Paul's gospel, we can find five principal elements or bases of appeal in the new Christianity: 1. There was the solid moral foundation of ethical monotheism inherited from two

---

2:6-11). To the Colossians, perplexed by the superstitious mystery religions all about them, Paul gives the fullest description of Christ as the likeness, or portrait, or image of the unseen God. In him "the divine Fulness willed to settle" (Col. 1:19); in him are "all the treasures of wisdom and knowledge hidden" (Col. 2:3); "in Christ the entire Fulness of deity has settled bodily" (Col. 2:9); since "you have been raised with Christ, aim at what is above where Christ is *seated at the right hand of God* . . . for you died and your life is hidden with Christ in God . . . Christ is everything and everywhere." (Col. 3:1, 3, 11.)

thousand years of experience of the world's greatest religious race; 2. There was the matchless character of the historic Jesus, in contrast to the unbelievable myths of Greece and of the mystery religions; 3. There was Christ crucified, with the good news of free forgiveness on the basis of his divine Atonement; 4. There was the might of the risen Christ, pouring forth his grace upon all the members of his Body, observable in the changed lives of slaves like Onesimus, in evidences which men could "see and hear"; 5. There was the good news of salvation for all, in its complete universality and immediate availability, with its free offer of individual and social redemption in the Kingdom of God. The gospel could challenge all and say to each: "Believe in the Lord Jesus Christ and thou shalt be saved." Amid the abstract religions of law and philosophy and surrounded by superstitious mystery cults and widespread illiteracy, Christianity came with its vernacular Bible, its stimulus of learning and widening education; yet it centered in a unique and matchless historic Person. It was indeed the almost unbelievably good news before which men could exult and say: "Thanks be unto God for his unspeakable gift!"[6]

We cannot better close this chapter on the Gospel of Paul than in the words of this grand old warrior himself, as an unconscious revelation of the portrait of Jesus and of the life of Christ:[7]

[6] The cynical Gibbon in his celebrated fifteenth chapter of the *Decline and Fall of the Roman Empire* attributes the spread of Christianity to: (1) The inflexible zeal of the early Christians. Christianity had the strength without the fetters of the Jewish law, which was better fitted for defense than for conquest; (2) Its doctrine of the future life with its vivid and great hope, richer than the pale immortality promised by the mystery religions and the animal worship and low ethics of the religions of Egypt; (3) The miraculous powers ascribed to the primitive church. It offered health and happiness, a meaningful cross of suffering and world conquest; (4) The pure and austere morals of Christianity, among the criminals of Corinth and Rome, with its passion for perfection, condemning worldly pleasure and luxury and offering an asylum from the wicked world; (5) Its organization in the union and discipline of a Christian republic which formed an independent state in the heart of the Roman Empire. Its doctrines of freedom and equality challenged the polytheism, pantheism, and skepticism of decaying Greece and Rome.

[7] I Cor. 9:17, 19; II Cor. 6:4-10; 11:23-28; Rom. 8:31-39; 15:19.

Woe is me if I preach not the gospel . . . By suffering, by troubles, by calamities, by lashes, by imprisonment; mobbed, toiling, sleepless, starving . . . amid evil report and good report, an "impostor" but honest, "unknown" but well-known, dying but here I am alive, chastened but not killed, grieved but always glad, a "pauper," but the means of wealth to many, without a penny but possessed of all.

With all my labors, with all my lashes, with all my time in prison, I have been often at the point of death; five times have I had forty lashes (all but one) from the Jews, three times I have been beaten by the Romans, once pelted with stones, three times shipwrecked . . . in danger from Jews and Gentiles, through dangers of town and of desert, through dangers on the sea, through dangers among false brothers—through labour and hardship, through many a sleepless night, through hunger and thirst, starving many a time, cold and ill-clad . . . From Jerusalem right round to Illyricum, I have been able to complete the preaching of the gospel of Christ . . . If God is for us, who can be against us? The God who did not spare his own Son but gave him up for us all, surely He will give us everything besides! . . . What can ever part us from Christ's love? Can anguish or calamity or persecution or famine or nakedness or danger or the sword? . . . No, in all this we are more than conquerors through him who loved us. For I am certain that neither death nor life, neither angels nor principalities, neither the present nor the future, no powers of the Height or of the Depth, nor anything else in all creation, will be able to part us from God's love in Christ Jesus our Lord.

11

THE INTERPRETATION OF JOHN

WHEN WE PASS FROM THE WORK OF LUKE THE HISTORIAN TO John the theologian, we enter into a different intellectual climate and into a new world of thought. The difference can best be understood if we recall the contrast between Aristotle and Plato. Aristotle was the realist, the born scientist and historian, who cared for fact, for classification and logical thought. Plato was the idealist, the lover of wisdom, the mystic philosopher and poet, who cared little for concrete fact, or for what seemed to him to be the lower world of nature or history, but was consumed by a passionate search for truth, beauty and goodness, in the higher invisible world of spirit. One was a son of fact, the other a candidate for truth. Each took a different path of approach to reality.

A similar difference is observable between the method of the first three writers of the Gospels and that of the fourth. The first three were more factual and tried to write down the acts and words of Jesus "in order." The Fourth Evangelist cared little for fact and little for history, save at the one crucial point that Jesus lived and died as a real man. He lacked a sense of time, and interest in the succession of events. But he had an immediate sense of eternity; he passionately sought the truth; he was a mystic, a theologian, a poet and a religious genius. He saw everything—all facts and events, all nature and history—*sub specie aeternitatis.*

Considering the secondary nature of Mark, Matthew and Luke, if this Fourth Gospel had been by the Apostle John, the son of Zebedee, it would have been immediately, enthusiastically and universally received. Instead, we have no evidence of the existence of the book before 110 A.D. and only by 180 A.D. are all four Gospels firmly established in the churches.[1] If one reads the last two verses of the Fourth Gospel (21:24, 25), he sees the marks of a later hand in the guarantee of the Ephesian elders of the authorship and general credibility of this Gospel: "*We know that his witness is true.*" But at the time the Gospel was first published, why was any guarantee of its credibility required? Apart from these last two verses there is not a word in the whole Gospel to suggest that it is, or claims to be, by the Apostle John. It is not only anonymous, like the first three Gospels, but it is the most anonymous book in the entire Bible.

It seems psychologically incredible that John or the author should refer to himself as "the disciple whom Jesus loved," for Jesus had no favorite. The writer of the obviously genuine Second and Third Epistles of John calls himself "the Elder" or Presbyter. We have historic evidence that there were two Johns in Ephesus, John the Apostle and John the Elder. The whole book and the relation between the four Gospels becomes intelligible if this Elder John, or some other Hellenistic Christian in Ephesus who had received the tradition of John the Apostle, and had realized the experience of Paul in his own life, wrote the Gospel. We can then look to the first three Gospels for materials for a history of Jesus of Nazareth, and to the Fourth Gospel and Paul's Epistles for the interpretation and experience of the living Christ.

We shall not have space to state all our sources[2] as we write on this seemingly simple but highly complex book; nor can we state at length the reasons which compel us to take the following position: We are convinced that the Fourth Gospel was not and could not have been written by John the son of Zebedee, but

---

[1] Theophilus of Antioch (c. 180) is the first unequivocally to quote John as inspired Scripture and expressly ascribe it to John the Apostle. This was more than a century and a third after the probable date of John's death by martyrdom in 44 A.D.

[2] The writer has read or reread Scott, Moffatt, Burkitt, Streeter, Bacon, B. W. Robinson, Schmiedel, Schweitzer, Baron von Hügel, MacGregor, and others, but he feels an especial debt of gratitude to Sir Edwyn Hoskyns for the two volumes of his commentary on *The Fourth Gospel* (Faber & Faber, London), and to C. J. Wright in *The Mission and Message of Jesus*, which seem to see equally the critical and spiritual sides of this Gospel.

was by a much greater man, perhaps John the Elder in Ephesus about 110 A.D. He was the author of the Gospel and the three Epistles of John. The Epistles should be read before the Gospel as they show the conditions in Ephesus and Asia Minor at the beginning of the second century when they were written. Jerusalem as the spiritual center of the church had been destroyed some forty years before and the original apostles and eyewitnesses had passed away. The immense majority of the Christians were Greeks, and the Jews were regarded as those who had rejected their Messiah. Many of the Jewish terms were misleading, or made little appeal to the Greeks. Some of the converts had grown cold, and some had been led astray by the heresies of false prophets as described in the letters to the Seven Churches of Asia Minor in the Revelation, written about 96 A.D.[3] There had been the growth of a particularly dangerous heresy described in the First Epistle (I John 2:18-22, 26; 4:1-4) which was incipient Gnosticism.[4] With their "many antichrists," "they withdrew from us." Asserting that they possessed "all knowledge" they denied that Jesus was the Christ or that he had come in the flesh as a real man. Claiming to be spiritual, prophetic, and Christian, they yet rejected Jesus Christ. But their boasted liberty

[3] See Rev. 2:1-4, 13-15, 20, 24, etc. There were false prophets, "the woman Jezebel," "Balaam," the "Nicolaitans" with their proud spiritual knowledge, and with their resulting sects, divisions, immoralities and hatreds.

[4] Gnosticism, which arose out of the mingling of religions and the Hellenizing of Christianity, was prevalent in the first two centuries, and at the close of the second century the church had to fight for its life against this heresy. It maintained that men were saved by higher knowledge rather than by faith. The holy God and the higher world of spirits could have no contact with base matter, save through a hierarchy of intermediate beings, angels and spirits. Man, imprisoned in the flesh, in the body as a tomb, must seek release from his lower nature by this higher esoteric knowledge, or enlightenment, or by an unethical redemption such as that offered in the mystery religions. The Gnostics or "knowers" denied that Christ had come in the flesh and they did not believe in his real humanity or his real death. To meet this heresy, John maintains with Paul that all the fullness of the Godhead bodily was in Christ and he omits all reference to angels or demons or the hierarchy of intermediate spiritual beings familiar to Paul. He denies the superstitions and myths of the mystery religions, for "salvation is of the Jews" (John 4:22). Much of his Gospel implies a polemic against the Jews and the Gnostic heretics, though he uses some of the Gnostic terms such as light and darkness.

had led them into immorality, into disobedience to the commands of Jesus, and into sectarian hatred and division so
serious that it seemed to the writer that his time might be indeed "the last hour" of the antichrist.

We saw that the teaching of Jesus in the Synoptics had two
foci: God the Father and the coming Kingdom; that Paul's
teaching had two foci in Christ crucified and risen; so John's
Gospel has two foci in the Father and the Son: the Eternal
Father above, manifested in the historic Jesus as the unique
revelation of God in time and place below. These two are frequently fused by John into one burning center which becomes
the text and theme of the entire Gospel, and this is the writer's
one contact with history: *God has once for all entered history in
Jesus Christ, who has come in the flesh in real humanity.* This
same Jesus was born, lived, died, and rose again as the Jewish
Messiah and the Greek Logos or Word incarnate. The Fourth
Evangelist forces his readers back upon the life and death of
Jesus in the flesh as the pivotal center, the one place for the
understanding of history, of man, and of God. Here God confronts man with the truth in Jesus; here he reveals himself
fully and finally, once for all; here he seeks to reconcile the
world unto himself, when Jesus is "lifted up" upon the Cross
to draw all men unto himself, and here he judges men by their
attitude to Jesus Christ. In Jesus men are confronted by eternity;
by life or judgment; by the love of God or the condemnation of
God; by his Kingdom and rule or by disobedience; by salvation
or death. This dualistic writer feels that men must see the two
ultimates: God or the power of evil, truth or falsehood, light
or darkness, life or death. And men must respond by obedience
or disobedience, faith or unbelief. Everything is either black
or white in this Gospel.

In a series of "we" passages more striking than those of Paul's
traveling companion in the Acts, the author identifies himself
with the continuation of the true original apostolic community
against the Gnostic heretics, haters and deniers. Nine times in
four verses in the first paragraph of his first Epistle, he repeats
this emphatic "we," and then carries it over into his Gospel.

That which was from the beginning—this Word, Life, Light, which was divine and became flesh, incarnate as real man—*we* heard, saw, witnessed, and touched; we testify and bring you word of this eternal life that was with the Father, that you may share our living fellowship with the Father and with his Son, Jesus Christ.

The devout Baron von Hügel points out that to attribute this Gospel to John the Apostle, or to an eyewitness who writes an historic document, is to force the four Gospels into flat contradiction with each other so that we lose historicity everywhere. In the first three Gospels, Jesus speaks prevailingly of God and his coming Kingdom; in the Fourth Gospel, his message is centered in himself. In the former, the Messiahship is a hidden secret revealed only to the Twelve, late in the ministry; in the fourth it is proclaimed from the beginning and argued with his enemies in almost every chapter. In the first three, he is a real man tempted in all points as we are; in the Fourth Gospel he is a supernatural being who knows all things and needs no information from any man. In the Synoptics, he faces the future and his speedy second coming on the clouds of heaven; in the Fourth Gospel he has come already—by the Spirit, saying repeatedly, "I came down from heaven," "before Abraham was I am." In the first three Gospels, salvation is a moral process in a life of obedience, in loving God and one's neighbors; in the Fourth Gospel, men are saved by a miraculous new birth, they are born of water and the Spirit in baptism; they eat his flesh and drink his blood in the sacrament of a later church. In the former, he is prevailingly the "Son of Man," a mystery, a problem to be interpreted. In John, he is the Greek Logos, the pre-existent Son of God who became flesh on earth. In the first and third Gospels, he is miraculously conceived and born of the Virgin Mary. In the Fourth, while he is the very Incarnation of God, no virgin birth is mentioned and he is spoken of as the "son of Joseph." These constitute only a fraction of the differences between the two in doctrine, in viewpoint, and in vocabulary. The reason that Christians have not recognized this is because they unconsciously read the Fourth Gospel in the light of the first three, and vice versa.

Consequently we look to the first three Gospels for the historic Jesus and to John for the interpretation and meaning of that history. John falls into place as the keystone of the four Gospels, if not of the entire New Testament, if we once recognize the nature of this great work. The author is passionately historic at one and only one all-important point: He sees that the whole life of Jesus in the flesh is indeed the interpretive center of all history, which shows its final meaning and purpose, so that John can say in substance: "Who is a liar but he who denies that the Word became flesh, and that Jesus truly lived, suffered and died to reveal God as Father and to save man?" This is the central truth of the Fourth Gospel. Once this is realized, it must be remembered that the author is not trying to write history but to interpret it, and that he has no more interest in a series of prosaic facts and details, as a succession of events in time, than had Plato.

He handles his tradition and historical materials with complete liberty, controlled and limited by his doctrinal convictions and devotional experiences alone. The close student will note that he has everywhere the mystic's love of a double or triple meaning. When he preaches and writes to the Christians of Ephesus, he knows that they are familiar with the oral tradition and some of them with the written Gospels, especially Mark and Luke, which he always takes for granted as his background. He is not trying to mislead them, and knows that they will not misunderstand him if he puts into the mouth of Jesus the teaching regarding his Incarnation and the message he is sure the risen Christ by his Spirit wishes to convey to all Christians in the second century.

The Hebrews had a sober historic sense and began writing history long before the Greeks, but in the Gentile world of John's day, the exact quotation of the words of a great teacher were not regarded as necessary if one was faithful to his spirit. Thus Thucydides, one of the most conscientious of Greek historians, had naïvely explained at the beginning of his history that where a speech had to be provided for any of his characters, he had supplied the same as it seemed fitting. In the same manner, Plato freely composed his dialogues so that it is impossible to tell which are the ideas of Socrates and which are those of Plato.

The Gentile readers of the Fourth Gospel would clearly understand that John was not claiming to give a verbatim report of Jesus' utterances but only to be faithful to his understanding of their meaning and spirit. The Gospel of John constantly uses the first person to retell the whole story as if Jesus were speaking in accordance with the "I" style which Dr. Deissmann shows was then common in Ephesus. He puts into the mouth of Jesus the whole body of his teaching as he understands it, in terms of the life in Ephesus and of the Greco-Roman world of that day. This made it more understandable and helpful for the whole Gentile world and for all succeeding centuries.

For illustration, though many believers were perplexed by the long delay, the Jews were still looking for the Son of Man coming on the clouds of heaven. John feels that this is obsolete and unhealthy and that the Greeks of Ephesus and the world must realize that Christ has come already in the Holy Spirit with the offer of eternal life. It is strange to think that this was the first "modernistic" Gospel, as an interpretation or explanation to the world in that period of transition, in order to transplant Christianity from Jewish to Gentile soil. Consequently it was held as suspect by conservatives for nearly a century. Hitherto the church had been speaking to the Greek world in a Jewish vocabulary; henceforth the gospel was in universal language that could make its appeal to the whole world.

The author of the Fourth Gospel had before him as he wrote several sources, oral or written: 1. He had received a strong tradition from one or more of the Twelve, perhaps from John the son of Zebedee, in Jerusalem or Ephesus. He had sources of a tradition of the early disciples and probably his own knowledge of the topography of Jerusalem, and his inside source of information of the closing events of Jesus' life in his Judean ministry. He was much closer to the events of which he wrote than we are, and perhaps some of Luke's "many" written documents and some of Paul's lost letters were known to him. As Professor F. C. Burkitt says: "The Fourth Gospel enshrines many true words of the Lord which would otherwise have been lost to us." In any case, with strong assurance of what he felt to be the apostolic tradition, he corrected or supplemented the first three Gospels at several points. 2. Paul had been in Ephesus for at least three years and had warned them that "grievous wolves" and false prophets would waste the flock with perversions of the truth to draw the disciples after them (Acts 20:17-29). This writer had an intimate knowledge of Paul's work and his theology, and had entered into the rich Pauline experience described in the last chapter. He tried to write just such a Gospel as Paul might have written.

3. The writer thoroughly knew Mark and was in literary dependence upon him, though he seldom quotes accurately from his written document. He had much in common with Luke, and was either in literary dependence upon him or his sources in the Sayings of Jesus, but he has few points of contact with Matthew whose viewpoint he did not share. 4. His chief source, however, was no outward tradition, oral or written, but his own rich, vivid, inner experience, and his long years of inspired meditation upon it. He had a sure faith in and an overwhelming experience of God as Father, of Jesus Christ as Saviour, and of the Holy Spirit who, he believed, was guiding him into all truth and speaking in and through him in this Gospel as Jesus had promised. He was certain that revelation had not ended with the death of Jesus. As confidently as the prophets proclaimed, "Thus saith the Lord," so he felt that the living Christ was speaking through him. He was saying things that *must* be said to the Greeks, to the Jews, and to the world, but that could not have been said intelligibly before Jesus was "lifted up," crucified and glorified. Only in the perspective of these later events could the life of Jesus be understood. Unlike the three Synoptic writers concerned with the birth, the baptism, the life and teaching of the historic Jesus, John, like Paul, centers his Gospel in the Incarnation, the Crucifixion, and the Resurrection as the acts of God in history. But where Paul emphasizes the death of Christ the Fourth Evangelist emphasizes his life.

In this Gospel especially, we realize the limitation of all language. How much does a word of three letters "God" convey to us of the ineffable reality behind the universe? The writer of the Hebrews says: "Many were the forms and fashions in which God spoke of old to our fathers by the prophets, but in these days at the end he has spoken to us by a Son." The three Synoptic Gospels speak of Jesus as the Jewish Messiah, the Lord's Anointed, but Jesus was more than any one or all of the meanings of this many-faceted but relative and imperfect word. Philo of Alexandria (c. 20 B.C.–50 A.D.), anxious to embrace the truth both of Hebraism and Hellenism, had borrowed from Greek philosophy the term Logos which he understood as the operative reason of God, identified with the creative Word of God in Genesis, mediator between God and the world, the first-born Son of God, the expiator of sins, the high priest who stands before God on behalf of the world. As the first monotheistic mystic, Philo allegorically interprets the Scriptures with Moses as the lawgiving Logos.

Strongly resembling Philo, the author of the Fourth Gospel in a striking Prologue, or Introduction (1:1-18), sums up his entire Gospel for the purpose of winning the attention of Greek readers to a message of Jewish origin. But to John, the Logos was not an abstract principle but a Person, not creative reason but the revealing Word of God, active in creation and in all history as the Light which lighteth every man, till the Word became flesh and dwelt among us for awhile. John recognized, however, that while this approach was the most helpful for educated Greeks, this term, like the Jewish word Messiah, was not fully satisfactory, owing to the obtuseness and the opaqueness of all language, where all words are narrowing molds, seldom luminous and transparent.

As Albert Schweitzer well says: "The names by which men expressed their recognition of him (Jesus) as such, Messiah, Son of Man, Son of God, have become for us historical parables. We can find no designation which expresses what he is for us." If man was made in the image of God, then God's fullest and most intelligible revelation of himself could not be in inanimate nature, or in language, or in a book, but in a Person who most completely revealed him. And how could relative language reveal completely the relation of God to man, of God to Jesus Christ, or of eternity to time?

Men have ever turned back to the inner mind of Jesus himself as the most perfect mirror of God, believing that the consciousness of Jesus was the clue to the mind and purpose of God. The writer of the Fourth Gospel was concerned with the unveiling of Jesus' inner life. He never equates Jesus with God, nor does the New Testament say that Jesus was God. When Jesus is made to say "Before Abraham was, I *am*," it does not necessarily imply that Jesus had a memory of a pre-existent life with God. But it does mean that in some unique way God was in Christ, that Jesus had a life transcending the categories of time and space, that the pretemporal life that was in Jesus was grounded in the eternal nature of the indescribable Being "I am that I am" or, according to Moffatts' translation, "I-will-be-what-I-will-be" (Exod. 3:14). Whatever metaphor is used in John or any other book, the mystery of life remains as it pertains to God, to man, and to Jesus.

Thus John speaks of Christ as the Way, the Truth, the Life, the Light of the World, the Door, the Good Shepherd, the Bread of Life, the Fountain of Living Water within, the True Vine, the crucified, glorified Lamb of God, the Resurrection and the Life—God incarnate in man. In a word, the union of Hebraism and Hellenism has begun and Christianity is now acclimatized to the Gentile world. In these bold metaphors, in the seven times repeated *I am,* the writer of this great Gospel is not striving for the correct definition of credal formulae to gain our intellectual assent. Rather he is doing just what Paul did and just what Jesus did before him; he is trying in the Gospel as in his first Epistle *to share with us a great experience.*

The writer of the Fourth Gospel is speaking throughout, not as a detached historian but as an evangelist, a pastor and a theologian. He confronts the world with his message as a challenge and a crisis as clear-cut as that which Paul placed before the Philippian jailer. God is offering a universal gospel to all by free grace in his great summary: "For God loved the world so dearly that he gave up his only Son, so that everyone who believes in him may have eternal life, instead of perishing." Once God is seen in Christ and his gospel is accepted, all history has meaning and all nature is sacramental. All the common things of life are redeemed; the fact of paternity, of speech, of light, water, bread, wine, life and death furnish the symbolic language to interpret the good news of the single, central, eternal manifestation of God in the sphere of redemption in history. God is spirit; God is light; God is love, fully and finally revealed only in Jesus Christ his Son, come in the flesh.

After allegorically selecting seven miracles as "signs" and making Jesus utter the seven "I ams," the author frankly states his purpose in writing this Gospel: "Many another Sign did Jesus perform in presence of his disciples, which is not recorded in this book; but these Signs are recorded *so that you may believe Jesus is the Christ, the Son of God, and believing may have life through his Name*." The writer is confessedly an evangelist. All the apostles and early Christians were witnesses and many were heralds of the gospel. Martin Dibelius has shown how much of the material of the first three Gospels was selected for the purpose of the evangelists in preaching. This John had probably long been preaching before he felt compelled to write. The Gospel seems to sum up his series of oral sermons which he had been preaching for years in Ephesus.

If we read the record not as a formal history but as a series of oral sermons, with illustrations from events, parables, and allegories, it will help us to understand it better. *Ten sermons taken together are now cast into the form of a great drama or Passion Play* by the dramatic mind of this writer, divided into vivid scenes and acts. This intuitive and mystical writer and preacher has an allegorizing mind like that of John Bunyan portrayed in *Pilgrim's Progress*. We do not complain that Bunyan's account of "Christian" is not history, or that Shakespeare's *Hamlet* or *Julius Caesar* or Milton's *Paradise Lost* are not prosaically factual, for neither Bunyan, Shakespeare nor Milton was trying to write history. It requires poetic imagination to understand either dramatists, poets or the writer of the Fourth Gospel.

After the Prologue, let us read these chapters as ten vividly

illustrated evangelistic sermons, and then view them as acts in a
great drama: 1. After the introduction concerning John the
Baptist and the first disciples, we have in the second chapter
an allegorical sermon on *Marriage*, with the contrast between
wine and water, or the Christian religion and its rivals. In this
first, and all of the seven "signs" in this Gospel, the writer sees
that God's "sign" is Jesus. The prosaic mind in reading Wordsworth sees only a "yellow primrose by the river's brim," or in
Tennyson the "little flower in the crannied wall" and nothing
more, while the poet is looking behind nature to "what God and
man is." The same prosaic mind will see in this allegory only the
enormous quantity of more than a hundred gallons of water made
into wine for guests who had already drunk the house dry. Literalism will see God displaying his mighty power in a trivial act
merely to help a host embarrassed by the thirst of his guests. It will
forget that when men are dying of thirst in the desert, in war or
peace, God works no such miracles. But let us note the possible
allegorical hints in a wedding which is often used as a symbol for
the Reign of God, and "the marriage feast of the Lamb." The six
stone jars for the Jewish rites of purification, which are explained
to Greeks in Ephesus, as Mark does to his Roman congregation
(Mark 7:3, 4), may represent the Jewish ceremonial religion. In
any case we are not obliged to transform a great allegory into
a cheap miracle. With spiritual freedom the fundamentalist will
insist upon literal miracle where the modernist will see allegory.

2. In the third chapter of John, we have a sermon not on marriage but on birth, the *New Birth dramatized through Nicodemus*.
The whole sermon teaches the necessity of a spiritual birth. John
probably is dealing here with some historical tradition but with
complete freedom for his own uses. He begins in a private inter-
view by night, only known to Jesus and to Nicodemus, but soon
is saying "we" testify, "we" are speaking and "ye" must be born
anew, "ye" receive not our witness. Nicodemus is soon forgotten and this Evangelist is preaching his sermon as eternal
truth to all in Ephesus and the world. In the same way this author
quickly forgets the Samaritan woman, John the Baptist, the
Greeks, and all other personalities as soon as they serve to intro-

duce his sermon or his dramatic scene. It is characteristic that we cannot tell when the words of Jesus end and those of the Evangelist begin; they are all in the same vocabulary. James Drummond suggests that an apostle may have "portrayed the Master of his heart's devotion in colors drawn from half a century of vivid experience of his indwelling spirit, and blended together the actual and ideal in lines no longer separable."

3. In the fourth chapter, a sermon on *the Water of Life* is illustrated by the woman at the well. This may be either creative allegory or a tradition of a real incident, dramatized to reveal the mind of the Master and the nature of his message, where the recurring theme, as throughout the whole Gospel, is eternal life. Much of the story is obviously symbolical. Jesus "must needs" pass through Samaria, geographically, providentially and scripturally, for his witnesses must carry the gospel to "all Judea and Samaria and to the end of the earth," even to the Greeks in Ephesus. But the eternal truth of Jesus' sublime message is timeless and placeless, addressed to all humanity: "Anyone who drinks this water will be thirsty again, but anyone who drinks the water that I shall give him will never thirst any more; the water that I shall give him will turn into a spring of water welling up to eternal life." Mark had been more accurate about facts, John was more concerned with eternal truth. Each has a place in a portrait of Jesus and a life of Christ.

4. We cannot study at length the Evangelist's sermon on *Sickness and Health*, illustrated by the man beside the pool, in the fifth chapter. There is apparently a free adaptation of some traditional incident and there may be some parallels to Mark's healing on the Sabbath where the man is told to take up his bed and walk (Mark 2:1-12). The "thirty-eight years'" sickness may be an allegorical or symbolical reference to the Israelites wandering in the desert for "thirty-eight years" (Deut. 2:14) in the period of spiritual impotency or "homelessness" of Judaism. In any case, the incident or allegory is only a text for another long sermon on sickness and health, the contrast between the Old Covenant and the New. Jesus is made to summon five wit-

nesses to himself: his own, John the Baptist, his mighty works, the Father in Heaven, and the Scriptures (John 5:31-40; 8:14).

5. The sermon or scene on *the Bread of Life* (John 6:1-71) is illustrated by the feeding of the five thousand. This is the one incident prior to the last visit to Jerusalem recorded in all four Gospels, but the Evangelist, as always, is free to alter the details to suit his theological purpose (Mark 6:30-44; II Kings 4:42-44). The story is an allegory of the spiritual ministry of Jesus, as the bread of man's inner life. The author is seeking apparently to spiritualize and ethicize the sacramental rites of the church (John 6:51-71). While the first three Gospels have emphasized the prophetic element in the religion of Jesus, John has emphasized the sacramental. There is an obvious reference to the eucharist, but to eat his flesh and drink his blood is clearly not material but means spiritually to "feed on him in thy heart by faith." Yet here are the beginnings of the essential sacramental doctrines which finally developed into Catholic Christianity.

6. Jesus' sermon on *Spiritual Blindness and the Light of the World* is illustrated by the blind man (John 8:12; 9:1-10:12). Light, like flowing or living water, is one of the central thoughts symbolized in the Feast of Tabernacles (mentioned in John 7:2). The Evangelist illustrates his sermon by an incident of healing which he uses with the freedom of a dramatic artist to show the mind of Jesus on spiritual blindness and spiritual sight.

7. The Evangelist's next sermon is on *Jesus as the Good Shepherd* (John 9:22-10:42). There are no parables in the Fourth Gospel, but this is an allegory, or an amplified metaphor, similar to the Door, the Bread, the Light, and the Vine. We may compare this with Jesus' parable of the shepherd and the lost sheep. Jesus had just been contending with the Pharisees as "blind guides" (Matt. 23:16) and false "hireling shepherds" who have no concern for the sheep (Ezek. 34:2-3). Jesus is the Good Shepherd who knows his sheep, one by one and every one, as the sheep know him: "My sheep hear my voice." The writer is constantly speaking out of his own experience. Throughout this Gospel, in a strange way if one has eyes to see or ears to hear, a hundred phrases of timeless and eternal truth leap from the

page, independent of any historic context of time or place. As with Paul and Plotinus, "He who has seen it knows what I mean."

Jesus is not only the Good Shepherd in contrast to false hirelings; he is *the* Door, *the* Way in contrast to other and false ways. John does not say that he is the *only* teacher or prophet, but that all teaching which is not inspired by the spirit of which he is the incarnate manifestation is not of God but is the defrauding work of thieves and robbers. The Evangelist has constantly in mind not the prophets of the Old Testament and conditions in Palestine, but the false teachers in Ephesus and Asia Minor. Jesus says to all and to us: "I have come that they may have life and have it to the full . . . I lay down my life for the sheep. I have other sheep which do not belong to this fold . . . so it will be one flock, one Shepherd" (John 10:7-11).

8. Jesus' sermon on *Death and Resurrection* is illustrated by Lazarus. Both the prosaic literalist and the critical historian will find this chapter very difficult. If this were the greatest miracle of Jesus' life, why is it that the three Synoptic writers never mention it? We must constantly remember that we are dealing here with a great mystic and allegorizer. We may recall the book of Job, or Jonah, or Daniel, or Milton's *Paradise Lost*. Here is the great Evangelist and preacher who has himself been raised from the dead spiritually. Possibly he knew a friend, Lazarus of Bethany, who had been spiritually quickened. Ever since Paul had spent three years in Ephesus, there were spiritually living men all over Asia Minor who had once been dead souls. The Evangelist knows of Paul, his experience of Christ, and the truth of his chapter on the resurrection (I Cor. 15). He is about to preach his great sermon in Ephesus on Life Eternal. He hears in his soul, like the sound of many waters, the words of the Living Christ, which constitute his text: "*I am the resurrection and the life*: he who believes in me will live, even if he dies, and no one who lives and believes in me will ever die" (John 11:25-26). John feels that if he keeps silent the very stones will cry out, for a whole waiting world of dead souls needs to be quickened and raised to life. The Fourth Evangelist is as certain of the fact of spiritual resurrection and of the future life as he is of his own

physical existence. Either there had been some incident in Palestine which had grown into a tradition before it reached the writer, or the Evangelist combines several elements into a synthetic parable of the raising of Lazarus.[5] Here again, with no Spanish Inquisition, the free man may see miracle or parable, according to his unconscious wishful thinking.

Now frankly here is a stumbling block for the scientific and historical type of mind. What lack of feeling for fact, or what lack of historical sense, could have led a mystic allegorizer to make the final, crucial moment of Jesus' life—the cleansing the Temple which brought about his death—the opening act in his drama to afford a text for his sermons and succeeding scenes? The cleansing of the Temple illustrates his theme that the new gospel of Christ is to supersede the old religion typified by the Temple, which is the background of all the opening sermons. The Evangelist must then finally make the raising of Lazarus the last act and the cause of Jesus' death (see Mark 11:15-18 and John 2:14-25). He thus pays the price of giving us a spiritual and allegorical but utterly unhistoric Gospel. As between Mark and John, one is history, the other is drama; one is fact, the other allegory; one is narrative, the other a vivid illustrated sermon of truth. And that is what this great Evangelist meant it to be, just as John Bunyan meant his allegory writen in Bedford jail. Neither writer ever dreamed that he was writing history; both knew they were writing truth.

The great Evangelist has still two more sermons for us, two more acts in his great drama. These are: 9. The drama of the Passion, or the sermon on *Sacrifice and Glory, illustrated by the Cross,* which occupies nearly half his Gospel, and 10. The *Last Discourse* of Jesus as the living Christ.

[5] There were two Synoptic traditions of "raising from the dead" (Mark 5:22f. and Luke 7:11f.). There was also the parable of the rich man and "a certain beggar named Lazarus," which ends with the words "if one rose from the dead" (Luke 16:19f.). There was the story of Mary and Martha (Luke 10:39) and of the woman who anointed Jesus' feet (Luke 7:38; John 11:2), and there was the clear teaching of Jesus and Paul on the resurrection. Whatever the source or sources may have been, Lazarus to the Evangelist symbolizes life transformed by the power of Jesus. The hostile Jews symbolize those who will not believe "even if one rose from the dead."

If we contrast the long discourses of Jesus in Jerusalem in conflict with his enemies, as narrated by John in the opening chapters, with Jesus' teaching in the three Synoptic Gospels, the former seem polemical, sententious, and dogmatic. They do not rise to the heights of the Sermon on the Mount, or the parable of the prodigal son. There is no love of one's enemies and no embodiment of Paul's great hymn concerning love (I Cor. 13). The polemic elements in these long sermons rather resemble Jesus' attack upon the Pharisees as described by Matthew, and it looks as if both Matthew and John had colored their narratives. But if we contrast the last discourse in the three Synoptics which seems to include garbled quotations from a Jewish document now known as the "Little Apocalypse," with the last discourse of Jesus as narrated by John, the latter is incomparably greater and is nothing less than sublime.

Anyone who has the imagination to understand Plato and the poets, and will read this great drama in ten acts, or these ten sermons on supreme spiritual themes, will see that it is "one of the greatest books of religion ever written—if not indeed the greatest." Jesus is known only in so far as he is loved. In John's Epistles, the central theme is love; he does not hate the Jews, but he hates their hate; he hates the sin but loves the sinner. The pure in heart, or those willing to amend their lives will see God. And that is the purpose of John's writing to interpret this Man of Mystery, who himself *wrote in lives, not in books*. John also seeks, like Paul, to write living epistles, to create living witnesses; yet from the point of view of sacred literature, there is "no composition that is a more perfect work of art." Whether or not he was an external witness, he saw with the inward eye and wrote what he saw. The closing discourses display an unconscious but incredible boldness in portraying "the mind of Christ" on the eve of the Crucifixion. Could any other writer so portray it? He is the finest embodiment of the Spirit of Christ continuing to speak and to guide into truth after the death of Jesus.

Our final concern with the Fourth Gospel is not with its tradition but with its truth, not with its author but with its subject, not with John but with Jesus. In the well-known words of

Thiersch: "If there were a great picture which tradition had affirmed to be painted by Raphael, and it was proved not to have been painted by Raphael, but by some otherwise unknown artist, the world would have not one great painting the less, but one great painter the more." We must apply Jesus' own text to this Gospel, "By their fruits ye shall know them." In the catacombs of Rome "St. John's Gospel is the leading factor in the entire field of catacomb symbolism," including pictures of the raising of Lazarus, the woman of Samaria, and the marriage at Cana. John was the chief comfort in the catacombs and in the centuries since. Is it too much to say that "these sermons originally preached by John in Ephesus have become the most popular and the most widely read literature in the world?" They have furnished the theme of thousands of funeral sermons. This Gospel has been the charter of Christian experience for eighteen centuries. It has brought light, life, comfort, and assurance to myriads.

Clement of Alexandria is quoted as saying that "John, last, having observed that the bodily things (the simple facts relating to the life and teaching of Jesus) had been set forth in the Gospels, on the exhortation of his friends, inspired by the Spirit, produced a spiritual Gospel." And Luther writes: "John's Gospel is the one tender, true chief Gospel, far, far to be preferred to the other three and placed high above them." Think what this Gospel meant to poets like Wordsworth, Tennyson, and Browning. In Wordsworth's account of the growth of his own faith, he says: "I meditate on the Scriptures, especially the Gospel of St. John, and my cry rises up of itself with the ease of an exhalation, yet a fabric of adamant." Robert Browning could have said the same and does say it in substance in his "Death in the Desert" and his poem on immortality. In response to a modern questionnaire sent to a wide circle of Christian leaders, about ninety per cent found the Gospel of John the most helpful, widely read and best liked of all the books of the New Testament. And by its fruits it may be known to the modern student.

In concluding this chapter, will the student, divesting himself as far as possible of all prejudice, read or reread the following passages: John 4:14, and then chapters 14 to 17,[6] asking one question: Whoever wrote the four Gospels and the Epistles and whatever the limitations of the writers, *was Jesus of Nazareth merely a Galilean carpenter, a good man fundamentally mistaken about God, or did he truly reveal the very nature of the God and Father of Jesus Christ?* If the answer is the affirmation of faith, will the reader ask himself whether he has entered upon the experience recorded in this and the other three Gospels as a follower of Jesus Christ, and if not whether he is willing to do so?

AUTHOR'S NOTE

If the reader will pardon a personal word by the author, he will see that the first verse noted above, John 4:14, well illustrates the fact that we can never have absolute certainty regarding any past historical event or oral teaching, and that our moral certainty lies in the Christ of faith rather than in the details of the Jesus of history. At Mhow in Western India in 1897, this passage brought to me on the darkest day I had ever known the greatest blessing of my life: "Anyone who drinks this water will be thirsty again, but anyone who drinks the water I shall give him will never thirst any more; the water I shall give him will turn into a spring of water welling up to eternal life." This promise has proved literally true for nearly half a century and I believe it will prove eternal truth so long as I keep drinking of this water of life (the life of God in the soul of man, shared with his fellow men).

When, years later, I visited Jacob's well at Sychar (modern Askar) and saw its stones deeply worn by the hands of pilgrims during the centuries, I was completely oblivious of the historic accuracy or inaccuracy of the incident, whether the Samaritan woman was an historical fact or an allegory. This I could never prove nor disprove and I cared as little for these details as did

[6] Several passages have been disarranged in this Gospel before it left the hand of the final editor. It will be most helpful to read these great closing chapters in the correct order, Chapters 15, 16, 14, and then 17, and if possible in a modern translation like that of Moffatt's.

the author of this great Fourth Gospel. But I could daily prove the timeless spiritual truth of this passage. The essential thing was not a question of Jacob's well, or the Samaritan woman, or the author of the Fourth Gospel. I can testify that in seventy-two years, here is the one and only completely satisfying source of life that I have found in this sinful world of war and suffering and sorrow. I care not who wrote this great anonymous work, whether John the Apostle, or John the Elder of Ephesus, or someone like the great unknown Prophet of the Exile. I shall always be deeply grateful to him that he himself had drunk deep of this living water, and that he had associated himself in the unbroken succession of the apostolic community that could say: "*We* bring you word, so that *you* may share our fellowship; and our fellowship is with the Father and with his Son Jesus Christ." The great essential is not the accuracy of historic facts or records but spiritual experience, verifiable anew in every age. That was the object of the early Evangelists, of the Gospels and the Epistles, and that has been the single object in the writing of this imperfect interpretation of Christ.

12

THE TWENTIETH CENTURY PORTRAIT

As WE COME TO THE CLOSE OF THIS BOOK, WE MUST GATHER UP the various threads of our study. The dedication to Albert Schweitzer was meant to suggest that at first Jesus comes to us as a mystery, "as One unknown." Only as we seek morally to obey the command, "Follow thou me," and attempt the tasks which Christ has to fulfill for our time—that is, only "to those who obey him will he reveal himself in the toils, the conflicts, the sufferings, which they shall pass through in his fellowship, and as an ineffable mystery, they shall learn *in their own experience* who he is."

In the Introduction, Professor Burkitt was quoted as suggesting that it was the duty of every Christian, each man for himself, to make a portrait of Christ. In order to do this with open minds, we began our study of the historic Jesus as recorded in the first three Gospels. Though we might crave more knowledge of him than we have, we found that we may actually know all that we need to know regarding the life and teaching of the historic Jesus. We can know practically all that Paul knew, and share the same experience which he and all the first disciples had, who came into living fellowship with God through Jesus Christ and then went out to win the Roman Empire and to turn the world upside down. The true follower of Jesus has, in principle, to endeavor to follow Jesus' way of living and to reproduce the kind of life which his followers record in the Acts of the Apostles. Though the religion of Jesus is not the religion of a book but of a Person, these Gospels and the Epistles of the New Testament are marvelously adapted to lead any honest seeker or follower of Jesus into this identical experience. We began our study of this life where Mark begins, with the baptism of Jesus by John, the Elijah or forerunner. The word from heaven "Thou art my beloved Son, in thee I am well pleased," in connection with the anointing of the Spirit, seemed to confirm the growing conviction of Jesus that he was called not only as the Lord's Messiah but as the Suffering Servant of Jehovah. "Behold my Servant, my chosen one, my heart's delight; I have endowed him with my Spirit to carry true religion to the nations." (Isa. 42:1.) The temptations in the wilderness which immediately followed Jesus' baptism were all obviously Messianic—"If thou art the Son of God"—but Jesus withstands them, refusing in turn the temptation to miracle, to magic, and to might, resolved from first to last only to do God's will, in his time and way, to seek God's ends by his means alone.

In the first two chapters, we accepted the view of the Synoptics that Jesus first appeared in Galilee with his gospel of God proclaiming: "The time has now come, God's reign is near: repent and believe the good news." We saw that there were five senses in which we might view the coming of God's rule or Kingdom: 1. It was already present in Jesus in whom God's will was perfectly done; 2. Jesus made a genuine offer that God was ready to bring in his rule and fulfill all the promises if Israel would repent and obey; 3. When Israel rejected God and crucified his Messiah this necessarily involved judgment in the destruction of Jerusalem, and since then we see God's judgments (not punishments) abroad in the earth, especially in times of man's flagrant sin and godlessness as in world wars; 4. We saw that the promises of God's rule were fulfilled in part at Pentecost, in the ever-imperfect Church Militant, in the unseen Kingdom of God in the hearts of men, like seed growing silently; 5. We also saw that, apart from an arbitrary miracle of God without human co-operation or response, the complete consummation of the Kingdom will doubtless be realized only beyond history and not perfectly within it.

Since we share with Christ the power of an endless life, we can have the same sure confidence that Jesus himself had about the coming Kingdom. If God be God, "he must reign," and his rule must ultimately be realized, however long-suffering he may be in bearing with man's sin. Remembering then the above five senses in which we may view its coming, *the Kingdom of God may be for us the same central spiritual reality that it was for Jesus.* We must patiently labor, as fellow workers with God, surrendering our lives to his rule in the ever-imperfect church of Christ on earth, while we continue to pray "Thy Kingdom come," having already received the earnest and foretaste of a Kingdom which cannot be shaken.

When we studied the teaching of Jesus, we found that the Sermon on the Mount was the charter of the Kingdom of God which was its theme, that the Sermon was the supreme description of the Christian way of living, and the great summary of Christian ethics. Christians are to love God, their fellow men and even their enemies. We found that Jesus not only seeks for himself but declares for his followers the pure, the perfect, the absolute will of God, irrespective of their ability or inability to perform it. We found that Jesus' teaching is not law but gospel; it is not a command to do something but to be something. The Sermon on the Mount cannot be performed in literal deeds, but we can so be transformed by the living Christ that, spiritually understood, this shall be our mirror of the perfect will of God, our divine frame of reference, our absolute standard of conduct.

But unless we wish to become fanatical bibliolaters, and modern Pharisees, we must remember that Jesus never legislates. The letter not only of the Law but of Jesus' literal teaching "killeth," while only the Spirit, ever guiding us toward all truth, giveth life. We are not under literal bondage to give to every beggar who asks us, to make no provision for the morrow, to relax "not an iota, not a comma" of the Law of Moses, nor one of its ceremonial commands with regard to "unclean" foods, or the strict observance of the Jewish Sabbath. We are not bidden in slavish literalism to turn the other cheek and to resist no evil and no evil man who would enslave humanity. With freedom did Christ set us free; he did not die and rise again to bring us into fresh bondage. On the other hand these "hard sayings" are not to be disregarded. They often furnish ideal guides for conduct or needed warnings.

After studying the crisis in Jerusalem, we asked what was the meaning of the Crucifixion, and what evidence there was for the resurrection of Jesus. We found that during the period when doctrine was rudimentary, the great body of believers accepted Jesus as the Christ, or Messiah, which was the highest term they knew for the revealer of God and the redeemer of man. The early Christians also agreed not only that God was in Christ but that in some way, in and through him, God was reconciling and winning back the world unto himself. Whatever theory or doctrine men have held, we found that the *fact* of the Crucifixion had, by the appeal of Christ's sacrificial love for sinners, brought men to repentance, and had moved multitudes of men over all the world throughout the centuries. Christ's death had actually brought about for many a reconciliation with God, an at-one-ment.

In the chapter on Spiritual Resurrection and Its Consequences, we found that, sure as the early disciples were that they had known Jesus in the flesh, just so sure were they that he was risen, that he was alive again, and that they had seen him. And much more important, they believed they were in vital and unbroken communion with him as their living Head, and they gave evidence of the fact in their daily experience and in their changed lives. During the short span of Jesus' earthly life, few had accepted his message and embraced his way of life. His mission indeed looked almost like utter failure at the Crucifixion. Yet within a few days something had happened. Not only had the wavering Simon become Peter, the Rock, and shortly after Saul of Tarsus, the persecutor, had become Paul, the great Apostle to the Gentiles, but a growing multitude, so changed that they were called "a new race of men," were "upsetters of the whole world" (Acts 17:6-7). And in every age since, each living believer can say: "*I know* whom I have trusted, and am certain that he is able to keep what I have put into his hands, till the great Day!" When we studied the Gospel of Paul, we saw that all that Paul found in Christ, which transformed his character and gave him power in service, is available for each of us. That is why we studied Christ in Paul. The end was always our own experience.

When we studied the Interpretation of John, we found that

the Fourth Evangelist reduces the whole gospel to a single truth: By whatever mode or manner, God once for all entered history in Jesus Christ, who came in the flesh in real humanity. To the Gnostics of Ephesus, John says that if they deny Jesus incarnate in flesh as a real man, they are in fact denying the Father who sent him. The three historic Synoptic Gospels are in general agreement on the facts and teaching in the life of Jesus of Nazareth. John writes not to add to those facts but to interpret them. In the light of the Cross, the resurrection, and the coming of the Spirit, John is able to see the significance of Jesus' life in true perspective. With a new vocabulary and new concepts necessary to reach the Greek Gentiles with a gospel of Jewish origin, out of a long life of deep experience of the risen Christ, John writes to show the one central truth of the Incarnation, that God was indeed in Christ. He writes with the single frankly avowed object "that *you* may believe that Jesus is the Christ, the Son of God, and believing may have life through his Name."

In mid-passage in Mark's Gospel, as in all the Synoptics, Jesus asks the searching and supreme question, which marks the climax of the whole record, "Who say ye that I am?" The issue was not what honor they would do to Jesus, nor was it one of credal orthodoxy regarding his person or work. The answer to his searching test of who he is, and of their relation to him, will reveal the disciples' conception of the nature of God, of the Kingdom or rule of God, of the way of salvation and the duty of man. Peter as the leader answers spontaneously "You are the Christ!" From this crucial moment there begins to appear in clearer outline the portrait of Jesus, who is to become the eternal Christ, the crucified Messiah and the Saviour of men.

And from this moment also, the one supreme duty of the follower of Jesus can be revealed. He says to his disciples of all time, in substance:

You say I am the Christ, the Messiah, and so I am. But I am to be a crucified Messiah, rejected by Israel and by man, spat upon, accursed, and nailed to a felon's cross. But there is no other way for me or for anyone who would be my follower. If anyone wishes to follow me, let him deny himself, take up his cross, and so follow me (as a cross bearer, daily denying himself and his self-centered life, to lead henceforth the God-centered life). For whoever wants to gain the world and save his own self-life will lose it, and whoever will lose his self-life for my sake and the gospel's will save it. My yoke is kindly and my burden light. I have come that they may have life and have it to the full.

Here is the great paradox and epitome of Christianity for all time. And it centers in our relation to Jesus Christ. He is the touchstone of destiny.

In a crisis in Jesus' ministry many of his own followers complained "This is hard to take in" (John 6:59-69) and drew back and would not pay the price of discipleship any longer. Jesus asked the faithful remnant, "Will you also go away?" Peter's reply was significant for all time: "Lord, to whom shall we go? Thou hast the words of eternal life." Let us ask ourselves the same question. Is there any other worthy way of life or of salvation for the individual and society except his way? If we ask for the Way, the Truth, and the Life, that we may find God as Father and all men as brothers, could we be satisfied with Moses, with Gautama Buddha, or Confucius, or Mohammed, or any of the founders or leaders of the world's other religions? Could we look with hope for final spiritual truth to any one or all of the scientists, philosophers, poets or moralists; to any modern statesman, economist or industrialist? Can we turn to any social system for complete individual and social redemption, whether capitalism, Communism, Socialism, Fascism or Nazism? Is there any other person who shows us the ideal standard, the perfect character, the highest teaching of truth coupled with the power of realizing it? To whom else can we go?

Is there not a sense in which the answer for many of us must be that it is Christ or nothing? Let us note carefully the inescapable alternative. All the lines of this book and all the life and teaching of Jesus focus upon a single point; they converge upon a single issue. It is not a matter of creedal orthodoxy, nor the acceptance of some elaborate statement of faith, bristling with difficulties. It is not a question of whether Jesus did or did not claim to be the Messiah, whether the Greek conception of the Logos, or Word, was adequate, whether or not we can believe in the Trinity, or in the pre-existence of Christ. It is not a question of our theory of the Atonement, or our doctrine of the Person of Christ. It is something much more simple and fundamental than any of these. The supreme question is: Can I come into such a relation to Jesus Christ that I may find God as my Father? Was Jesus right in his teaching of God as Father; was he sent to reveal God, and may we form an adequate conception of God in Jesus Christ, and in him alone? *Or,* was Jesus, however good a man, fundamentally mistaken about God, so that we have no "God and Father of the Lord Jesus," but are left merely with the beautiful, sentimental memory of a deluded man?

After all he had claimed for God and his Kingdom, if the death of Jesus were merely the end of his life and nothing more, then for many of us ethical values cease to exist. Either this horrible tragedy of Golgotha had a further meaning, or we must abandon faith in a righteous and a loving God. If the life of the most perfect goodness known to man should close not only in physical and social disaster, but in the lowest abyss of spiritual despair, it would mean that goodness was a complete failure and the love of God and one's enemies meant moral shipwreck. It is not merely the worth of man and the moral order of the universe that are at stake here. God himself is the issue. Jesus had staked everything upon the Kingdom of God, but he had finally seen that perfect obedience would cost a Cross of vicarious suffering. If that suffering, however, meant desertion by God and final spiritual failure, then the Kingdom was a delusion and God himself a failure or a nonentity. Thus in and through the Cross and resurrection of Jesus we have everything—or nothing.

Either God is the Father of Jesus and we are joint heirs of eternal life with the living Christ, or Jesus is a dreamer who is dead and God is unworthy of our worship or even of our respect. In the latter case Jesus, even though a failure and defeated by death, would be infinitely better than God; but he could be of no help to us. We do not crave a model failure. Our avid hunger is for life. No demonstration of logic, science, or philosophy is possible here. Jesus brings us face to face with ourselves, with the meaning of life, with the final significance of history, and with God. In Jesus and the whole epic of his life, his teaching, his death, and resurrection, we confront God in his last and uttermost manifestation. Either by an act of faith we must say: "My Lord and my God, who loved me and gave himself for me in Jesus Christ," or by an act of unbelief we must reject him. Jesus makes final moral neutrality before God impossible.

Let us note that it is not we who arbitrarily raise this issue. Jesus raised it himself. He came to save the world, to declare the gift of the all-loving Father, to proclaim the good news of the beneficent rule of God and call men to repent, to change their whole way of self-centered life and turn them to God. But inevitably this offer of the free grace of God in complete salvation brought a challenge and a judgment with it. If men refused to hear Jesus' message and rejected God, they thereby not only passed judgment on Christ, they judged themselves as well. For the time being at least—the only time which they were sure was theirs—they were separating themselves from his way of life and from his direct way to God. They were, for the time, rejecting Christ and God who sent him. Jesus clearly saw the issue and warned the Pharisees and leaders of their danger. In the end they had either to accept him—and the God who sent him—or they had to crucify him, and in doing so reject God. This was the sin of which the Spirit of God was to convict men— "because they do not believe in me." And this is the same inescapable issue which is presented to each one of us today.

WHO SAY YE THAT I AM?

This book is being written in one of the greatest crises in all history. We are in the midst of the second world war of this generation, already raging over five continents and the seven seas. After slow ages of evolutionary development and ten thousand years of struggle to achieve civilization, the leadership of the race farthest advanced in science, philosophy and music has been seized by the most demonic force yet known in history. Under the pretentions of a superman, a super-race, superstate, supermorality-and-religion, a nihilistic revolution aiming at world conquest has swept over much of the earth. With venomous hate, it seeks the persecution and the avowed extermination of the Jews, the people of Christ. The war will leave millions dead, crippled, starved, demoralized, degraded, or bereaved. The rector of the University of Athens—the city of Pericles, mother of Hellenic culture—is pleading for bread for thousands of students who are starving as we write. Once noble countries are now slave states. The forces of lust, greed, and hate loosed in the world have found expression in the torture and massacre of the Gestapo. A "new order" of barbarism has menaced almost every value built up after three thousand years of the Judeo-Christian religion. All human freedoms have been threatened, all moral standards defied.

The World War is a fresh revelation of the guilt and sin of man—not merely of Germans and Japanese, but of all men. Many eagerly seek an alibi and a scapegoat and maintain that this is a conflict merely of evil against the good, of sinners against the righteous. But the whole war is but the military phase of a world-wide revolt against the evils of our "civilization," whose cancerous growths we will neither admit nor cut away. The only nation that had tried completely to destroy economic injustice, and which has fought most heroically against this invasion of evil, is solidly and proudly atheist in its party leadership. The leading "Christian" nations have been characterized by imperialism, flagrant economic injustice and race prejudice. Something like a quarter or a third of their people have been "ill-fed, ill-housed, and ill-clad," in the two richest countries on earth. Yet the one thing we will not admit is our sin—*our* sin. And what we do not yet realize is that the war has shown that the world had forgotten God. The secular world had been living without God and without spiritual hope or life. We want victory in the war, but there is as yet no evidence that we are willing to pay the price of a just and lasting peace—not at least if it means any abridgment of our sovereign selfishness, or any guarantee of equal justice for all. When a plan is proposed for postwar employment for all, justice for all, security for all, it is not even seriously considered by Congress or the press, except as it may become a political campaign issue.

Jesus is the only character in history who, once our relation to him has been determined, so affects our own destiny. With no other is our relation to God so identified. It matters little what we think of any of the men mentioned above when we asked to whom else we could go. Our destiny does not depend upon our opinion, or definition of, or relation to, Moses, or Socrates, or Buddha. But it is inextricably bound up with Jesus Christ. We shall have to pause for a moment to survey an even wider area of life before we can realize the inescapable significance of Jesus. We shall find that without Christ a final keystone is lacking in our converging human experience. Whatever our approach to truth—in science, art, morality, philosophy, or religion—we rise toward some hoped-for goal, or end, or summit; some final principle by which we seek to unify all life and give it ultimate meaning and value.[1]

If we turn first to science for the solution of our moral or spiritual problems it must reply, "the answer is not in me." To ultimate questions of why, whence, whither, confessedly science can give no answer. Science cannot create, finally explain, nor satisfy the deepest hungers of humanity. Science can harness power from a cataract or the lightning, it can build or destroy a material civilization. With all its brilliant inventions to improve our material welfare it can flash its messages round the world—yet it has no saving message today for a frustrated humanity. It cannot create character or culture, or brotherhood, or human happiness, or final hope. It cannot save or make whole the individual or society.

Human reason can show that the world is coherent, that it forms a single system, but it fails to find the actual principle of unity which holds the world together and which makes it a cosmos instead of a chaos. The crown of the edifice of science and reason, if there be such, would be in a loving, omnipotent

[1] We ask the liberty of rewriting at this point several paragraphs from *Man Discovers God*, pp. 247-248. For the thought here we are indebted to Archbishop Temple in his *Men's Creatrix*, pp. 92-128; 255-260; 351-366.

Will. But science never finds God in its test tubes, nor within the range of its microscope or telescope, nor in the conscious or subconscious of psychology. It rears a mighty palace of truth but finds no keystone for its completing arch. All the sciences begin to build their vaulting tower to heaven, but they still stand incomplete, a conflicting Babel.

If we turn from science to art, similarly its goal is never reached. We enjoy a picture, a poem, a symphony, a cathedral, but it does not prompt us to any action, or policy, or reform. The aesthetic emotions and the loftiest feelings of love and devotion do not yield to any logical or philosophical treatment. They may yield a mystical experience that seeks at the summit the immediate apprehension of an absolutely satisfying object in "the moment eternal." But the moment does not last. Art, like science, confessedy falls short of the goal of life and even of its own goal. It points toward an ideal experience of the contemplating soul of some image truly adequate as an expression of the whole world's ruling principle. It seeks the absolute and ultimate in beauty, but it does not of itself give us God, or life, or lasting satisfaction. The keystone of its lofty arch of beauty and promise is still lacking.

If we turn from science and art to ethics, its goal is never reached. The troubled conscience stands in awe before the moral law within. Ethics shows that the highest moral good for man consists in a perfectly integrated character and in a life of love and fellowship with one's fellowmen. Ethics tells man what to do but leaves him powerless. Agonizing after good works or moral perfection only drives one toward the shipwreck of self and the seeking of supernatural aid. Duty-doing never by the utmost of human capacity reaches the possession of God. The warring world today is the consummation and demonstration of man's selfishness, sin and moral impotence. Ethics suggests a Will which is perfectly self-determined, and yet is active altogether in love, and such a Will, if it controls the universe, is the very principle of unity sought by science, art, and morality; for only if there be such a Will is the universe fully rational, yielding ultimate truth, beauty, and goodness. But ethics, everywhere under the limit of relativity, can only fitfully disturb man's conscience. Its mounting arches confessedly have found no keystone of completion. Each miserably repeats Paul's experience in the seventh chapter of Romans. *All* have sinned, all continue to sin and no man can save or perfect himself. Ethics is as impotent as was the Law of Moses.

If we turn from science, art, and ethics to philosophy, least of all do we find any final solution there. Philosophy of itself can only show at most that God must exist if the world is completely reasonable, and that he is the ground of the possibility of all certainty. But of itself it can never give certainty in anything, nor refute ultimate skepticism. It reaches noble heights in Socrates, but in the end "it knows that it knows nothing." Philosophy of itself finds no goal or satisfying end, some twenty-five centuries after its beginning. Therefore science, art morals, and philosophy seem to require for their own completion, and for their unity with one another, the existence of an adequate God which none of them can prove or reveal or bring to man.

Similarly all the great religions of the world reach out toward the belief in a single ruling power, toward a God of righteousness and love, transcendent and immanent, creator and redeemer, unseen yet incarnate, a plenary God, adequate to the whole universe, to humanity's suffering and hope, and to each man's need. But is this goal ever fully reached save in the God and Father of our Lord Jesus Christ? Socrates and Buddha tell men to look to themselves, but in the end each awakened man cries: "O wretched man that I am, who shall deliver me?" Jesus does not mock men by telling them to save themselves. He calls them to follow him that he may make them life himself. He is himself the way to the Father's heart and the Father's home for every wandering prodigal or lonely soul. As Augustine found, with Francis, Luther, John Wesley and other unsatisfied lives, the human soul can only find rest and completion in a God of absolute power and of absolute love.

All these mounting arches of which we have spoken rise in converging lines of hope, but each by itself is incomplete. Of themselves they never reach their meeting point. There is always lacking a completing keystone as the crown and summit. If this completion and consummation of life is not found in science, art, ethics, philosophy or the great ethnic religions of the world, is it possible that the one missing keynote of life may be found in "the stone which the builders rejected," a stone of stumbling and a rock of offense? Jesus is both cornerstone and keystone, both alpha and omega. To man's self-sufficient reason, to his proud science and its glittering achievements, to his skillful arts, to his Stoic morality and pharisaic self-righteousness, to his vain philosophy, to his most costly treasures in his personal, tribal, and national faiths, which one and all fall short of completion and lasting satisfaction, is not Christ himself the possible answer—the only possible answer?

Jesus left no book, no tract or written page behind him. He bequeathed no system, no philosophy, no theology, no legislation. He raised no armies, organized no institutions, held no office, sought no influence. He was no scholar, and yet he is more quoted than any writer in all history. His sayings at times are on almost every tongue, and his words have literally gone out into all the world. No man ever laid down his life in Asia or in Africa to translate Plato or Aristotle, Kant or Hegel, Shakespeare or Milton, but hundreds have died to carry Jesus' priceless words to the ends of the earth. Several hundred languages have been reduced to writing in order to transmit his life-giving message. Savage tribes have been uplifted, cannibals civilized, head-hunters converted, schools and colleges founded, and the character and culture of individuals and of peoples have been changed as the result of the influence of his words which are creative spirit and life.

At the time of the first World War, the Scriptures had been translated into some 600 languages. At the outbreak of the second World War, 1,039 languages and dialects had been conquered. In the decade preceding this war, portions of the Bible had appeared in a new language at the rate of one every five weeks. Some 26,000,000 volumes of Scriptures are now being issued every year. A hundred best sellers together do not equal this circulation of the Scriptures. The Bible was the first and most important book ever printed, and over a billion copies of the Scriptures, as the one universal book, have been issued to date, or one for every two of the world's population. Yet it is Christ who is the consummation and completion of Scripture and by him we judge the whole. Clement of Alexandria glories that the gospel of Christ "was poured out over the whole universe."

We see that Jesus has made a terrific impact upon history. Not only religion and ethics but all literature, and almost every area of life has been profoundly affected by streams of influence that flow from Jesus Christ. Literally a hundred thousand volumes have been written about him or have attempted to explain him. But something inexplicable always remains. No human mind by the most exhaustive research can trace all that he has done for man, for woman, for the child; for the slave, the serf, the criminal, the pauper, the sick, the defective, the despairing sinner. No one can comprehend all that he has done for the home, for the church, for the state, for international relations and their future, for human co-operation and ultimate unity, for moral reformation, for the cause of peace.

If one reads a work like Sir James Marchant's *Anthology of Jesus* and reviews the testimony to Christ of saints, theologians, preachers, and writers, ancient and modern, in poetry or prose, he soon sees that all confessedly fall short of fully expressing him and his meaning for them. Jesus emerges and remains greater than tongue can tell, too great for our small minds or hearts. We have found that he is ever greater than his disciples, the four Evangelists, the New Testament writers, the framers of the creeds, his followers across the centuries, or than we ourselves can express in words. We hear Dostoievski say: "There is in the world only one figure of absolute beauty; Christ"; and Renan: "Jesus will not be surpassed. His worship will constantly renew itself"; or we might quote the noble words of Goethe regarding Jesus. But we are reminded of the saying of Aristotle regarding the character of his master Plato, as one "whom it is blasphemy in the base even to praise." We call none of these men base, nor can any of us cast the first stone at another, but we know enough of the moral failure of each of these men to feel that no one of them was worthy even to praise Christ—nor are we. It is not a question of panegyric, or fulsome praise, or creedal exaltation, or apotheosis. "Why callest thou me good?" "Why call ye me Lord, Lord and do not the things which I say?" We have seen that Jesus cannot be accounted for by calling him a "man of genius." We could name a hundred men of genius who leave us cold. The distinctive thing about Jesus is that in some absolutely unique way, God meets us in his life. And our response to him must also be unique:

> Who answers Christ's insistent call
> Must give himself, his life, his all.

If we survey humanity's major human ills, our most desperate areas of need, and our unsolved problems, we may find, in a very strange and unaccountable way, that there is just one key that fits every lock, one ultimate solution for every spiritual problem. And that is Jesus Christ. We may enter Jesus' way of life as simply as did the first four disciples in Galilee. They were asked nothing about themselves—no tests, no profession, no promises, no creed. But no other makes such an imperative moral demand upon us as does Jesus. No other so convicts us of our complacency and our sin. No other so calls us to a complete change of life by returning to God in the full surrender of our lives to him. We may long be indifferent to him, or even to ourselves, to life, and to God. But when once we come to ourselves and recognize what we are and who he is, we cannot in the end be neutral to Christ.

Now let us face the supreme, the searching question which Jesus asked of his followers at the great crisis of his life: "Who say ye that I am?" After reviewing his entire life, let us ask ourselves if the following points are true, and if so, let us think of the significance of these stupendous implications:

1. *Jesus Christ reveals God as Father to man.* Standing at the very summit of ethical monotheism, Jesus gives us our highest revelation of God in his experience, his character and his teaching. He alone combines the fullest disclosure of the character of

God, both as righteousness and love; he relates the mystery of the divine "wrath" and the divine mercy to man's sin. It is significant that man's highest conception of deity as "the God and Father of our Lord Jesus Christ" cannot be stated except in terms of Jesus. It is equally significant that the habitual formula at the beginning of the great New Testament Epistles is: "Grace and peace to you from God our Father and the Lord Jesus Christ." Without any attempt at theological explanation, the worship and experience of the early church held to the closest relationship between the divine Father and the Son. As one writes: "The greatest spiritual fact that has ever emerged in the long story of the human race is Jesus of Nazareth's consciousness of God." If Jesus' revelation of God is true, and if he has given humanity its highest, deepest, and most intimate conception of God and its most vital relation to him, this alone sets him forever apart.

2. *Jesus is the highest embodiment of human character.* It is not only that his is the highest religious experience known to man and the supreme personal force in the moral history of humanity. It is not only that he stands highest in the highest sphere, first in the moral and spiritual realm. In a very real and creative sense, he is a "second Adam." He gives humanity a fresh start. Jesus' own life was so passionately surrendered to the will of God, so consecrated to the Kingdom, that he makes imperative ethical and religious demands upon men. The absolute character of his ethic seems not only harmonious with the will of God but in conformity to the actual constitution of man and history.

Of Jesus, Carlyle exclaims: "Our divinest symbol. Higher has the human thought not yet reached." And Emerson can say that his name has been "not so much written as ploughed into the history of the world." If Matthew Arnold was right in holding that "the outward proof of the possession of greatness is that one excite love, interest and admiration," then Jesus is surpassingly great. H. G. Wells asserts that "he is easily the dominant figure in history . . . A historian . . . simply cannot portray the progress of humanity honestly without giving a foremost place to a penniless Teacher from Nazareth"; he "finds the picture centering irresistibly round the life and character of Jesus."

Albert Schweitzer gives his own life in sacrificial service in Africa to Jesus as "the one immeasurably great Man who was strong enough to think of himself as the spiritual ruler of mankind and to bend history to his purpose." Such quotations could be extended to fill several volumes the size of this. We have already seen that in some strange way Jesus seems in every age "our eternal contemporary" and one who maintains his incomparable position through all the vicissitudes of changing circumstance and fortune. He holds the allegiance of the greatest galaxy not only of scholars, thinkers and writers, but of martyrs, missionaries, and sacrificial servants known to history. Though deprecating their unworthiness and inconsistency, already a third of the population of the world confess their faith in him and take his name upon them.

3. *Jesus realizes our highest thought of humanity.* Through his character and teaching, through his relation both to God and man, we gain our highest conception of the worth of man, the dignity of man, the priceless value of human personality. Even the lost finds a friend of sinners. The least and lowest becomes "the brother for whom Christ died." Christ also provides the highest conception and possibility of human brotherhood. In the light of Jesus' thought of God's universal fatherhood, the word brotherhood also takes on new meaning. Jesus rejects Hebraic legalism and all nationalistic particularism and proud racialism. His parable of the Good Samaritan transcends the conception of an exclusive Jewish Messiah. Paul, who interprets what Jesus had achieved, turns to the Gentiles with a universal gospel and substitutes the ecumenical church for a particularistic nation. Christ achieves and makes possible a new universalism as wide as humanity. Henceforth in him there can be neither distinction of race, color, sex, nor creed. He condemns all pride of man as man, all pride of class, all glory of wealth or knowledge, of reputation or self-righteousness, or anything which exalts itself against the love of God or the humility of Christ. Jesus Christ can promise and provide the only hope of any final unity or brotherhood of man.

4. *Christ offers salvation to man.* When a Philippian jailer

needed to know the way of salvation, it was instantly and fully available—as for all men—in Christ crucified and risen: "Believe in the Lord Jesus Christ and thou shall be saved." Jesus Christ alone so reveals God and so convicts of sin that he makes men fully aware of their need of salvation and of the impossibility of saving themselves. It is Jesus who reveals that man's primal sin is pride, selfishness, and the self-centered life. It is Jesus who shows that repentance alone is the gateway to the humble, the Christlike, the God-centered life. As the great Kierkegaard says, the existing individual is shattered in his self-esteem at the very center of his being. The most prolific secular writer of our generation says: "Religion is the first thing and the last thing. And if a man has no religion he begins nowhere and ends nowhere."

It is only to the convicted and repentant soul that Jesus can speak for God with full authority: "Thy sins are forgiven thee." And he can say with power to the forgiven man: "Go and sin no more." Jesus Christ alone fully justifies and in the end completely sanctifies. The believer is saved already and united to Christ by faith, yet "we are saved by hope," knowing that we are not yet like him. Thus every Christian is a joint product of God and man, of Christ and his disciple, of divine sovereignty and human freedom: "Work out *your own* salvation with fear and trembling; for *it is God* which worketh in you both to will and to do of his good pleasure." It is ever a mystery but Christ as Saviour offers full salvation to man.

5. *Jesus Christ is unique in his relation to time and eternity;* he claims the past, the present and the future. "Jesus Christ is always the same, yesterday, today, and forever." He forgives the past, he saves for the present, he is the hope of the future. There is an aspect of his person and work that is absolutely unique, so that we can speak of his "finished work," something that has been done "once for all." With seeming intolerance we say with the apostles to the Sanhedrin: "There is no salvation by anyone else, nor even a second Name under heaven appointed for us men and our salvation." Yet what unmeasured tolerance we Christians should have, guided as we are by the "Light that

lighteth every man"—every man on earth, good or bad, in all religions and in no religion. We, like our Master, with boundless compassion are meant to be friends of sinners.

If Jesus came not to destroy but to fulfill, then he can build upon all the partial good of all the past and all incomplete individual characters as in the case of St. Paul or St. Augustine. We can accept not only Jewish scriptures as our Old Testament, but all partial truth, beauty and goodness in all systems. Christ alone could say "It is finished"; our work is not yet done. The future is wide open with infinite and eternal possibilities: "When the Spirit of truth comes, he will lead you into all the truth." What is there that we cannot learn, what is there that we cannot do, what that we cannot attain to if we have both time and eternity, if we have the power of an endless life and are guided by the God of all truth?

6. *Jesus Christ triumphs even in the unsolved problem of evil, in the face of unmerited human suffering, and over man's last enemy, death.* Who has made so deep a revelation of sin yet is so without despair? Who so fearlessly sounds the depths of evil yet so triumphs over it? Who so passes through seeming annihilation yet cries "O Death where is your victory? O Death, where is your sting?" There were a million martyr deaths, but only one Cross of Christ. There was only One who could give the unmerited sufferings of Israel a triumphant meaning. There could be but One who made vicarious suffering the final revelation of the nature of God. If God entered history and suffered for man's iniquity, then the Atonement is not some irrational remnant of superstition, but what the wise and proud count "the foolishness of God" far transcends man's utmost wisdom. The Crucifixion shows that God cannot finally triumph over evil by destroying it, but only by bearing it himself.

We glory only in the Cross of Christ. Here we see the deepest wrong made to right the world, the climax of vicarious suffering achieving man's redemption, the deepest shame made man's greatest glory, the darkest despair transfigured into humanity's highest hope. In the Cross of Christ we see the final meaning of suffering. Here we see the very heart of God. For if God was in

Christ, then he is always and everywhere all that Jesus was. And here we see the destiny of man: "We know that in *everything* God works with those who love him, whom he has called in accordance with his purpose, to bring about what is good . . . predestined to be made like his Son." Thus all things may in the end be worked together for good—every circumstance, every limitation, every sorrow, every suffering. And the last enemy that shall be abolished is death. In some inexplicable way, this Man is mediator and he is final. Nontheistic humanism can give no reason why Jesus and not some other "good" man is the world's one hope. In Christ we have the final assurance that no evolutionary development of the future can produce any higher form of "goodness" than the Cross, any higher revelation of God or any other world Saviour.

Especially in time of war and its aftermath, the problem of evil, of sin, and of suffering is so desperate that only one who has suffered with and for us can meet humanity's deepest need. Gautama Buddha faces the problem of suffering negatively, seeking a way of escape from existence and telling men to save themselves by an arduous discipline of which few are capable. But Jesus seeks no escape from life, whatever its evil. He meets it, he triumphs in it and over it, for us. Across the centuries witnesses multiply to Jesus' ministry to us in our suffering, as in the words of Gladstone: "If asked the remedy for the heart's deepest sorrows, I must point to 'the old, old story,' told in an old, old book, and taught with an old, old teaching, which is the greatest and best gift ever given to mankind."

7. *Jesus Christ alone makes life whole and his gospel is for the whole world.* He alone can integrate all life, individual and social. He calls all men to follow him and summons all his followers to final unity through his ultimate principle of love. Wherever his gospel has been denied or ignored, wherever it has been perverted or misrepresented by fanatical followers or by worldly Christians, we have seen sad results. But wherever it has been incarnated, lived, and proclaimed by his true disciples, it has won individual and social triumphs.

Jesus' true followers have always heard the ringing command:

"Go into all the world and make disciples of all nations . . . And all the time I will be with you, to the very end of the world." The new religion was contagious. Christians were called "upsetters of the whole world." Pliny as a governor in Asia Minor might well complain to Trajan that "The infection has spread not only through the cities but into the villages and country districts." Justin Martyr can claim: "There is not a single race of human beings, barbarians, Greeks, nomads or herdsmen living in tents, where prayers in the name of Jesus the crucified are not offered up." Tertullian declares: "We are but of yesterday. Yet we have filled all the places you frequent—cities, lodging houses, villages, townships, markets, the camp itself, the tribes, town councils, the palace, the senate, and the forum . . . . No race now lies outside God, the gospel flashing over all the earth and to the world's boundaries." Eusebius claims great churches of tens of thousands of men in "Rome itself, in Alexandria, in Antioch, in all Egypt, in Libya, in Europe, in Asia, and among all nations. I am compelled to confess that they could not otherwise have undertaken this enterprise, than by a divine power which exceeds that of men."

Professor Kenneth Latourette in his great work *The History of the Expansion of Christianity* [2] shows how the movement that Jesus inaugurated has swept over the world in ever-widening circles and in ever-deepening influence upon individuals and society. The first great tidal wave from apostolic times carried the movement for five centuries through the whole Graeco-Roman world, until Christianity became the religion of the Empire and outlived the fall of Rome. The second wave of revival from 950 to 1350 A.D., embraced the Middle Ages, evangelized Europe, and carried Christianity through Scandinavia to Russia, India, China, and the East. The third wave from 1500 to 1750, which included the Reformation and the Counter Reformation, carried the gospel to North and South America, to Africa and the islands of the Pacific. Though there was a relapse, or kind of ebb tide

[2] K. S. Latourette *History of the Expansion of Christianity* projected in seven volumes and summarized briefly in *Anno Domini* and *The Unquenchable Light*. See also Dr. Henry P. Van Dusen's *What Is the Church Doing?*

after each of these gains, the fourth and last tidal wave saw the greatest advance of all during the "Great Century" of modern missions, from 1815 to the present.

It is impossible to summarize the results of modern missions in a paragraph. Students of today can hardly realize the passion of the missionary crusade that uprooted and tore some fifteen thousand students of the last generation from the colleges of North America, Great Britain and Europe and sent them out to the ends of the earth under the fervid watchword, "The evangelization of the world in this generation." Unfinished and imperfect though the work was, these emissaries of Christ founded churches, schools, colleges, printing presses, model farms, industries, co-operatives and humanitarian institutions, and tried to build a whole new Christian civilization throughout the entire world. The writer himself, who first saw China under the degenerate Manchus, and Turkey under the tyranny and massacres of Abdul Hamid, witnessed the rise of Sun Yat-sen, Chiang Kai-shek and Madame Chiang in China, Kagawa in Japan, and the Christian leaders of the new Asia. Whatever its shortcomings and inadequacies, it is not too much to claim that the Christian movement "is today the greatest power for the uplifting of the life of humanity in its every aspect and for the building of a fairer world which this planet has ever seen." Its achievements it owes to Christ; its defects it owes to his imperfect followers. In China, for instance, while only one in a hundred has as yet professed to follow institutional Christianity, in the *Who's Who* of that nation, one in every six is a Christian, and of the score of outstanding leaders who are shaping every phase of China's national life, at least half of them confess the Christian faith.

Now let us gather together the various strands of our thought, and focus our attention upon the answer to Jesus' searching personal question: "Who do *you* say I am?" In the light of his whole life that was lived from the cradle to the grave seeking, as no other, solely to do the will of God, in his time and way, by his means alone, in the utmost service to man, in a life consummated by a sacrificial death—who do we say he was and is? Was he merely a good man, or was he sent by God as the revelation of the Divine to meet the deepest need of man? Why has he become the center of the religious history of the human race?

If it is not we, but Jesus himself who propounds the question, "Who say ye that I am?" what shall be our answer? If Jesus Christ, as no other, reveals God as Father to man; if he furnishes for us the highest ideal, the most perfect example and the noblest embodiment of human character; if he realizes our highest thought of humanity and our greatest hope of human brotherhood; if he alone offers complete spiritual salvation to the individual and society; if he stands in a unique relation to time and eternity, to the human and the divine; if he alone before the unsolved problem of evil, before unmerited human suffering and tragedy, before man's last enemy of death, triumphs in his Cross; if Jesus Christ alone completes and fulfills our life; if his gospel is thrilling good news for the whole world and for each and every individual, who then is this?

Life cannot be truly integrated about the false center of self, either individually or socially. Life can only be fully integrated when it becomes God-centered, for he is the only real center of the real world, and he only can bring all toward any ultimate approach to the final harmony of love which is the Kingdom of God. Man's first and final problem then becomes that of the shifting of the center of life from self to God. It is Jesus who calls us to "repent," that is to change our mind, our way of life, our center from self to God. And it is he who enables us to do this. He has asked us the inescapable question, "Who say ye that I am," but this is not the final question. That is raised by the words of Pilate, "What am I to do with Jesus the so-called 'Christ?'"

Eternity and judgment impinge upon the present moment. Now is the accepted time. And I am living in this momentous present. Every day I am living with Christ or without him; for or against him. However unconsciously, every day I am crucifying him afresh or crowning him as the Lord of my life. Our position is strangely similar to that of Pilate. He had to judge Jesus, but in so doing he was judging himself. Jesus was standing before Pilate, but all unconsciously, Pilate was standing before the eternal judgment seat of Christ—as every man must stand, though he be as blind as Pilate. And in the end Pilate had to do something with Jesus—just as we must do. He had to condemn or acquit him, to crucify or release him. No postponement, no evasion, no compromise was ultimately possible for Pilate—or for you and me. Unwilling or indifferent, evasive or procrastinating, blind or cowardly, or like Peter following "afar off," *I must do something with Jesus Christ*. In the end I must either crucify or crown him.

What then shall I do with Jesus?

APPENDIX I

The Four Gospels as Historic Documents

We cannot understand the life of Jesus without knowing something of the four Gospels as historic documents.[1] The simple believer might expect an infallible revelation from heaven recorded in an inerrant book, such as devout Moslems believe they have in the Koran. A moment's thought, however, will show that such a record would be not only impossible but undesirable. Such a Bible would require not only writers miraculously inspired, but inerrant language, infallibly transmitted—instead of the more than twelve thousand widely varying manuscripts and translations of the Gospels that we have—and the whole revelation would have to be infallibly apprehended and interpreted. Such a process would not be human and, as a matter of fact, we have no such record. No single extended saying of Jesus is recorded in the same words in any two Gospels, and there are single sayings of Jesus and of Paul of which we have several hundred varying interpretations.

Nevertheless we make no apology for the Gospels as historic documents. In a sense we know more about Jesus than about any other character in ancient times. The Gospels soberly record a series of epoch-making events that happened "under Pontius Pilate." We have better manuscripts, both as to quality and quantity, written nearer to the events described, than we possess of any other ancient character or writer. Of the plays of Aeschylus we have some fifty manuscripts; of Sophocles about a hundred; of Euripides, Cicero and Virgil some hundreds. But of the four Gospels and of the New Testament in the original Greek, we have over three thousand manuscripts and, with their ancient translations, more than twelve thousand copies. Moreover, these stand chronologically nearer the events they record than the manuscripts of the classics. The earliest surviving manuscript we have of Sophocles was written fourteen hundred years after his death; of Euripides sixteen hundred years, and of Plato, thirteen hundred years after he lived. Of the manuscripts of Aristotle, the earliest were not written within two and a half centuries of his death. Yet none of us seriously doubts the worth

[1] We are indebted throughout this section to C. H. Dodd, F. C. Burkitt, B. H. Streeter, E. F. Scott, James Moffatt, Edgar Goodspeed, Kirsopp Lake, Maurice Goguel, and Albert Schweitzer.

and authenticity of these classic writers.[2] We have their essential message and can estimate its value. As John Stuart Mill says: "It is of no use to say that Christ, as exhibited in the Gospels, is not historical, and that we know not how much of what is admirable may have been added by the traditions of his followers. Who among them was capable of inventing the sayings ascribed to Jesus, or of imagining the life and character revealed in the Gospels?" In the same vein Rousseau writes: "My friend, such things are not invented; the matters told of Socrates—whose existence no one doubts—rest on far slenderer evidence than do those told of Jesus of Nazareth." The oldest books of the life and teaching of Gautama Buddha were not put completely into writing for four hundred and fifty years, yet we do not doubt his historicity.

Though Christian documents are, compared to other ancient historic records, remarkably sober and trustworthy nowhere do they make any claim to infallibility. The earliest writers ascribe no supernatural inerrancy to any of the Gospels. Luke only claims that he has the necessary qualifications for writing an accurate history. He treats Mark and all his sources with great freedom. The writer of the Fourth Gospel plainly corrects Mark and Luke. No writer of the four Gospels had any idea of literal infallibility. When the Christian church formed a canon of the New Testament and placed it beside the Old Testament the idea of literal infallibility was adopted from the Jews by some Christian writers but by no means all. As Bishop Gore wrote: "The three first gospels do not always agree in details. The proposed reconciliations of their apparent discrepancies are often forced and improbable. On such grounds we have felt constrained to give up the theory of miraculous infallibility. And it should be borne in mind that the church never committed itself to, or made a dogma of, this theory."

The Apostle Paul refers to a number of facts concerning the life

[2] Professor Shirley Jackson Case writes on *The Historicity of Jesus*: "When all the evidence brought against Jesus' historicity is surveyed, it is found to contain no element of strength. All theories that would explain the New Testament literature by making it a purely fictitious product fail."

Dr. Joseph Klausner, the Jewish scholar, writes: "It is unreasonable to question either the existence of Jesus . . . or his general character as it is depicted in the Gospels." He adds that there are reliable statements in the *Talmud* that his name was Yeshu (Joshua, or Jesus) of Nazareth, that he performed miracles ("practiced sorcery"), that he beguiled and led Israel astray, that he expounded Scripture in the same manner as the Pharisees, that he said he was not come to take away from the Law or to add to it; that he was hanged (crucified) as a false teacher and beguiler on the eve of the Passover which happened on a Sabbath, and that his disciples healed the sick in his name: "They never doubted that he worked miracles."

and death of Jesus, and several times quotes from the recognized oral tradition of his teachings. The whole body of Paul's ethical teaching seems to indicate that both he and his converts were familiar not only with the oral tradition but with some of the written Sayings of Jesus. He has a clear conception of the character of Jesus, emphasizing his righteousness, obedience, humility, gentleness, forbearance, love and uttermost sacrifice. His converts are bidden to imitate Jesus as Paul himself seeks to do, and his whole moral ideal is derived from Jesus' life and teaching.

Thus we have a continuous living tradition as a central strand of testimony embodied in the *teaching* of Jesus, and in the *preaching* of the church as recorded in the early chapters of the Acts. The former was gradually recorded, about the time of the Pauline Epistles, in varying and growing copies of the Sayings of Jesus, different collections of which are extensively quoted by Matthew and Luke. Matthew and Luke drew their material from Mark and from different editions of the written Sayings of Jesus no longer extant. These lost documents are designated by scholars as Q, from the German word *Quelle*, or source. The literary style of the Sayings is simple, concise, and direct. Dramatic contrasts abound. The whole emphasis is placed not on what later generations thought of the messenger, but on his message. The oral tradition, on the other hand, representing primarily the gospel story, which goes back to the primitive preaching, and which records not chiefly the sayings but the doings of Jesus, was first recorded in the Gospel of Mark.

More than a century of devoted modern scholarship in several countries has been concentrated upon the life of Jesus, as upon no other character in all history, and this has yielded noteworthy results. Following textual criticism and literacy criticism, this study has included both "source-criticism" which deals with the written documents, seeking to establish their sources and dates; and, more recently, "form-criticism,"[3] which seeks to reconstruct the oral tradition lying behind the written sources from a study of the forms or patterns in which the material is presented.

While we owe an incalculable debt to this century of scholarship, even a layman may see for himself something of the nature of these

[3] Dibelius, Schmidt, Albertz and Bultmann in Germany, R. H. Lightfoot and C. H. Dodd in England, and B. S. Easton, F. C. Grant, D. W. Riddle and others in America, have made a study of the forms, types, or categories of the preliminary traditions of the life of Jesus. They seek to put each saying or incident in the life of Jesus back into its concrete setting or "life-situation," to show how each has been affected by the growth of tradition, to find which of these belong to Jesus' own lifetime and which have been colored or produced by the life of the early Christian community. Form history studies the literacy forms in which the oral tradition took shape.

four documents if he will read the opening verses of the Gospels in the order in which they were written, Mark, Matthew, Luke, and John. If he looks closely he will see that these are not four objective histories written to satisfy the curiosity of succeeding centuries, but that they are confessedly the work of believers for believers, with a frankly avowed religious purpose.

Mark, the first record, thus opens: "The beginning of the good news of Jesus the Messiah." The author does not say the beginning of the biography or history of Jesus of Nazareth. This first realistic record does not profess to be an objective history but thrilling good news. It is a gospel story of how a young Galilean prophet or carpenter-rabbi who was hurled into history, summoned his people to repent before the near approach of the Kingdom or Reign of God on earth, called his first disciples, launched a growing movement, and met increasing opposition until he was done to death on the charge that he was a false Messiah. The Jewish Matthew begins characteristically with the ancestry of Jesus, descended from Abraham and David, who came to fulfill the Law and the prophets.

Luke's remarkable preface reveals five successive stages of historical strata: 1. There was a religious movement founded upon certain established facts—the life, death and resurrection of Jesus; 2. There were original eyewitnesses of the facts, who became teachers of the gospel message; 3. "Many" had already drawn up narratives including the Sayings of Jesus and we have the informal story of Mark; 4. The anonymous author, having investigated the course of things accurately from the beginning, seeks to write the first connected or orderly account in what we call a biography or a history, though not in a modern sense; 5. This good news is written for contemporary or later readers, dedicated to a representative official, "your excellency Theophilus." Luke was an historian as truly as Herodotus. Like him he was not a scribe of dry facts but a dramatic narrator of vivid stories. But, unlike him, he writes with the avowed purpose that his readers may know the "solid truth" of what they had been taught, and share in the great spiritual experience of Jesus, of Paul, and the little groups of believers throughout the Roman world. We call the first three the Synoptic Gospels because they are in general agreement and present a common view of the ministry of Jesus so that they could be printed as a synopsis in parallel columns.

Much later John writes with the frankly confessed aim that his readers "may believe that Jesus is the Christ, the Son of God, and believing may have life through his Name" (John 20:31). His Gospel is not a history but rather a spiritual philosophy or interpretation to show the eternal meaning of the earthly life of Jesus. In his mystic philosophy he traces this life to the very "beginning" in the being of God, down through the "beginning" when God created the heaven and the earth (Gen. 1:1), to Mark's "beginning" of the good news, when the Word became flesh and lived for awhile among men. Then the writer depicts through a series of scenes or parables the drama of salvation as he sees it enacted on earth. Without the historic sense of Luke, he seems, like Plato, to be often casual or oblivious with regard to fact, but passionate in his vision of truth. Luke tries to record the facts, John seeks so to interpret them as to help us find the Way, the Truth, and the Life. In this book we draw our portrait of the historic figure of Jesus exclusively from the first three Synoptic Gospels. In later chapters of the book we deal with the interpretation of the person and work of Christ as conceived by Paul and John.

A general consensus of the results of a century of devoted and critical scholarship has yielded certain evaluations concerning the four Gospels. Between 50 and 62 A.D., the Apostle Paul had written most of his invaluable letters, spiritually the greatest that history records. During that and the following decade, various editions of the Sayings of Jesus had been recorded on perishable papyrus. Soon after 70 A.D., the epoch-making date of the destruction of Jerusalem, Mark records the gospel story which goes back to the primitive preaching of the apostles. It is the oldest and historically the most valuable of our records. There is a strong tradition that John, surnamed Mark, was the interpreter and reporter of Peter and had translated his vivid Aramaic reminiscences of Jesus into Greek for the Roman congregation. Mark's abrupt and crude Gospel, jotted down in terse, vivid language, doubtless offended educated Greeks; but as Dr. Goodspeed observes, it "was written in the popular Graeco-Jewish vocabulary of demon and marvel and was lightly esteemed in the ancient church in contrast with the later, richer works of Matthew and Luke, but no more dramatic and convincing account has ever been written of the heroic effort of Jesus to execute the greatest task ever conceived—to set up the Kingdom of God on earth."

Mark, the least literary but most historical of the Gospel writers, tries to give a connected narrative of the general course of the life of Jesus. His object is to supplement but not to replace the oral gospel, or memorized tradition of the acts and teachings of Jesus. He intends his readers to recognize that Jesus was the Son of God and also the Messiah, or Son of Man, who was to come in glory at the end, though according to Mark, Jesus never made this claim in his public teaching. Explaining Aramaic and Jewish terms, he writes for Gentiles, probably in Rome, basing his work on notes or recollections from his memories of Peter's conversation. Though Mark's Gospel is the oldest and is the basis of the records of Matthew and Luke, the writer apparently had before him several earlier documents such as a rudimentary edition of the Sayings of Jesus and an account of the Passion which covers almost half of his Gospel. This first Gospel consists of a series of anecdotes, scenes, or tableaux presented with vivid dramatic force and with convincing candor.

Matthew and Luke, probably written between 80 and 95 A.D., are both combinations of Mark and the Sayings of Jesus, supplemented by other written and oral material to which each had access. Matthew had apparently arisen in the more Jewish and Luke in the more Gentile wing of the church. The book of Matthew stands out in "massive unity" as it unfolds from a Jewish standpoint the life of Jesus as the Messiah, yet also as the universal head of the world-wide church. With consummate literary skill, the writer lays special emphasis upon the teaching of Jesus, gathering all the scattered fragments into five or six great discourses which form the framework of his Gospel. Five of these end with the same formula or rubric in conclusion. While Mark shows Jesus as a man of action, Matthew portrays him as the great teacher in language of depth, beauty, and understanding.

Matthew gives no personal reminiscences of Jesus but his Gospel is based upon the work of Mark. He handles Mark and the Sayings with veneration yet with freedom, improves upon the rougher and more abrupt style of Mark and often condenses his narrative. He habitually gathers the Sayings of Jesus under a single theme. He subjects the Pharisees to much more scathing criticism than does Luke. Matthew quotes profusely from the Old Testament to show where Jesus fulfills prophecy. He often modifies the apparent rigor of hard sayings, attempting to improve upon Mark by eliminating the demons' confessions of Jesus as the Christ, and omitting references to anger or other questionable moods in Jesus. He combines Catholic universalism with Jewish particularism, making Jesus say that "not an iota, not a comma will pass from the law," though Jesus had swept away the ceremonial Law and criticized Moses. He emphasizes the eschatological hope of the early coming of the Son of Man and dwells upon, or adds to, the teaching of judgment and eternal punishment. Matthew is an enlarged edition of Mark, adding the Sayings of Jesus, and was the most widely read in the early church. The author of the First Gospel remains unknown; it could not have been written by one of the Twelve if it was so completely dependent upon Mark.

When Luke wrote the Christian movement was spreading rapidly over the Greek world, challenging Judaism, the national cults and the new mystery religions of the Mediterranean. The need arose of unifying the accounts of Jesus' life and teaching, and of recording the rise and spread of Christianity from Jerusalem to Rome and throughout the Roman world. To this end, Luke and Acts were written as two parts of one work for the information of Christians and the defense of the new religion against the serious charge of disloyalty and agitation in the Roman Empire, resulting in the persecution of Christians. Luke, like Mark, makes no claim to being an eyewitness. He also handles his sources freely and does not hesitate to edit and correct the material of Mark and even more the Sayings of Jesus. He abhors Pharisaic bondage to the letter and his methods are an encouragement to modern critical scholarship. We writes in good Hellenistic Greek, with literary finish, with the feeling of a poet and an artist, with wide and versatile vocabulary. He has an eye for dramatic, personal and historical elements. He is catholic and cosmopolitan and has wide sympathy for Gentiles, for women, and for the poor. His is the Gospel of repentance, forgiveness, and faith. He is strongly humanitarian and his interest is always with the needy rather than with the rich and powerful. He is keenly interested in social reform, he thinks of the contemporary social order as fundamentally bad and eagerly records Jesus' condemnation of hoarded wealth. He tells twice over the story of the experiment in voluntary spiritual communism in Jerusalem.

Luke, like Paul, sometimes shows a bias in favor of asceticism and the single life. He often emphasizes both the authority and tenderness of Jesus. He gives prominence to prayer, to the work of the Holy Spirit, to thanksgiving, to the love of Jesus and the universality of the gospel. While Mark and Matthew emphasize the eschatological hope of the early coming of Christ, Luke shifts its importance and makes it possible indefinitely to postpone its fulfillment. Luke thought of Jesus as the founder of a movement which had become a growing and powerful church; and this in time gradually eclipsed the immediate expectation of the end. His emphasis furnishes a natural transition to the Fourth Gospel which no longer looks for Christ's early return.

Originally all four Gospels were impersonal if not anonymous; no writer mentioned his own name. No author is visible in Mark or Matthew, while in the Third Gospel the author uses the first person only to address Theophilus. The Fourth Gospel was originally impersonal; only a later editor refers to the unnamed disciple "whom Jesus loved" in order to authenticate the tradition he had followed. All four writers wished the light to fall on Jesus only, and in a remarkable way they succeed in fastening every eye upon his portrait. Although each of the four has its own marked individuality and although in many details they contradict, yet, as a whole, they richly supplement each other. Mark's is the popular, evangelistic, active Gospel, Matthew's is the teaching Gospel, Luke's the historic, human, social Gospel, while John's has not the historic but the doctrinal, divine and "spiritual" emphasis.

In the case of all four Evangelists, by the time we have finished each Gospel, we have, as the writer would have wished, completely forgotten the author, who falls into a Rembrandt shadow. As on the Mount of Transfiguration, we see no one save Jesus only standing in our midst. Hence we have four anonymous and mutually supplementing Gospels. No one of them is perfect and complete, else we would not need the other three; yet not one of them could be spared. Providentially none was omitted, though Professor Burkitt wonders that Mark was included in the canon considering the poor opinion held of it by the early church. Archaic, crude and mutilated without its closing chapters, it was yet the treasured possession of the church of Rome. Modern scholars rejoice that it was preserved, while the saints of the centuries prize most the "spiritual" Fourth Gospel.

We seek to learn a lesson from these four anonymous writers in the way they handled their records and sources, freely and critically, yet reverently. And also in the way they looked upon this mysterious central figure of all history. In the end we hope to find a portrait of Jesus, human, vivid, and essentially true. After stripping away all later accretions, it is possible that each may see what Robert Browning saw:

> That one Face, far from vanish, rather grows,
> Or decomposes but to recompose,
> Becomes my universe that feels and knows.

APPENDIX II

HISTORICAL BACKGROUNDS OF THE LIFE OF JESUS

To understand the life of Jesus, we must recall the background of Jewish history and conditions in Palestine at the time of Christ. The Jewish people were to become the bearers of ethical monotheism for the world. This deeply religious people lived their religion and their religion alone enabled them to survive. In an unaccountable way also they were marked for suffering, until, as no other people, they had to grapple with the problem of evil, of unmerited affliction, and of vicarious suffering. For six centuries they had been a conquered people.

To understand the mission and message of Jesus, we must recall the dark tragedy of Jewish history. The hopes of the people had centered in the Messiah and they had been promised not only independence but dominion. Yet for weary centuries this world appeared to the despairing Jews to be ruled not by God but by the evil forces of all the great heathen empires in turn of Assyria, Babylon, Persia, Egypt, Syria, Greece, and Rome with their idolatry and cruel oppression of the Hebrews. No wonder the Jewish world outlook became pessimistic. In 722 B.C., within two decades after the warnings of Amos and Hosea, came the fall of the northern kingdom of Israel before Assyria. In 586 B.C., when the southern kingdom of Judah fell before the armies of Nebuchadrezzar, as foretold by Isaiah and Jeremiah, came the destruction of Jerusalem and the Babylonian captivity.

Then Palestine lay prone under Persian domination for two centuries, from 538 to 330 B.C. When the Persian empire fell before Alexander the Great, the Jews experienced no liberation but only a change of masters, and for a century and a quarter they were under the rule of the Ptolemies of Egypt, from 320 to 198 B.C. When Palestine passed as the spoils of war to Syria, Antiochus Epiphanes, in order to accelerate the Hellenization of Judea, endeavored to stamp out the Jewish faith with unspeakable abominations, such as the sacrifice of swine on the sacred altar of their holy temple. He forbade the Jews to remain Jews, to worship the God of their fathers, and by force compelled them to sacrifice to Zeus. This seemed indeed "the abomination of desolation" in the holy place.

For a time a successful rebellion led by Judas Maccabaeus and carried on by his brothers achieved the independence of the Jewish state under a Maccabean theocratic dynasty. But the later Maccabees degenerated to ambitious, inefficient and cruel rulers, indifferent to the Jewish religion, and civil war was followed by the intervention and the domination of invincible Rome. In 63 B.C., Jerusalem was captured by the Romans when the Roman general, Pompey, brought to an end the century of Jewish freedom inaugurated by the Maccabees, ushering in Roman rule by a massacre of twelve thousand Jews, slaying the priests at the altar. The Great Rebellion, or Roman War, lasted from 66-70 A.D. In 70 A.D., a futile rising led to the capture of Jerusalem by Titus. The inhabitants were delivered to the sword, crucified, and sold into slavery. Tacitus tells us that Titus burned and destroyed the Temple "to root out the superstition of the Jews."

Sixty years later, in 132-135 A.D., another desperate outbreak under Bar Cocheba, led to the destruction of the Jewish state, and the final dispersion of the remnants of the nation as they were scattered to the four corners of the earth for centuries to come. Thus the history of the Jews for more than two thousand years was a tragic drama. In a way unique in all history, whether consciously or unconsciously, a people and a Person were prepared to be the Suffering Servant of all humanity. During more than a century and a quarter that began sixty years before Jesus' birth and continued until 70 A.D. scarcely a year went by without wars, rebellions, outbreaks and riots, during which more than two hundred thousand Jews who were the flower of the nation perished by the sword. Jesus could not but be concerned with the central problem of his people under the Roman yoke. His own intellectual and spiritual life had its development in the gradual solution which he sought to find for it.

Palestine was strategically located for the birthplace of a world religion. It was at the crossroads of three continents, as a land bridge between Asia, Africa, and Europe. It was the meeting point of Orient and Occident, where the divergent civilizations and religions of the East and West met and mingled. In point of time the world had been prepared for the Christian Era by the contribution of the Jewish people of the religious basis of ethical monotheism; culturally and linguistically the world was made ready by the civilization of Greece, spread by the conquests of Alexander the Great, and it was being unified by the law and order of Rome and communications made possible over the growing network of Roman roads. Both in time and place, therefore, Palestine marked the birth of a moral crisis in a restless and troubled world as the Christian Era drew near.

Palestine was "the least of all lands," only half as big as New Hampshire. "From Dan to Beersheba" was only 139 miles. At the time of Christ, Palestine, as part of Syria, was under Roman rule and included three political divisions. In the south lay "gloomy Judea" whose Judaism produced John the Baptist. In the north lay the flower-strewn sunny hills of Galilee which brought forth Jesus and the Gospels. The northeast, beyond Jordan, was under the rule of Philip, the third Herod. Galilee lay in the "Circle of the Gentiles," a tiny land, only some fifty by twenty miles in extent, with its mixed population. Here mingled Semitic Arabs, Phoenicians, and Greeks, with the Hebrews who were more open and less strict and bigoted than the Jews in Judea. The Galileans were reputed to be gay, optimistic, kindly and generous, but they were hardy patriots. This northern part of Palestine has changed little from the time of Christ, and the traveler today may enter a carpenter's home in Nazareth, as the writer has done, and watch him making primitive plows and yokes.

From the hilltop above Nazareth which Jesus as a boy must often have climbed, one can see the white sails on the Mediterranean and overlook the historic battlefield of Esdraelon. Near by was the great highway from Egypt to Damascus and Babylon as well as to Greece and Rome over which passed the Roman legions and the commodities and cultures of many nations. In plain sight, an hour's walk away, was Sepphoris, the second most important city in Palestine, a thriving commercial center and the capital of Galilee. Three-quarters of a century before Jerusalem fell, Sepphoris had tried to throw off the Roman yoke under Judas of Galilee. Revolutionaries had seized the royal treasures and arms, but the Romans burned the city and sold the inhabitants into slavery. Villages around Samaria and Emmaus were burned, and two thousand men were nailed to crosses about Jerusalem. When Jesus was a boy, he had probably seen the city of Sepphoris going up in smoke, and all in Nazareth had heard of its tragic fate.[1]

At the time of the census, a decade after Sepphoris was seized, Judas instigated a fresh revolt (Acts 5:37), but Sepphoris knew by bitter experience that the cause was hopeless and would not join the rebellion. The city stood firm against the revolt in 66 A.D. as it had done for half a century, and this bitter experience of the folly of rebellion against mighty Rome may well have made an indelible impression upon Jesus in his youth, and left him permanently out of sympathy with the Zealot movement.

Jesus had spent his childhood under the memories of the bloody rule of Herod the Great (47-4 B.C.), who had adorned Judea with buildings to Caesar. Herod was an ambitious Idumean, appointed by Caesar as governor of Judea, with the title King of the Jews. He ruled in

[1] Jesus doubtless formed the conviction that the Kingdom of God or the Messianic rule could never be advanced by the sword, while Peter, James, and John were from the region of Galilee where the psychology of revolution still flourished. S. J. Case's *Jesus: A New Biography*, p. 211; and *Journal of Biblical Literature* XLV (1926), pp. 14-16.

splendor, with infinite energy and adroitness, with Solomon's taste for magnificence and women. He built new cities, making Jerusalem the finest in the East. The restored Temple was a proverb of magnificence, begun in 20 B.C., though not quite completed until 64 A.D. A large Roman eagle made of gold had been erected over the principal gate of the Temple in defiance of the Law against all images. When this was pulled down and cut to pieces by young patriots, Herod ordered all of them to be burned alive. The Jews now faced the one supreme problem of their very existence. Their only hope was in the national salvation, but where was the promised Messiah? It seemed to most Jews that a Messiah was desperately needed, not to preach a Sermon on the Mount about nonresistance and loving their enemies, but for violent emancipation and deliverance from their oppressors.

The Jews detested Herod for his ferocious cruelty, his heathenizing policy, and his oppressive taxation which Josephus says "reduced to penury a people he had found in great prosperity." Under tyranny and corruption, with the extortion of the Roman taxgatherers, the Jews under the Romans had to pay a city tax, a house tax, road tax, water tax, meat tax, salt tax, etc. This did not include the double taxation exacted by the high priests. The misery of the poor was intensified by their emotional resistance to Roman rule. Many writers maintain that there was widespread tension and a prevalence of neuroses, or nervous maladies, whose sufferers frequently interrupted Jesus' preaching. There is evidence for the tradition that Joseph had died during Jesus' boyhood, and that a heavy burden rested upon Jesus as the eldest son. The care of four younger brothers and at least two sisters, in addition to his widowed mother, meant that Jesus had to support a family of at least eight persons (Mark 6:3).

Upon Herod's death, his kingdom was divided among his three sons as tetrarchs. Herod Antipas in Galilee, who was called a cunning "fox" by Jesus (Luke 13:32), caused a scandal by marrying Herodias, and put John the Baptist to death for denouncing it. Philip who ruled in the northeast founded Caesarea Philippi near the source of the Jordan, where Jesus in retirement drew forth Simon Peter's confession of his Messiahship. When Archelaus, the other son of Herod, was banished in 6 A.D., Judea was placed under Roman procurators, of whom Pontius Pilate was the fifth (26-36 A.D.). According to a letter from Agrippi I to Caligula, Pilate was "inflexible and stubbornly relentless," guilty of "acts of corruption, insults, rapine, outrages on the people, arrogance, repeated murders of innocent victims and constant and most galling savagery." The Roman governor usually resided at Caesarea on the coast, going up to Jerusalem at the great religious festivals, or in time of riots to the castle of Antonia overlooking the Temple. His chief concern was to collect the taxes and keep the peace, but he was the guardian and supervisor of both the Jewish state and cult. With a mere handful of Roman troops, he was always afraid of revolt by these fanatical Jews.

The Law and the prophets represented two complimentary and necessary sides of religion. The rabbis believed they stood in succession to the prophets as well as to Moses. At the time of Christ, the *Torah*, or the Law, was the foundation of the Jewish religion. The prophets, who taught that "to obey is better than sacrifice," and who were often opposed to the conservative priests, had kept religion free, but after the Exile the Law held almost absolute sway. Judaism gradually became "the religion of the Book," with the increasing danger of the formalism, legalism, and bibliolatry which Jesus challenged. The priest and the legalist always hate and fear the prophet, the mystic and the unorthodox element in religion, and even Nehemiah places the prophets in the enemy camp (Neh. 6:14). The religion of the *Torah* had been alive until the Law was canonized, hardened and sometimes fixed in "the letter that killeth." Then the future belonged to the scribes or doctors of the Law, who were later called rabbis, or masters, fathers, or guides. By adding rule upon rule, they earnestly sought to prevent the secularization and disintegration of Judaism. They tried "to make a fence" for the Law by ritual minutiae, externalism and rigidity, and this tended to obscure the weightier matters and spiritual essentials of their faith. Each leading scribe, or expert scholar, who could interpret the letter by the oral tradition applying it to contemporary life, founded a school and gathered a group of devoted followers.

The scribes and Pharisees represented the Law and the synagogue, which had become the center of religious teaching; the priests and Sadducees maintained the Temple and its sacrifices. The synagogue was a meeting place for the pious, for services of worship on the Sabbath, for religious instruction, for the village school, for the study of the Scriptures, and for unrestricted public use as the meeting place of the community. The leader was often a rabbi or a doctor of the Law, but the synagogue was democratic, without a minister, with the recognition of laymen as teachers. It was the natural place for Jesus to begin his ministry, and for Paul at a later time. With endless casuistry, the scribes and Pharisees quoted multiplying precedents so that when Jesus came as a prophet, speaking with moral authority from his immediate experience of God, he necessarily challenged all the leaders: scribes, priests, Pharisees, and Sadducees. Until the new life could burst the chrysalis of the Law and the Temple, it could never fly forth, free and beautiful.

Josephus, the great Jewish historian (c. 37-95 A.D.), speaks of the four principal Jewish parties as the Sadducees, the Pharisees, the ascetic

Essenes, and the Zealots. Each sought a solution of the central Jewish problem of their plight under the yoke of Rome.

The Sadducees adopted the technique of compromise and appeasement toward the Romans. They were drawn from the Jerusalem aristocracy, the wealthy merchant class, public officials, the priests and officers of the Temple. They represented the old conservative priestly traditions and with the aristocratic scribes, they opposed the more democratic lay Pharisees drawn from the ranks of the people. They were pro-Roman in sympathy. The enormous Temple income derived from the sale of sacrificial animals, the system of exchange and the various ecclesiastical taxes and lucrative contracts with traders from all over the Empire, added to their wealth. They differed from the Pharisees in denying the bodily resurrection of the dead, personal immortality, a future life and retribution, and a Messianic Kingdom on earth, as well as the existence of angels and demons. They rejected determinism, or fate, and maintained the freedom of the will. They were orthodox believers of the old school, accepting the original religion of Jehovah and the Law, but rejected all innovations, oral traditions, and sacred books not included in the *Torah*. Though some were pious, as a group they were characterized by complacency, arrogance, and greed, and had no concern for the poor. They were conservatives both in religion and politics, afraid of dangerous enthusiasms and seditious revolts like the Zealot movement. As the possessing class, they were often ready to compromise in order to maintain the existing order and their privileges under Rome.

The Pharisees were the holy or "separated ones," characterized by their zealous legalism. Moral life was reduced to the observance of the sacred Law. They held themselves aloof from the common herd or people of the land, whose laxity in keeping the Law made contact with them defilement. The minute ceremonial requirements of legalism had made the faithful observance of the Law impossible for the masses of the poor who were looked down upon as what we would call "the unwashed multitude" or "the unclean rabble." Fellowship with them made Jesus an outcast. The best of the Pharisees, however, enshrined the noblest ideals of the Jewish people. They were the most deeply religious and, according to the best Jewish evidence, Matthew has not given a fair picture of them. When his Gospel and that of John were written, the Pharisees and the Jewish nation as a whole were regarded by the Evangelists as the crucifiers of Christ.

Though dominantly legalistic, the Pharisees were the teachers of the written Law and of the oral tradition, which was necessary to apply the Law to the conditions of daily life. The Pharisees were also the fervid defenders of monotheism against the Hellenizing, or heathenizing, movement. While the Sadducees would concentrate on the sacrifices of the Temple, the best of the Pharisees developed religious individualism, spiritual worship, and carried religion to the home. They sought to improve the status of women, they strengthened belief in the future life and were strong missionary propagandists.

There were many conflicting schools among the Pharisees, especially the opposing schools of Hillel (c. 70 B.C.-c. 6 A.D.) and Shammai, either of which Jesus might have joined if he had become a rabbi. Instead, as merely one of the "people of the land," this young artisan, Joshua of Nazareth, was counted "ignorant of the Law." The school of Hillel [2] was more humane and tolerant than that of the harsher Shammai, though his lenience in the matter of divorce led to scandalous laxity which Jesus sought to correct. The school of Shammai was usually more strict and fanatical and this sometimes led to formalism and hypocrisy. The conflict with Jesus over some of his disciples' eating with ceremonially unwashed hands, precipitated by the Jerusalem Pharisees who had come to Galilee to investigate his work, was probably led by strict members of Shammai's school. Some of Jesus' most scathing condemnation was probably against this intolerant group.

The Essenes followed the method of escape from life. Pliny tells us that their membership was recruited from those who were "wearied of life's struggle with the waves of adversity." They were a remarkable monastic order living a religious and communistic life in small villages on the shores of the Dead Sea. Dr. James Moffatt describes this

> little Jewish order of over four thousand souls, a league of virtue, with their agricultural settlements, their quaint, semi-ascetic practices, their strict novitiate, their silent meals, their white robes, their baths, their prayers, their simple but stringent socialism, their sacerdotal puritanism, their soothsayings, their passion for the mystical world of angels, their indifference to Messianic and nationalistic hopes, their esoteric beliefs, and their approximation to sacramental religion.

The Essenes sought to flee the world, while Jesus came "eating and drinking," in the home and in the world. They were destitute of money and possessions, they abhorred arms, though they would sell their cloak to buy a sword for self-protection upon a journey; they abjured animal sacrifices, the taking of oaths and all falsehood. They repudiated marriage and like the modern Gandhi practiced strict continence. Their three rules were the love of God, the love of man, and the love of

[2] Hillel of Babylon of the family of David was the most brilliant of the rabbis, a "prince" of the Sanhedrin, and leader of the Pharisaic scribes. More gracious than his sterner opponent, Shammai, he practiced the virtues of charity, humility, patience and piety. Many of his teachings bear resemblance to those of Jesus, such as his negative version of the Golden Rule, and his "Judge not thy neighbor until thou art in his place," and "He who wishes to make a name for himself loses his name."

virtue. Described by Philo and Josephus, they are not mentioned in the Bible and despite many close parallels probably did not appreciably influence early Christianity.

The Zealots, or "the zealous," were fanatical Jewish nationalists who advocated violent revolt as the solution of the Jewish problem. They opposed foreign domination and foreign thought with its laxity toward the Law. The pro-Roman and pacifist party was represented chiefly by the Sadducees, the anti-Roman party was composed chiefly of the Zealots and the populace. The majority of the Pharisees were pacifists and fatalists; only a minority on the left wing favored the sword of the Zealots. One of Jesus' disciples was Simon the Zealot (Luke 6:15), though probably Jesus would not have chosen him if he had been a member of a political party advocating violence. When Pilate offered the option between "Jesus Bar-Abbas or Jesus the so-called 'Christ'" (following Moffatt's translation), Barabbas, guilty of murder and insurrection, was probably a Zealot leader.

The Zealots arose when Quirinius, the Roman governor of Syria, attempted to take a census (c. 6 A.D.), which Luke connects with the census at the time of Jesus' birth. Simon of Galilee led the radical and desperate of the people to try and stop the census and to resist all godless Roman authority. It is uncertain whether these fanatic nationalists of the extreme anti-Roman political party had the definite appelation of political Zealots for the first sixty years (6-66 A.D.). Their motives were partly religious but growingly political. They resented Roman taxation as disloyal to the theocracy, as "nothing else than downright slavery." Their object was to throw off the Roman yoke, by force if necessary, in order to restore the theocracy of the rule of God. Their party was a combination of noble and base elements, of fanatical martyrs, superstitious enthusiasts and political assassins.

Jesus with his deeply spiritual sanity could not agree with the policy of the worldly self-seeking Sadducees, the monastic, ascetic Essenes, the fanatical legalist Pharisees, nor with the revolutionary, militarist Zealots, whose program would inevitably lead swiftly to the destruction of Jerusalem as he foretold. The lure of these fatal policies he had rejected from the three temptations in the wilderness until his last trial when the high priest asked him: "Art thou the Christ, the son of the Blessed?"—i.e., in the high priest's view, a heretical, false Messiah— "And Jesus said I am." (Mark 14:61.)

Dr. Klausner in his *Jesus of Nazareth* shows why most Jews of the first century and of the twentieth could not accept Jesus. The Maccabees had freed the people and built up a Jewish Palestine: the Herods had destroyed it and Rome had enslaved the nation once again. The burning desire of all loyal Hebrews was freedom from the hated Roman yoke, and the chief hope of this was the Messianic promise of national glory. This hope Jesus did not fulfill. He believed himself to be and claimed to be the Messiah, but that this carpenter was the glorious Son of Man prophesied in Daniel, or that the Messiah must be put to death as a criminal, "was impossible of comprehension" to most contemporary Jews and seemed sheer blasphemy. "Jesus was crucified as 'King-Messiah.'" But the Jews could not accept him as Messiah.

Jesus was more Jewish even than Hillel, yet his teaching contained a kernel of opposition to Judaism, disregarding ritual separatism. Jesus, in his teaching of God as Father and the love of individual and national enemies, introduced something new into the idea of God which Jews could not accept. He both annulled Judaism as the life-force of the nation, and also the nation itself as a nation, in breaking down the barriers of nationality and making religion acceptable to all mankind. "The Jews as a whole could not, therefore, accept Jesus." He remains for the Jewish nation "a great teacher of morality and an artist in parable . . . . In his ethical code there is a sublimity, distinctiveness and originality in form unparalleled in any other Hebrew ethical code." From the standpoint of general humanity he is "a light to the Gentiles." There can be no question but that some of the ardent Galileans saw their Lord and Messiah in a vision. The nineteen hundred years' faith of millions is not founded on deception, but the Jews cannot accept Jesus as Messiah to this day. Such is the verdict of Dr. Klausner.

APPENDIX III

CHRONOLOGICAL TABLE [1]

167 B.C.-135 B.C.	Revolt of the Maccabees
165 B.C.-120 A.D.	Apocalyptic literature, Jewish and Christian
c. 70 B.C.-c. 6 A.D.	Rabbi Hillel, and his contemporary Shammai
c. 20 B.C.-c. 50 A.D.	Philo of Alexandria
c. 6. B.C.	The birth of Jesus
6 A.D.	Judas of Galilee leads revolt of the zealous, stamped out by Quirinius
27	The baptism of Jesus; the beginning of the ministry in Galilee
28	Murder of John the Baptist by Herod Antipas
29	In April, Jesus under ban of the authorities, disappointment of zealous patriots, growing opposition and partial failure of Galilean mission
29	In summer, Jesus withdraws from Galilee to Tyre and Sidon
30	In spring, to Caesarea Philippi
30	Last week in Jerusalem, from April 1, triumphal entry, April 6, Thursday, the Last Supper; April 7, Friday, the trial before Pilate and the Crucifixion (fourteenth Nisan, according to John, or fifteenth according to Synoptics)
30-40	Gamaliel I
c. 32	Conversion of Paul
c. 45	First missionary journey
47	Council at Jerusalem
50	I and II Thessalonians, Paul at Corinth
54	I Corinthians, from Ephesus (Paul in Ephesus 52-54)
	II Corinthians, comprising parts of three letters

[1] There are but few dates in New Testament chronology known with certainty; most of the rest are approximate. In this table we have followed chiefly James Moffatt's *Introduction to the Literature of the New Testament*; and his *Everyman's Life of Jesus*; E. F. Scott's *Literature of the New Testament*; Morton Scott Enslin's *Christian Beginnings*; Maurice Goguel's *The Life of Jesus* and Hastings' *Bible Dictionary* on "The Chronology of the New Testament."

54	Galatians, probably from Ephesus
	Accession of Nero (reigning 54-68)
55	Epistle to the Romans, from Corinth
56	Arrest of Paul in Jerusalem
c. 60-62	Epistles of the Imprisonment: Philippians, Colossians, Philemon and Ephesians, from Rome (or from Ephesus 54-55)
64	Burning of Rome, under Nero, persecution of Christians
	Death of Paul, death of Peter
70	Destruction of Jerusalem (Roman War 66-70)
c. 70-75	Gospel of Mark
80-95	Luke and Acts, and Matthew
90-110	Epistle to the Hebrews
95	Revelation, in reign of Domitian
c. 110	Gospel and Epistles of John, written probably in Ephesus
100-125	Pastoral Epistles in present form
100-115	Pliny's correspondence with Trajan on Christians in Bithynia
c. 117	Epistle of Polycarp, martyrdom of Polycarp 155
115-156	Irenaeus, Bishop of Lyons
132-135	Insurrection of Bar Cocheba
150-175	II Peter
367	Athanasius enumerates all present books of New Testament

The Roman Emperors
Julius Caesar—100-44 B.C. (Dictator)

Augustus—27 B.C.-14 A.D.

Tiberius—A.D. 14-37

Caligula—A.D. 37-41

Claudius—A.D. 41-54

Nero—A.D. 54-68

Civil Strife—A.D. 68-69

Vespasian—A.D. 69-79

Titus—A.D. 79-81

Domitian—A.D. 81-96

Nerva—A.D. 96-98

Trajan—A.D. 98-117

Hadrian—A.D. 117-138

Antoninus Pius—A.D. 138-161

Marcus Aurelius—A.D. 161-180

Herod the Great, king, 37-4 B.C.; Herod Antipas, Tetrarch in Galilee, 4 B.C.-39 A.D.; Pontius Pilate in Judea 26-36 A.D.; Herod Agrippa, king, 41-44 A.D.; Josephus, historian, c. 37-c. 95 A.D.

BIBLIOGRAPHY [1]

ABINGDON COMMENTARY. *Abingdon Bible Commentary*, in one volume
ABRAHAMS, ISRAEL. *Studies in Pharisaism and the Gospels*
ANGUS, SAMUEL. *The Mystery Religions and Christianity*
AUBREY, E. E. *Present Theological Tendencies*
BACON, BENJAMIN WISNER. *The Story of Jesus*
———. *Jesus and Paul*
———. *The Fourth Gospel in Research and Debate*
———. *Studies in Matthew*
———. *The Beginnings of the Gospel Story*
———. *The Gospel of Mark*
———. *Introduction to the New Testament*; etc.
BAILLE, JOHN. *The Place of Jesus Christ in Modern Christianity*
———. *The Interpretation of Religion*
BOSWORTH, E. I. *The Life and Teachings of Jesus*
BOUSSET, J. F. W. *Jesus*
*BRANSCOMB, B. HARVIE. *The Teachings of Jesus*
———. *The Gospel of Mark*
———. *Jesus and the Law of Moses*
BULTMANN, RUDOLF. *Jesus and the Word*
———. *Form Criticism*
BUNDY, WALTER E. *The Religion of Jesus*
———. *Our Recovery of Jesus*
BURKITT, F. C. *The Gospel History and its Transmission*
———. *The Life of Jesus*
BURTON, E. D. *The Teaching of Jesus*
BUTTRICK, G. A. *The Parables of Jesus*
———. *Prayer*
———. *Jesus Came Preaching*
CADBURY, HENRY J. *The Peril of Modernizing Jesus*
CADOUX, A. T. *A New Orthodoxy of Jesus and Personality*
———. *The Parables of Jesus*
BOWIE, RUSSELL. *The Master: a Life of Jesus Christ*
CASE, SHIRLEY JACKSON. *Jesus, a New Biography*
———. *The Historicity of Jesus*
———. *Experience With the Supernatural in Early Christian Times*
———. *Evolution of Early Christianity*
DEISSMANN, ADOLF. *Paul*
———. *The Religion of Jesus and the Faith of Paul*
———. *Light From the Ancient East*
DENNY, W. B. *The Career and Significance of Jesus*
DIBELIUS, MARTIN. *The Sermon on the Mount*

[1] The most important recent books are starred.

DIBELIUS, MARTIN. *From Tradition to Gospel*
——. *A Fresh Approach to the New Testament*
DODD, CHARLES HAROLD. *History and the Gospel*
——. *The Parables of the Kingdom*; etc.
*EASTON, BURTON SCOTT. *The Gospel Before the Gospels*
——. *Christ and His Teaching*
——. *What Jesus Taught*
——. *The Gospel According to St. Luke*
EDERSHEIM, A. *The Life and Times of Jesus*
*ENSLIN, M. S. *Christian Beginnings*
FAIRBAIRN, A. M. *The Place of Christ in Modern Theology*
FARRAR, F. W. *The Life of Christ*
FOSDICK, H. E. *A Guide to the Understanding of the Bible*
——. *The Modern Use of the Bible*
——. *The Manhood of the Master*
——. *The Meaning of Prayer*
GLOVER, T. R. *The Jesus of History*
——. *Paul of Tarsus*, etc.
*GOGUEL, MAURICE. *The Life of Jesus*
——. *Jesus the Nazarene*
*GOODSPEED, EDGAR J. *An Introduction to the New Testament*
——. *The Short Bible*
——. *The Formation of the New Testament*
——. *The Story of the Bible*
——. *A Translation of the New Testament*
*GRANT, F. C. *The Growth of the Gospels*
——. *Form Criticism*
——. *The Gospel of the Kingdom*
——. *The Economic Background of the Gospels*
——. *The Earliest Gospel*
*GUIGNEBERT, C. A. H. *The Jewish World in the Time of Jesus*
——. *Jesus*
HARNACK, ADOLF. *What is Christianity?*
——. *The History of Dogma*
——. *The Expansion of Christianity*
HEADLAM, A. C. *The Life and Teaching of Jesus the Christ*
*HOLTZMANN, OSCAR. *The Life of Jesus*
*HORTON, WALTER. *Our Eternal Contemporary*
——. *Realistic Theology*
*HOSKYNS, SIR EDWYN. *The Fourth Gospel*
——. *The Riddle of the New Testament*
KENT, CHARLES FOSTER. *Great Teachers of Judaism and Christianity*
——. *The Life and Teachings of Jesus*
*KLAUSNER, JOSEPH. *Jesus of Nazareth*
*KNOX, JOHN. *The Man Christ Jesus*
LAKE, KIRSOPP. *An Introduction to the New Testament*
——. *Landmarks of Early Christianity*
*LATOURETTE, K. S. *History of the Expansion of Christianity*
——. *The Unquenchable Light*

*LATOURETTE, K. S. *Anno Domini*
*McCOWN, CHESTER C. *The Search for the Real Jesus*
———. *The Genesis of the Social Gospel*
MACGREGOR, G. H. C. *A Commentary on the Gospel of John*
MACKINNON, JAMES. *The Historic Jesus*
MACKINTOSH, D. C. *Social Religion*
———. *The Reasonableness of Christianity*
———. *Religious Realism*
MACKINTOSH, H. R. *Doctrine of the Person of Jesus Christ*
*MANSON, THOMAS WALTER. *The Mission and Message of Jesus*, by Major, Manson and Wright
*MANSON, WILLIAM. *The Gospel of Luke*
MATHEWS, SHAILER. *New Testament Times in Palestine*
———. *Jesus on Social Institutions*
*MOFFATT, JAMES. *Translation of Old and New Testaments*
———. *An Introduction to the Literature of the New Testament*
———. *Every Man's Life of Jesus*
MOULD, E. W. K. *The World-View of Jesus*
———. *Essentials of Bible History*
MONTEFIORE, C. G. *The Synoptic Gospels*
———. *Some Elements of the Religious Teaching of Jesus*
MOORE, GEORGE FOOT. *Judaism in the First Century of the Christian Era*
MURRY, J. MIDDLETON. *Jesus—Man of Genius*
*NIEBUHR, REINHOLD. *The Nature and Destiny of Man*, two volumes
NOEL, CONRAD. *The Life of Jesus*
*PAGE, KIRBY. *The Personality of Jesus*
PATTERSON-SMYTH, J. *A People's Life of Christ*
*PORTER, F. C. *The Mind of Christ in Paul*
———. *The Message of the Apocalyptical Writers*
*RAWLINSON, A. E. J. *The Gospel According to Mark*
———. *The New Testament Doctrine of Christ*
RICHARDSON, ALAN. *The Miracle-Stories of the Gospels*
ROBINSON, B. W. *The Gospel of John*
———. *The Sayings of Jesus*
SANDAY, WILLIAM. *The Life of Christ in Recent Research*
*SCHWEITZER, ALBERT. *The Quest of the Historical Jesus*
———. *The Mystery of the Kingdom of God*
———. *Out of My Life and Thought*
*SCOTT, E. F. *The Literature of the New Testament*
———. *The Fourth Gospel*
———. *The Nature of the Early Church*
———. *The Validity of the Gospel Record*
———. *The Kingdom of God*
*STREETER, B. H. *The Four Gospels*
TAYLOR, VINCENT. *The Formation of the Gospel Tradition*
TITTLE, E. F. *Jesus After Nineteen Centuries*
WARSCHAUER, J. *The Historical Life of Christ*
WEIGLE, LUTHER A. *Jesus and the Educational Method*
WEISS, BERNHARD, *The Life of Christ*

INDEX

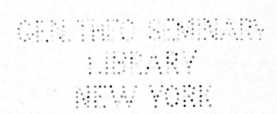